GREATER THAN
Empowered For a Purpose

A Study of Spiritual Gifts by

BY DAVID CASE

Copyright © 2019 by Live Free Ministries, Inc.

First Edition.

ISBN: 978-0-9662598-8-9

Library of Congress Control Number: 2019909393

Printed in the United States of America.

For inquiries, Live Free Ministries can be reached at livefreemin@gmail.com or through the website at livefreemin.com. Information on the Omega Project is available at omegaprojectks.com. Books, blogs, and videos by David A. Case are available at effectiveheartchange.com.

Contents

Introduction

I was lost in a world of confusing thoughts and emotions. What should I do with my life? Did God have a purpose for me? How could I know what to do and where to go? At the time, I was studying a model of the spiritual gifts often called the motivational gifts. The motivational gifts are not about what we are called to do, but about who we are as a person. They are more of a personality profile.

It's been over thirty years since that particular time of self examination. I still have my moments of wondering about my reason for being. What am I supposed to do? What is my purpose?

In case you haven't figured it out, I am an introspective person. On the motivational gifts profile, I am an exhorter. In ministry gifting, I am a teacher. That may not mean anything to you, but what it means is that I think about everything. I ask a lot of questions, and I examine life from just about every angle.

What it also means is that I can very much relate to people who are struggling to find a purpose and a place in life. Do you know who you are as a person? Do you understand what God wants you to do with your life? One of the best ways to answer those questions is through an understanding of spiritual gifts. God knew what your purpose in life was before He ever created you. He placed in you the very talents and desires that would enable you to complete what He wants you to do.

Spiritual gifts are a kind of road map for your direction in life. You are what you care about in the deeper places of your heart. Your core values tell you who God created you to be. You do have a purpose and a place in this world! This book will help you identify who you are. Once you know that, it is simply a matter of being the person God created you to be and staying on the path.

This book will help you identify who you are.

Once you see who you are, the next step is to rest in the work of God. That's the part I struggle with. Resting. I look around. I see others. I compare. Either I am pleased because I am "ahead" or I am frustrated because others are accomplishing so much more. I feel inferior and begin to think that I am out of God's will. That is, I feel that way until I stop, go back to the basics of who God created me to be, and rest in His work.

The contents of this book could be best described as a model. There are concepts in Scripture that are based on a few verses here and there. These concepts can't truly be taught as something solid or universal that all people of faith should accept. The idea of how spirit, soul, and body interact is a place where we have no clear, agreed upon picture. There are many ideas but there is no consensus as to what is taught by Scripture.

When there is no clear, agreed upon teaching, we create a model of what we think the picture is like. If the model is truly Scriptural, it should bring a greater understanding of Scripture in general. It will not contradict what we know to be true, but it will shed new light on concepts that are difficult without the model.

In teaching this model of the spiritual gifts, I see the "lights go on." People "get it." They understand themselves, one another, how God interacts with them, and life in general at a deeper level. My hope is that this model will have a similar positive impact on your life!

This model emphasizes that we are not mere human beings but a home for God. It is the presence of God that will take the ordinary to a whole new level. It is this mixture of the divine and the human that will add a sense of hope, meaning, and purpose to life.

There is so much to discover! I hope you will join me on the journey.

Greater Than?

Chapter 1

- ### How are we greater than what our DNA would predict?

The whole is greater than the sum of the parts.

You are not just you. You are designed to connect with God and to connect with others. You are completed by God and completed by others. That is the essence of spirituality. Connection. Completion.

[handwritten: WHAT ARE THEY   6/20/22   -FAMILY   -IDENTIFY - Community   - CLEARIFY   -MULTIPLY - Diversity]

When science takes inventory of you, it measures the physical components. It misses the deeper understanding of you. You are made up of deep desires and drives. You have a heart that cannot be defined by science, nor is it limited to your DNA. Your heart is more than just a physical something that is handed from one generation to the next.

Because we are temples of God, we have the capacity to house more than just the breath of God that makes us a living being. God can breathe on our minds and quicken its capacity beyond our normal level of understanding. He can multiply our strength. He can even move through us in supernatural ways. We are greater than dust because of the breath of life. We have the capacity to live in a way that is greater than what our natural body could ever accomplish because we can walk directly in partnership with God.

[handwritten: WHEN YOU WALK IN COVENANT YOU WALK IN SUPERNATURAL POWER!]

- ### Who is the real you?

The deepest part of you is what you care about. Your passion. The place of vision for you. Whatever holds your attention. That is also the part of you that is most easily wounded. It is the place of your greatest pleasure, but it is also the place of your greatest pain.

When wounding enters in, the place of your passion can be taken captive. The very thing you were created to be or to do becomes obnoxious. The tender person rages because of the pain. The one who desires to understand will become caustic and closed to new information. Your passion can drive you into pain and bondage … or it can connect with God and be the place of ultimate fulfillment.

The deepest part of you is what you care about!

- ### How do I keep my passion in a healthy place?

God has actually created a number of different passions that on face value don't seem to be that compatible. The thinker and the mercy person don't necessarily have much in common.

The organizer can quickly clash with the more spontaneous person. Each of these descriptions is a "value" created by God. Each has a purpose and a place.

Most people pursue an understanding of spiritual gifts to find "their" place. The healthiest way to pursue spiritual gifts is to learn to value people that are not "like" you. Even if a person's value does not ring true to you, that doesn't make it less important to God or to the body of Christ. Should we not show honor for values that God has put inside of people?

God has created us so that we need each other to be whole. The only way that happens is for us to value those who are different from us. Here is another "greater than." A group of people walking with God will always demonstrate the life and love of God more fully than a single individual. That is, a group of people will demonstrate the image of God if they value those who are not like them. That is love—to get outside of yourself and love others who are not like you.

Many times, Christians tend to group around value centers. Many of the denominations emphasize one of the particular values that we will be covering in this study. Jesus said, **"By this all will know that you are My disciples, if you have love for one another" (John 13:35)**. Instead of forming camps built around our value centers, we need to embrace those who are different from us.

- **If love means we learn to honor those different from us, how do we know when it is our time to "shine"?**

We are designed for fit. Every person has a place and a time. Those who try to compare themselves among themselves miss the purpose of life *(2 Cor. 10:12)*. The great orator is nothing without a crowd of people who are willing to listen. A person can run fast or jump high. What is that worth unless there is a need for that skill or there are people to appreciate the accomplishment?

Fit is a great word to better understand spiritual gifts.

Fit. It is a great word to better understand spiritual gifts. We fit with God. We fit with others. We get the opportunity to shine … or to appreciate someone else who is bringing something of value. Is it more important to be the speaker? Or the listener? The healer? Or the one being healed?

I have coined the phrase "Stand up; sit down" to describe how spiritual gifts should work. We each get to be a piece of the puzzle. We each have a place and a time. Sometimes, the most significant role we can play is to observe and appreciate. That is the time to "sit down." Sometimes, God is using us to bring something to His people. It is our turn to "stand up."

The problem, is that too many people become addicted to standing up. They want to be the center of attention—always. At all times! They want to be right. They want to be the best. They don't understand stand up; sit down. They don't understand spiritual.

To be spiritual is to connect. It sees the whole. It values others!!! It learns that to be the completer is just as important as to be the star. To sit down is to cooperate with the body in a way that makes us a part of a beautiful whole. When one person dominates, there is not unity. There is an ego demanding its attention. The spiritual picture of that is grotesque, when it should have been the love of God.

Greater than. The whole is greater than the sum of its parts. When human beings join together in unity, the outcome is amazing. [Too often, studies of spiritual gifts become a study in "MY" gifts. It is not about learning to appreciate others. It is not about finding "my place to fit." It is not about learning to sit down and acknowledge what God is doing in others. Team gets lost.] *When you see the value in others youll clearly see how you fit with them. If you see them as a threat youll always be wondering "were do I fit in?"*

- **How do we discover and grow in our gift?**

Stand up; sit down. We all have gifts and callings from God. There are frequently extended times of preparation if we are to live out our moment to stand. During the preparation phase, we sit down. We watch others. We learn to appreciate what God is doing in others. We grow. We prepare.

Those who get in a hurry to step into their place of giftedness often destroy the work God would have done. A woman's desire for a husband can be lived out in a healthy way. She can be growing in character and preparing herself for the day she is a wife and mother. Or she can be fearful that she will never marry and can begin to chase after that desire in very unhealthy ways. Each day she does that, she destroys her ability to be the very wife and mother that she could have been. Each day that her desire doesn't come to pass, she becomes a little more frustrated with life and angry with God over her unfulfilled desire. However, if God were to give her the desire of her heart at this point in her life, her now perverted character would destroy the very gift God gave her.

> **Those who get in a hurry to step into their place of giftedness often destroy the work God would have done.**

You RUSH
You MISS THE JOY OF
PROCESS AND
END UP

During the sit down phase, we need to more accurately see who God has created us to be. Our desires and our talents are the two most important indicators of who we are. Desires get easily twisted into something they should not be. *WHERE YOUR IMPATIENCE LEAD YOU AND YOULL FEEL EMPTY AND UNSATISFIED*

To stay in a healthy place, we must get desires fully surrendered to God. The very thing we want the most must be completely surrendered to God. Otherwise, that deep desire within us becomes our god. We forcefully move toward fulfilling that desire in a way that overpowers our ability to hear God speak what He wants in that area of our lives. Without surrender, our passions take over in a way that is outside of the will of God for our lives. If we want the best chance to see who we really are, we must be willing to "sit down"—to be in an accountable relationship with a group of people who are seeking God and giving feedback to one another.

- **How does a talent become a spiritual gift?**

In the area of talent, we act like the 3-year-old, and we try to do life "by myself." Spiritual gifts done God's way are done in partnership with God and with people. Talent, by its very definition, seems to be something I have. So it would make sense that I should use my talents? Right?

No. Talents also need to be fully submitted to God. Our best talent effort will always fall short of what God wants for our lives *(Rom. 3:23)*. God wants partnership. He wants to spiritually breathe on our talents in a way that we will be able to do much more than we could have done with mere talent. Partnership with God is the *Greater Than* lifestyle.

Partnership with God is the *Greater Than* lifestyle.

Those who are in love with their own talents will never live a partnership with God lifestyle. They can't. They believe that what they have is good enough. That is why Peter's boldness had to fail him before he could truly walk with God. That is why Paul's intellect had to take him to a sick place before he would submit to the "mind of Christ."

In *1 Corinthians 1:26*, it says that not many talented are called by God. Why not? Because they don't ever get to the point of being able to hear God's voice in the area of their calling. They are too in love with what they can do. Peter did eventually submit his boldness to God. Paul likewise. It can happen, but most people need to go through a severe test before they will submit their talent areas to God.

- **What is the x factor that God wants in our lives?**

Truly, God means for the outcome of every one of our lives to be greater than the sum of the parts. There is supposed to be an x factor. What we could do with our natural talents is so pitiful compared with what God has for us. In *John 14:12–14*, Jesus tells us:

> *Most assuredly, I say to you, he who believes in Me, the works that I do he will do also; and greater works than these he will do, because I go to My Father. And whatever you ask in My name, that I will do, that the Father may be glorified in the Son. If you ask anything in My name, I will do it.*

Imagine that! Greater works shall we do. Greater than Jesus' works? Possibly … but not if we merely live in a talent zone.

Are you willing to wait on God during the sit down phase? If not, you might not ever get past talent. You might not ever get your desires surrendered to God to a point where He can use you in a significant way.

The greater than lifestyle understands that we play a significant role in the Kingdom of God, but we only play that role when there is genuine partnership and genuine appreciation of the total work God is doing. Spiritual gifts are not a competition to see who has the most, but a lifestyle of learning to draw each and every person into the place God has for him. Fit. Learning to blend your gift with others.

Many people are in such a race to find their spiritual gift that they run right past the clues God would have given them about who they are.   When you begin to see and value the giftedness of others, you are more likely to respond to God and others in a way that God can flow through you. As God flows through you, you can better see who you were created to be.

Even if you never gained any sense of your own spiritual gift, this study would be worth it if you would grow in appreciation for what God is doing in others and through others. Sit down. Learn. Appreciate. If you do, God will speak to you. You will find yourself walking in ways that bless others without even knowing that you are walking in your spiritual gift.

God, open our eyes to first see Your life at work in others!

Many people are in such a race to find their spiritual gift that they run right past the clues God would have given them about who they are.

Activity for Understanding

List the areas of your most talent:

- Networking
- Speaking publically
- People skills

List the areas that you care about the most or that bring you the highest levels of satisfaction when they go well or disappointment when they do not go well: (Note: Talent and values may or may not overlap with one another).

- Teaching/Mentoring youth and young adults
- Creating new programs, trying new things

Water, Ice, or Steam?

Chapter 2

- ### What does the breath of God look like in our lives?

If spiritual gifts are about a walk with God, how does the Spirit show up in our lives? Most people I know (myself included) spend the majority of their days feeling very human and not so much like a temple of the Holy Spirit. We get up. We go to work. We act. We think and feel. But where is God?

In a culture that doesn't understand spirit or spiritual flow, how do we understand spiritual gifts? It is no wonder that most people take it one of two ways: either they make the gifts magical and impossible to understand or they describe the gifts as merely talents.

A more biblical understanding of the gifts begins with **Romans 8:16, "The Spirit Himself bears witness with our spirit that we are children of God."** The Holy Spirit does not take over. *He does not eliminate human function.* He connects with the human spirit and "bears witness" with it. The result of God's bearing witness with us is that we cry "Abba, Father."

Normal 2 thought processes

Third option BIBLICAL one

Our spirit is quickened by God. It is energized. There is a new spring in our step. We suddenly have a sense that God is with us and the desires of our hearts are changed so that they line up with what He is thinking and with what He would want. All of this comes because there is a point of interface between God's Spirit and our spirit. When we connect with God, things change. If we don't connect with God, all that is left is human talent. We work for God and battle against the spiritual pride that comes with our accomplishments.

When we connect with God, things change.

- ### Why do we often miss the moving of the Holy Spirit?

While the supernatural can be very powerful, it often happens at a mostly subconscious level. The **"Abba, Father"** from above is often missed by the new believer unless someone who understands the process calls the attention of the new believer to what is happening. **John 6:44** tells us that no one comes to Christ unless he is drawn by the Father. Many people are not aware of the drawing work of the Holy Spirit. These people believe that they have made their own decision to come to Christ completely apart from the work of God. They believe that they made their decision "by myself." Just like the three year old.

One of the greatest works of the Holy Spirit is conviction of sin *(John 16:8)*. What does that look like? Again, for most, it starts as a subconscious tug. Over time, if a person gives the Holy Spirit the space to work, that tug will grow and grow until it comes to a place of conscious awareness. This is a picture of the Spirit's primary way of moving in our lives. It is a subconscious tug that pulls us from one place to another at the spirit level.

It could be described as a transfer of energy. We have a new sense of life and a new ability to think thoughts or make decisions that we could not have made without the help of the Holy Spirit. All of this can easily happen without us even recognizing that God did anything. We can easily claim credit for all that is happening.

We are spiritual beings. We are designed to connect with the Holy Spirit. If we give God space in our lives, there is a transfer of peace, joy, or patience (*Gal. 5:22-23*). Or there is conviction or an *"Abba Father."* In the end, recognizing that God is at work becomes necessary for the work of God to both grow and continue in our lives.

If we give God space, there is a transfer of peace, joy, or patience.

For those who don't give God space, we are under the power of sin and Satan. Because we are designed to spiritually connect on a continual basis, it is all but impossible to block out the spiritual energy transfers of the demonic realm. We get offended and the power of bitterness grows. One glance in the wrong direction and lust seems to take over with an unbelievable power. We don't have to recognize the spiritual energy transfer to be under its power!

Even so with the moving of God. The biggest reason we shut down the flow of the Holy Spirit is because we don't recognize He is even there. We take credit for the good things happening in our lives. We gradually move away from His energizing into a place of pride … and the power of the Holy Spirit is shut out. Satan slides into that place to energize the pride. The work of God is stillborn for a season.

If we recognize the work of God and give thanks for it, if we meditate on what He is doing, we give space to the Holy Spirit to continue His work. While much of the moving of the Holy Spirit is subtle, eventually the mind, the will, the emotions, and the body have to cooperate or the work of the Holy Spirit will be shut down. A person can even shut down conviction for a season by jumping back into sin.

Many people make the spiritual gifts about the miraculous—meaning the obvious supernatural encounters like healing or tongues or deliverance. The majority of the time the Spirit's quickening is not a lightning bolt, but more like the air we breathe. It is the *"Abba, Father"* much more often than it is the fire falling from heaven. Unless or until we become attentive to this kind of moving of the Holy Spirit, we will seldom get to experience the more miraculous side of the supernatural in our lives.

- ## What are the different ways the Holy Spirit shows up in our lives?

In the book of Acts, the miraculous seems to be flowing at an amazing clip. If we account for the number of years the book covers, the miraculous events were not every day and all the time. Paul spent weeks on mundane journeys that ended up being dead ends (*Acts 16:6-10*). This same Paul had incredible words of knowledge about the future, yet he couldn't even figure out where to go on his ministry trips without taking long and arduous detours. Even

I struggled with this if not must can go back unhealthy to place.

the great men of God have seasons when God is doing something much more subtle, and the miraculous seems to be on vacation.

As water, ice, and steam are all different forms of water, His subtle presence shows up in our lives in three different ways. *First of all, He transforms our very person into the character and nature of God.* There is a group of spiritual gifts that I believe has to do with our inner nature. These gifts are about who we are much more than they are about something spectacular that happens to us or through us. In this group of gifts, a gift we call mercy is more about who a person is than it is about a specific act a person does.

Secondly, the Spirit begins to change what we do. *He moves on our desires and begins to establish His callings in our lives.* These callings are not just related to the church. A person is called into a specific job just as clearly as he is called into the pulpit. The Spirit's moving impacts both what we do and how we do it. What we are called to do is a second category of spiritual gifts.

Finally, the Spirit speaks to us in a very clear and intimate voice. Those who become familiar with the still small voice tend to be the ones who are the channel for God to release the truly spectacular. God speaks. We respond. A miracle takes place. In a society that seldom hears God speak, it is no wonder that we see few of His miracles. Certainly, some healings occur just because of prevailing prayer and the mercy of God. But the supernatural will happen only on a very limited basis until we learn to hear and act on what God speaks to us.

This third group of spiritual gifts is known as the power gifts or the supernatural manifestations. This category of gifts describes points at which God intervenes. I believe the key to these gifts is an intimate walk with God. Individuals connect with God and become the release point for a miracle to take place. We become a *conduit for the supernatural acts of God.* We make the invisible God visible as we pray, speak, and act!

• **Who is a candidate to receive the working of the Holy Spirit? How does it happen?**

> **God doesn't have favorites who are endowed with greater spiritual gifts.**

God doesn't have favorites who are endowed with greater spiritual gifts *(Gal. 2:6)*. He has children who walk with Him. He moves through His children when He wants and how he wants to bring the greatest amount of good to all *(1 Cor. 12:11)*. However, many of His children limit the work of God because they are not aware of the subtle working of the Spirit. These people only live in the world of human talents and human works. They hope that they are accomplishing something for God but have minimal true communion with God or communication from God.

Instead, God wants us to walk with Him, recognizing almost moment by moment His quickening—which is the essence of the spiritual gifts. The Spirit changes who we are, and God calls that a spiritual gift. The Spirit changes what we do and how we do it, and God calls that a spiritual gift. The Spirit gives us encounters of intimacy and power that bring the miraculous into being, and God calls this moving of His Spirit on people spiritual gifts.

This simple step of acknowledging different types of gifts is a first step toward clearing up some of the confusion in the area of spiritual gifts. (Spiritual gifts are the result of living connected to the Holy Spirit.) There is more than just one way that the Spirit moves in our lives. Spiritual gifts are not special talents endowed on special individuals. They are the domain of every man on every day at every hour. Spiritual gifts are how we do life in the Spirit.

The biggest issue will not be identifying your gifts so much as it will be sensing the Spirit's moving in your life. No matter who you are as a person, God has one common goal: to transform you into the character of Jesus Christ and then to engage you as a godly person to demonstrate His love to others—ultimately bringing glory to Himself.

- ## Why would it be in the interest of God to shut down the flow of the miraculous?

When miracles happen, people can get caught up in the miracles and lose track of pursuing God. God has no interest in being the side show when He should be the main event. He wants to manifest His glory in order to change lives. Too often, when miracles are flowing, they become the object of attention. When this happens, the purpose of God is no longer being accomplished, and not surprisingly, the supernatural manifestations fade away.

> **God has no interest in being the side show. He wants to change lives!** ☆

Unfortunately, many people do some crazy things in the name of trying to keep the miracles flowing. How much better off would we be if we learned to see God's purpose and pursued that with our whole heart?

A proper understanding of the gifts brings a better understanding of how we fit into His plan to change lives. Each one of us has a special place. Each one of us is a key to seeing a life changed. Each one of us has unique and special spiritual gifts, but the greatest gift of all is the call to walk with God. When we do that, everything else takes care of itself.

- ## What are the water, ice, and steam forms of God's moving?

In order to better understand spiritual gifts, I will be taking one grouping at a time. We will begin with those spiritual gifts that identify the core of who we are as a person. I call these gifts the *character gifts*. Next, we will take a look at those gifts that describe what we are called to do with our lives. I refer to these as our *callings*. Finally, I will talk about the intimacy walk which releases the power gifts. These power gifts need a release point—a person who is a *conduit or channel* if they are to go forth. These are the healings or the word of knowledge that often comes at a point of desperate need.

- Character gifts
- Calling gifts
- Power gifts

In many ways, it is artificial to break these gifts down into separate categories. They are all part of the complex and individual way that each of us walks with God. None of us ever fully fits a cookie cutter category. However, I do find that it is helpful to break them down into the artificial groupings to grow in our understanding.

For those who desire to know the Scriptural foundations for this model, I encourage you to read the appendix next. The main text of the book will describe the giftings and how they function in real life. The appendix will cover the basic theology behind the model. Feel free to read the appendix now or later, whichever best suits your learning style.

The water of life—the very presence of God can show up as water, ice, or steam in our lives. It can manifest in our character, in our calling, or using us as a conduit. Are you ready to more fully drink of His water?

Activity for Understanding

Imagine you could be any personality type that you wanted to be. What would that person look like?

Imagine that you could do anything that you wanted to do in life. What would you do?

— Travel to meet and work with people

Does the person you would like to be match up with the actions that you would like to do? How to they fit with one another? How are the two different?

List times that you have experienced or been used in the supernatural:

"I Am"

Chapter 3

- ## **What is the difference between a "being" gift and a "doing" gift?**

Most studies on the spiritual gifts focus on either the miraculous gifts or the ministry callings listed in the Scriptures. I believe that the most significant of the gifts are actually the being gifts or as I call them the character gifts. Another common name for them is the motivational gifts. This category of gifts is listed in *1 Corinthians 12:6* and is commonly translated as "activities." However, the Greek word is *energema*. We are all energized by different core values. The fact that we care deeply about different things means that there are multiple character types created by God.

What do I mean by the being gifts or the character gifts? It is easy to get confused by the language. The very same words are used to describe both the being gifts and doing gifts.

Let's start with the example of a teacher. There are many who are called to do the work of a teacher. Some teachers are deep thinkers, some are more into communicating information, and others teach because of the impact it can have on students. A number of different personality types have the ability and even the call to be a teacher. Those who do the activity of teaching we call teachers, but not all teachers have the same inner desire driving them to teach. Their "energies" are different.

Much of the time, a study of spiritual gifts focuses on what a person does. However, the same word teacher can also describe the being of a person. Some people are wired more toward the intellectual. They are energized when they understand the world around them and they want to teach others about that world. A detailed understanding of life is important to them. They value things that make them instinctively and naturally a teacher. It is who they are.

However, that same "teacher" person might be called into the business world. In his "doing" life, he might never be given the title of being a teacher. Yet, a person cannot deny his being. Even though he is a businessman, that person will approach the world of business as a thinker, collecting detailed information about all that goes on in that particular industry.

- ## **Where are spiritual gifts to be in operation?**

Spiritual gifts are about the Holy Spirit quickening our created person in such a way that His light shows through our daily life. A person in business could be a teacher, a servant, an encourager, or any of many other personality types. God wants to breathe on who we are in whatever setting He has called us to live.

The way many people see it, the only place to exercise a spiritual gift is in church. The teacher uses his gift in Sunday school or to lead a small group. The servant cleans the church. The encourager might be a counselor. Biblically, God wants to use whoever you are wherever you go.

- **What is the most valuable spiritual gift?**

I believe that the most significant and abiding of the spiritual gifts are actually the being gifts. You are what you care about. Deeply held core values are the best definition of any person.

Each value is created by God and has a special place in the Kingdom of God.

A person is a knowledge person, a relationship person, a "get the job done" person … and the list goes on and on. None of those values is "the" value for all situations. Each of them is created by God and has a special place in the Kingdom of God—but stand up; sit down. There are times when taking time for relationship needs to stand up and other values need to sit down. There are times when getting the job done needs to stand up and other values need to sit down.

Every value is needed at the appropriate time. Every value needs to give way to other values for a season. Sometimes the right mixture of two or more values is needed. What a person cares about deeply is the most significant part of that person. For a person to offer his passion to others in the right time and the right way is truly a spiritual gift.

- **What does it look like for God to show up in the areas of character, calling, and conduit gifts?**

A major difficulty in understanding spiritual gifts is that the same words are used for being and doing gifts. A teacher is a teacher whether he is a deep thinker or whether he has the job of teaching. In most cases, the same word is used to describe a person's character or his calling.

One example is that of the prophet. The word prophet actually describes all three types: being, doing, and God intervention.

An Example

Being or Character	Doing or Calling	Miraculous or Conduit
Prophet: One who responds to situations with a strong sense of what is right and what is wrong.	Prophet: A person called to consistently correct and challenge a people towards holiness.	Prophecy: A specific word from God to a person or group of people at a given time.

From this example and from the illustration of the teacher, hopefully it is becoming clearer that a single word might have multiple uses. For the prophet, we usually change the word to prophecy for the God intervention. For the teacher, a close parallel gift for the God intervention gift would be either a **"word of wisdom"** or a **"word of knowledge" (1 Cor. 12:8)**.

Character transformation is the foundation. Walking in our calling builds on that base. Both of these then give God an open door to bring glory to His name at a point of crisis when a supernatural intervention is needed. Think about it. Does God get the glory He deserves when the only person He has to work through is being a total jerk?

Character transformation is the foundation!

BALLANCE

For the purpose of God to be accomplished, He needs people who will walk with Him *and* believe in the supernatural. Far too often, there are those who pursue the supernatural but don't develop godly character. There are also those who care about being holy but don't believe they can or should walk in the supernatural. God has called us to both.

A person in business should be able to expect God to give Him the supernatural insight he needs to be successful. That is, he should be able to expect that help if he is truly walking in both the calling of God and the character of God. God's Spirit is the key that unlocks all doors. Oh how we need to grow in our walk with the Spirit of God! We need Him in parenting. We need Him in business. We need Him in the church.

Hopefully, the three ways that the Spirit intervenes in our lives are becoming clearer. Below is listed a basic definition for each of the categories of gifts.

Definitions

Being or Character	Doing or Calling	Miraculous or Conduit
The inner workings of how you think react and experience a situation; core values	Something that you are called to do on an ongoing basis	A supernatural work of the Holy Spirit done with the cooperation of the believer

- ### How does a person's "I am" shape his direction in life?

As I stated, I believe that the most significant of the gifts and often the most neglected of the gifts are the being gifts. In **Exodus 3:14**, God tells us about Himself:

> **And God said to Moses, 'I AM WHO I AM.' And He said, "Thus you shall say to the children of Israel, 'I AM has sent me to you.'"**

One of the names for God is simply **"I AM."** There is no greater gift to mankind than the beautiful and glorious character of a loving God. There is no greater gift from God to man than the unique personality He gives each person. Each person is his own "I am."

In **Romans 12:6-8**, God gives us a list of gifts in which every gift could easily double as either a being or a doing gift. I have already mentioned both the prophet and the teacher from this list and how both can serve in a kind of dual function.

If we focus on the being side, it is easy to see that character traits tend to come in clusters. The Old Testament prophet is a great example of a package of traits that tend to fit well together. Some of the traits of a prophet are being bold, out-spoken, immovable rocks that persist in the face of intense persecution. The prophet character type would never be confused with a person described as a mercy person. Prophets agonize over sin, and often separate themselves from men in order to get closer to God to hear His voice. They are intolerant of imperfection anywhere, and whenever they see sin they are greatly agitated.

Few of these traits match up with the character type of a servant or even a person who has a gift of giving. No, the prophet is a distinct type, and the other six gifts listed in **Romans 12** will become distinct types as we study them. From these types you will gain an understanding of your own tendencies in many situations. You will have a being gift. Your "I am" will become more evident to you as well as your "I am not." As we study types in Scripture, you will see some who think and respond to life much like you do. You will also find that you are unique, not quite fitting any pre-defined category, but that you are not alone. Character traits truly come in clusters.

The passage in Romans says to live according to the "grace" (or gift) given to us. In other

Live according to the grace given to you! words, each of us will react differently to different situations according to the gifting that God has given to each one. In the case of a car accident, one person might remain very calm and begin to immediately take care of the

physical needs of the situation (servant). Another might be drawn to the emotional needs of people in the situation (mercy).

The seven gifts represent an interesting combination of people, task, intellectual, emotional, truth, and experience combinations. Very simply put, different people respond differently to the same situation. Or to say it another way, one situation that may really affect a certain person, may hardly even faze the next person. We react according to the "gift" God has given us.

- **Review the seven gifts below and think about which one(s) most closely resembles who you are.**

Below is a quick sketch of each of the seven gifts. Again, remember that these are talent type of tendencies. The person who walks with God will have what he needs to perfectly complete his calling in any given situation. It is when we don't connect with God and depend on Him that we are limited to our talent tendencies.

Prophet: Prophets primarily react to "the truth." In any given situation, who's right or what's right becomes a major issue. They are willing to force the issue any time they think right and wrong is at stake. They tend to be visionary people who set the standard high, and thus are often perceived as being negative in that the standard is difficult to achieve.

Servant: Servants serve. They consistently focus on physical needs and as such are often not especially verbal people. They love a general closeness or being "with" people and hate contention. Much of their expression is through the things they do. Because of that, they can seem to prefer being or working alone.

Teacher: The teachers are the "intellectual" respondents of the group. They love to analyze the situation and to respond consistently and fairly. It is best and easiest if there is a written standard for them to react to in order to render the best possible judgment in a situation. They love to understand and enjoy the occasional chance to share it too.

Can you identify someone who fits one of the categories from just a basic summary?

Exhorter: The exhorters are the ultimate people person. The best definition of exhorters is that they study the faces of people and respond accordingly. As such, they are unpredictable unless of course you know the given people and the situation. They love to take on the impossible.

Giver: Givers are also interested in relationship with others, but they are more oriented towards seeing others prosper. They love to take things that are of no value and to turn them into a gold mine. They often see themselves as the provider for others which easily translates into being a father or mother figure. They love to nurture others. They also greatly value loyalty in their "extended family" of close relationships.

Administrator: Administrators are organizers. They value efficiency of task and especially like to see everyone doing his or her fair share. They love to start projects, but prefer to parcel out the remainder of the task to those who ought to be involved in the project anyway.

Mercy: Mercy persons are also people oriented, but are more primarily focused on people's emotions. When an emotional overload hits, they can take the quickest escape route, or they can choose to show "mercy." They tend to value heart intent, whether or not the job gets done. Self discipline is hard but forgiveness is easy—unless or until they hit woundedness overload.

- **What are some other things that will help shape our core values?**

That was a fast sketch. Tendencies of all kinds are mixed in any given individual. Ministry callings, parents' gifts and emphases, birth order, life experiences, and mentors all have a tremendous impact on any individual. However, the character gift of a person will tend to dictate how that person feels on the inside. The final outward reaction will then be altered by other influences.

We each have an "I am" that is our starting point. It is an internal values system that stays with us throughout our lives. It can be reprogrammed from selfish to godly. It can be surrendered to the Spirit of God and bring Him glory. Or it can be selfishly honored as a talent at the expense of others.

It will be your choice. Will you choose to exalt your "I am"? Or will you walk with God? You will never feel so alive, so real, so energized, so completely comfortable with "you" as when you choose to walk with God. It is your created destiny to be His temple. Your glory will shine brightest when His glory shines through you.

Activity for Understanding

For most people, the "being" and "doing" part of them is hard to separate from one another. Try to think about somebody that you know well whose "being" part is different from his "doing" part. Examples: A very quiet and non-assertive person who actually tends to take on significant leadership role or someone who is a very hyperactive, outgoing person, but yet often plays the role of listener or counselor.

Describe some people you know who have very different "being" and "doing" parts.

The Prophet: Establishing Truth

Chapter 4

Throughout the rest of the study on the character gifts, I recommend that you mark key character traits by underlining them or marking them with a highlighter. It might be helpful for you to write down names of people that come to mind as you read the different sections.

- **In what ways do core values drive people's responses to others?**

I always like to start the study of the spiritual gifts with the "being" gifts or "character" gifts because they represent the core values system of the individual. Every one of us has an internal sweet spot. When life lines up with that sweet spot, it is high five time. It is "Yes!" It is celebration time.

That sweet spot is somewhat predictable according to the character gift of the person. The prophet values truth and being able to discern what is right and what is wrong. The servant is very attentive to anything that might cause pain and suffering, and enjoys shaping things to make this life better. The teacher's focus is understanding. The exhorter is jazzed when he is able to help others achieve their potential. The giver thrives on being able to nurture and provide for an inner circle of key persons. The administrator loves order and fairness. The mercy person just wants people to be careful with and to care for the emotions of others. When two people of the same character gift get together, there is an immediate sense of "I like this person." Or maybe a sense of "finally, someone understands me!"

Because our character gift is a being gift, it is the deepest and most abiding of the gifts. Core values seldom change significantly. A person might go from a negative expression of a core value to a positive, but the core value is still the same. A mercy person can change from a general disposition of bitterness to one of forgiveness, but the core value of both the negative expression and the positive expression is still relationship.

A mercy person hurts because he values relationship. Out of that deep hurt comes the bitterness. Or the mercy person chooses to forgive and connects in relationship despite the hurt. Each time he forgives, he takes on more of the mercy character. He seems to be a totally different person, and he is … but whether responding positively or negatively, he is still responding to his "I am." He is still living out of his core value.

- **How should a study of the gifts move us toward a greater unity in the body of Christ?**

Learning to cooperate with your core values system can be a huge help in growing toward maturity. Learning to accept the core values systems of others can be a great help in getting along with others and showing them the honor and respect they deserve.

That is perhaps one of the greatest benefits of studying the gifts: it teaches us to value others who are not like us. We generally want to have a camp meeting with those who are like us, with our tree house sign up of "NO GIRLS ALLOWED!" We merely change the sign, saying that anyone with a different values system will not be allowed. All black and white, truth persons come here. All mercy persons, go over there. That is the way we want to function as human beings. That is not the will of God.

The will of God is for us to realize that our set of values are just one point of view. Any single point of view is always out of harmony with truth, with God, and with humanity as a whole. Our values can be submitted to God and used mightily by Him. Or they can slide into selfishness and be used in token ways by Him. As we study Biblical examples of each of the gifts, we will see both the good and the bad. We will see the God-placed values and we will see the human folly that comes when we fail to walk with God. Ultimately, it is walking with God that will keep us in balance and that will bring glory to His name.

- **Who are some examples of prophets and what do you see in each of them?**

The first character gift we will be studying is the gift of the prophet. Again, a prophet can be a calling (or ministry) gift. A person can do the work of the prophet. These uses of the word prophet are not what we are talking about in this chapter. The character gift of a prophet describes those people who have an internal values system that lines up with the work of the prophet. Jeremiah is a great example of a person whom God asked to do the work of a prophet but did not have the heart of a prophet. He would chastise the people and then cry about having to be hard on them. In heart, Jeremiah was a mercy person. In ministry, he was a prophet.

One of the best examples of a prophet in character (as well as in ministry calling) was Elijah. He was a prophet's prophet. His heart was that of a prophet. His ministry was that of a prophet. No Jeremiah type of conflict with Elijah. He valued black and white, right and wrong, and he lived black and white, right and wrong. You can almost hear the lion roar every time that Elijah speaks. He is bold and brassy, and there is nothing to temper that boldness anywhere in his person.

The prophet is a good character type to start with since it is a very clear type. Elijah, John the Baptist, and Peter are all definite prophet types. The story of Elijah is especially clear in illustrating the character of the prophet. I would suggest that you begin by reading 1 Kings 17-19. Notice Elijah's interaction with people and with God.

The very first picture we get of Elijah is him marching up to the King of Israel and saying, *"As the LORD God of Israel lives, before whom I stand, there shall not be dew nor rain these years, except at my word" (1 Kings 17:1b).* This guy is bold and very self assured. Notice, he does not say, "at God's word." He says, *"at my word."* Prophets are power persons. They like to know who's in charge and what's the bottom line. Elijah was letting the wicked King Ahab know that a prophet of God was on the scene and the prophet was taking charge. No wicked king would have sway over this prophet.

- **How do we learn to see each gift according to God's purpose for that gift, instead of trusting our instinctive response to that gift?**

Again, it is important to remember that Elijah is a type. He has the character gift of a prophet. He is not the first with this character, and he will not be the last. We have our share of individuals today who are just like Elijah, and they are created that way by God. Because of the mercy person's sensitivity in the area or relationships, he might ask, "Why would God create such a bold and intimidating person? Why would he allow someone to so completely walk over the feelings of another?"

This will be one of the most significant insights we can gain out of this study. God created prophets just as they are. He created mercy persons just as they are. The core values of these two gifts frequently clash (the core values of many of the gifts to clash!). No matter what our core values are, we need to learn to value the prophet for whom God created him to be. And the prophets need to learn to value those not like them, so that we can all walk in harmony.

> **We need to learn to value the prophet for whom God created him to be.**

The prophet, perhaps more than any other gift, doesn't particularly care about harmony, but cares about right and wrong. In a time of a wicked king, his gift shines. Confrontation is needed. In another time, his gift might not shine quite as bright. We need to learn to release the right gifts to function in the right way and at the right time. We need the whole body!

- **What does it look like for a person to have a higher level of spiritual perception? When is it healthy? When is it not healthy?**

In *verses 3-7 (of 1 Kings 17),* we get another picture of the prophet. Elijah ends up by the Brook Cherith with nobody to talk to except the ravens, which God commissions to feed him. An exhorter would go completely crazy without anyone to talk to. People are life for an exhorter. Not so for the prophet. Solitude and the voice of God are enough. Yes, prophets like to have a few close, intimate relationships. But for the prophet, that is usually enough.

The prophets need less relational contact because they value the voice of God over the words of man. For them, the spirit realm is incredibly real, and the voice of God is consistently clear and real. Our society tends to treat people who "hear voices" as psychotic, thinking it is a form of mental illness. I have found that many times these persons who "hear voices" have this prophetic character gift.

Prophets see and hear things in the spirit realm more easily than others. Those with this gifting do pick up on the spirit realm and can see and hear things that the rest of the world does not see and hear. Because our culture is "scientifically" based, we write these people off as insane and those who have a higher awareness of the spirit realm often come to believe that they are flawed. In Biblical days, these people were actually exalted as "oracles of God." Those societies recognized spiritual perception as being valuable. Our culture scorns it.

I do need to point out that spiritual perception is just that. It perceives things happening in the spirit realm. If a person doesn't learn the difference between spiritual activity that is of God and spiritual activity that is demonic, he will be at the mercy of the dark spiritual realm. If he is connected to and controlled by darkness, the psychotic description can be very accurate. But just because a person has a spiritual perception does not mean we should be skeptical of him, nor should it cause us to hold him in high esteem. It is how he responds to his ability to perceive that makes the difference.

Prophets latch on to a world that is unseen by the rest of us. That is why Elijah can be so bold with the king. He has heard from God. It is also why he can be so perfectly at home by the brook without another person around for months. He has God for fellowship and to him that fellowship is very real.

• How can a "testing" of relationships be a good thing? What makes it unhealthy?

In most cases, prophets view relationships according to a power paradigm. Who's in charge? Where do I fit on the pecking order? Do I have the respect of this person? What would I have to do to get the respect of this person? These questions illustrate a power paradigm. They illustrate the values and the thinking of a prophet.

Relationships tend to fit into the same kind of thinking of what's right and what's wrong. It doesn't take much for a prophet to shift from what's right to who's right and who's wrong … and who's in charge. To a prophet, life is about power. An unhealthy prophet feels very good when he has his share of it. A healthy prophet lives to see the authority of God established in a situation.

The whole picture of a prophet in relationship is further illustrated when he meets the widow in *verses 10-11*. Notice that there is no social chit chat in these verses. The prophet tests the widow from the start to see if she will respond to him. Again, prophets like to know the pecking order. They want to know where things stand on the power profile. So they test. They test not to be malicious but because of what they value, which is a sense of order through proper distribution of power. Others are often offended by the idea that the prophets test people, but for the prophet, that is how life is done.

It would be easy to look at these verses and criticize Elijah for an uncaring demeanor toward the widow. Elijah asks for the very last flour and oil that she has for himself, but adds a promise, that the oil will not run out nor the flour bin go empty as long as she continues to feed him. The prophetic boldness comes through. The woman responds to the request and is blessed. The words of the prophet do come to pass. He is validated by God.

- **When is the prophet's desire for validation a proper test and when is it an egotistic response?**

Oh, by the way, a sense of being validated is very important to the prophet. The words "I told you so" can very easily cross their lips, sometimes in ways that are not well received. While this can seem to be selfish, we need to remember that the prophet is oriented towards truth and toward bringing forth the word of God. In the prophet's mind it is "truth" or the "word of God" that is being validated. It is not personal. It is not selfish. It is righteousness and justice and holiness. We would all do well to take things a little less personally and to be a little more concerned with doing the right thing.

As we look at **verses 19 and 20**, we see another trait of the prophet: focus to the point of seeming to be a bit rude. Notice how abrupt Elijah seems when he says to the woman in **verse 19**, **"Give me your son."** Elijah is not much better in **verse 21** when he says to God, **"O LORD my God, have You also brought tragedy on the widow with whom I lodge, by killing her son?"** Prophets get to the point. They focus in and all else becomes unimportant. That kind of focus helps produce results. The boy was healed, but those who want a gentle, loving atmosphere will likely be disappointed.

Intense focus helps get results!

These same verses also illustrate the very deep emotions of the prophet. Elijah cries out in anguish to God. He stretches himself out on the body of the dead boy. He throws himself totally into the prayer. Though oriented towards truth, the prophet cannot be described as being on an even keeled intellectual pursuit. For him, truth is very personal and is the basis of all that he stands for. He either has heard from God or he hasn't. If he hasn't, he has failed. The prophet is very much emotionally invested in all he does. Accordingly, life is often lived at a fervent emotional pitch.

- **What do prophets find repulsive? When is this kind of strong response healthy and when is it harmful?**

Moving into **chapter 18**, we see Elijah meeting Obadiah, one of the few remaining servants of the Lord. Again, there is no social interaction. Elijah simply says, **"It is I. Go, tell your master, 'Elijah is here'" (1 Kings 18:8b)**. I may be reading a little too much into the statement, but it almost seems like there is a bit of a dig toward Obadiah in this statement. Prophets hate compromise. Obadiah may be a servant of the Lord and may have done good things, but he still is working for the wicked King Ahab. Throughout the conversation, it seems like Elijah is hardly willing to give the time of day to Obadiah. That actually would be a typical response of a prophet to Obadiah, if the prophet sees Obadiah as a compromiser.

In *verses 17-18*, we see the meeting between Elijah and Ahab. Ahab accuses Elijah of being the *"troubler of Israel."* Prophets are not afraid to correct, confront, or argue. In fact, they actually thrive on it because it is their way of trying to establish the truth of the kingdom of God. Thus Elijah's response:

> *"I have not troubled Israel, but you and your father's house have, in that you have forsaken the commandments of the LORD and have followed the Baals. Now therefore, send and gather all Israel to me on Mount Carmel, the four hundred and fifty prophets of Baal, and the four hundred prophets of Asherah, who eat at Jezebel's table" (1 Kings 18:18b-19).*

Notice the argumentative and challenging tone of Elijah's response. He will back down from no man, especially when he feels like God's point of view is being misrepresented. If a prophet doesn't feel like he is representing God's point of view (or at least an "I am right" point of view), he will be much less likely to take this kind of stand.

- ## How is a prophet's view toward arguing or fighting different from some of the other gifts? Describe how they respond to struggles.

Most of the time, the prophet doesn't see the argument as a personal thing as much as it is an opportunity to establish truth. Prophets value truth and one way to get to the truth is to fight it out. If God is truly supreme, and if He is backing up the prophet, the prophet surmises that he will win the fight and then establish the authority and truth of God.

Prophets don't see arguments as a personal thing.

The whole next scene takes the desire for a fight to a new level. Elijah taunts the false prophets and escalates the drama of the battle. Prophets often make good humorists since they are not particularly worried about what people think and since some of the best jokes are simply truth with an ironic twist or cover.

We see some of that in Elijah when he tells the false prophets that surely their god is meditating, or on a journey, or asleep. Can a god be God who is not awake, aware, and available? It is veiled humor. Because prophets are oriented toward power relationships, the thrill of being able to move an audience with humor or with confrontation is something that can jazz a prophet.

Elijah also escalates the battle by digging a trench around his sacrifice and pouring water in the trench. This is not just a battle, it is overkill for the sake of demonstration that God is God. Elijah had set the whole challenge up to force the people to recognize the One who is truly God and then follow the One who demonstrated Himself to be God. Elijah wanted no ambiguities.

Look at the level of energy Elijah pours into this fight. Prophets live to establish truth and thus can anticipate a battle with joy. Because they see the positive purpose of establishing and clarifying truth through a power confrontation, living life as a fight can become addictive for a prophet. The adrenaline rush and the sense of self vindication can become every bit as controlling as any drug that could be taken. When disconnected from God, prophets will fight for fighting's sake. They fight to get their fix. This, of course, is a perversion of their created purpose.

Prophets are so committed to truth and establishing the authority of God (or what they perceive as being right), they would rather die trying than not try at all. Martyrdom is not a scary thing to a prophet, but compromise is. To be a compromiser totally flies in the face of what they value. They like to set up opposites and force a choice. That is all well and good if it is truly a black and white situation.

- **What are ways that the prophet can get into the flesh when engaged in a "fight"?**

Many times there are multiple right choices—or multiple wrong choices. Sometimes, the prophet has latched on to what he thinks is right when he is wrong. When this happens, it can be a very difficult day in the life of those around the prophet. It will likely take a power struggle to bring any kind of a change in the prophet's thinking. Prophets respect power. Power comes from God. That can be respected.

In this battle scene, we also see the fleshly side of Elijah beginning to show its head, a side that will take him through a difficult journey. In *1 Kings 18:22b*, Elijah declares that, *"I alone am left a prophet of the LORD."* That statement simply is not true. God rebukes him for it later, saying that there are 7,000 who continue to serve Him. In the midst of this challenge, Elijah is on a roll and he continues on with the fight to establish God as God. A hint of the flesh surfaces here, but it will show itself to a much greater degree later.

Prophets are susceptible to an "I am the only one" complex. This is a combination of spiritual pride and self pity. Because they see most people as compromisers, and because they see themselves as having a zeal unequaled by others, they truly begin to feel that they are the only ones left serving God. Often, they are the only ones willing to go to open warfare for truth, but that does not mean they are the only ones serving God. Not every time is a time to fight.

Prophets are susceptible to the "I am the only one" complex.

Some of the best "fighting" that the prophets do is in the spirit realm. Because they are very sensitive to the spirit realm, they treat what they sense at the spirit level with a great deal of certainty. When Elijah prays for rain, he prays until he sees just a small puff of a cloud. As soon as his servant sees that cloud, Elijah says to his servant, *"Go up, say to Ahab, 'Prepare your chariot, and go down before the rain stops you'" (1 Kings 18:44b).* Signs are important to the prophet to give them a sense that they are on the right track, but once confirmation happens through some kind of a sign, they become super focused and super energized in faith.

Speaking of super energized, Elijah takes off in the energy of the Lord's anointing and gets to Jezreel running on foot before Ahab can get there in his chariot. Prophets are like that. In the thrill of the battle, or in pursuit of the anointing, they can seem almost superhuman. That kind of burst of energy does have its consequences. The energy burned during a high time is very likely to plunge them into a season of burnout, possibly leading to a sense of despair.

This is one example of what I will repeat over and over about all of the gifts. When taken too far, the greatest strength of a gift will become its greatest weakness. In Christ, a person's gift is awesome. Outside of Christ, it has the potential to become perverse and destructive.

- ### How does the prophet's approach to life make him vulnerable to depression?

Chapter 19 validates that some flesh had begun to surface during the battle. A person doesn't just jump from the anointing to depression. There are transitional steps. "I am the only one" surfaced during the battle and comes back even stronger the day after. In fact, it comes back so strong that Elijah pleads with God to kill him. Elijah sends away his servant and wallows in the low that is the day after the battle. This once mighty warrior is scared to death of Jezebel and seems resigned to the fact that she has the upper hand. Where did that come from?

It came from taking on the prophets of Baal single handedly. In the battle, he not only drew from the strength of God, but he also burned up all of his natural energy. When the flesh creeps in, that happens. We battle in our own strength.

Exhaustion comes when self has crept in, and God is squeezed out.

There is a battle that we fight when partnering with God that leaves us tired. When that battle is done, we feel good and we able to go to bed and sleep. There is a battle that consumes us and at the end of the day leaves us exhausted: mentally, physically, and spiritually. Exhaustion comes when self has crept in, and God is squeezed out. We see that with Elijah in these chapters. It is nearly impossible to tell if a person is on this burnout track during the battle, but on the day after, it becomes very evident.

- ### Starting with the fight with the false prophets all the way to Mt. Horeb, how does the self pity of Elijah continue to grow?

On the day after, Elijah is suddenly weak and full of self pity. He runs for his life from Jezebel. He prays that he might die. He sends away his servant so that he can suffer isolated and alone. That self pity did not surface out of a vacuum. The isolation is not new. He had lived in isolation for months when first in hiding from Ahab and Jezebel. This time, however, the isolation is not one where he is drawing on his God given ability to commune with God. This time the isolation is self imposed because he is the "only one" left serving God. Obviously, that is not true that he is the only one left serving God. The self pity flowing in Elijah is able to create those thoughts and make them seem to be true. Later, in the cave, God tells Elijah that there are **"seven thousand in Israel"** who have not **"bowed to Baal" (1 Kings 19:18)**. Elijah may have felt alone, but he is definitely not the only one left in Israel who is still serving God.

Every character gift is like that. Its greatest strength is its greatest weakness. The prophet is excellent at shutting himself in with God, not needing much in the way of human relationships to survive. He is great in battle. He is great in fervency. He is great in vision for what needs to happen. He is great until he stops walking with God and tries to let the strength of his own character be enough to face the trials of life. It is when we drift from God that we see the fleshly side of the spiritual gift. And it is not pretty, not even in a spiritual giant like Elijah.

Even in **chapter 18**, there were other signs that Elijah was close to going over the edge. The taunting of the false prophets is at least pushing the line. God hates evil and will destroy evil, but God's judgment always has a ring of compassion to it. There is a tear in His eye as He executes the needed judgment.

By putting water on the sacrifice and taking the battle to the point of overkill, Elijah pushes himself near the edge. He is still doing the work of God. He still has the anointing of God. But he is flirting with the edge. He is starting to mix in the flesh in his mission. Prophets love to dominate and annihilate evil. Some of that display of power is a picture of the character of God, but Elijah loses sight of God's compassion in his zeal to dominate. There is also a little too much human vengeance involved, and human vengeance burns human energy. When the human energy is gone, what's left? It is Elijah in **chapter 19**.

> **Human vengeance burns human energy.**

Elijah is wasting away under the broom tree. Sometimes, when we burn all human energy, we get to a point of being so tired that we cannot even sleep. In God's mercy, He gives Elijah divine food and drink, not once but twice. God is like that. He knows we are but dust and that we will burn all of our human energy. Yet, He has mercy on us when we do.

In **verse 8**, Elijah takes off for Mount Horeb. Nothing in Scripture gives us the idea that this is a journey God wanted Elijah to take, but it is one God knew was coming. God gave Elijah the food and drink he would need for the journey, yet when Elijah arrives, God's first words are **"What are you doing here, Elijah?" (1 Kings 19:9b)**. God knows our weaknesses and works with them to move us back into what He wants for us. Sometimes we have to burn off our natural strength and hit a place of weakness before we are willing to reconnect with God and to depend on Him again.

Next, God takes Elijah through the wind, earthquake, and fire experiences. These power experiences are the stuff of prophets. Prophets like high drama. Elijah had created high drama just a few days earlier. Not this time though! This time it was God creating the drama, but the Scriptures tell us that God was not in the drama. No, He didn't speak through the drama but through the still small voice. When He spoke, it was a bit of a rebuke to Elijah, telling him to go and anoint his successors. No, he was not the only one left. And yes, God could continue to get His work done without him.

In the end, Elijah only obeys one of the three orders from God. He anoints Elisha as his successor, but leaves it to Elisha to complete the other two anointings. When he does anoint Elisha, Elijah continues his distant, non-relational style. Listen to the account:

> *So he departed from there, and found Elisha the son of Shaphat, who was plowing with twelve yoke of oxen before him, and he was with the twelfth. Then Elijah passed by him and threw his mantle on him. And he left the oxen and ran after Elijah, and said, "Please let me kiss my father and my mother, and then I will follow you." And he said to him, "Go back again, for what have I done to you?"*
> *(1 Kings 19:19-20).*

If the account is giving us all the details, Elijah doesn't even speak to Elisha initially. When he does speak, all he says is, ***"Go back again, for what have I done to you?"*** Elijah is truly a prophet's prophet. He is a prophet in character and a prophet in calling which makes him more extreme in all of the prophetic traits.

What is interesting is that this greeting (or lack thereof) doesn't seem to negatively impact Elisha. He understands the calling of the prophet and the extreme honor it is to be God's representative. There are times when the message of God must be given priority to the normal social interactions of man. It seems to me that Elijah is still in a bit of a pout in this scene. He may just be acting out his gift and call, but it appears to me that the flesh is still hanging around from the events of previous chapters.

• What is the prophet's view toward correction? How do others often respond?

Prophets need to realize that sometimes things are best left unsaid or undone.

Prophets need to realize that sometimes things are best left unsaid or undone. When they are in God's time, they are possibly the greatest of gifts, but out of His time—the worst. Also, one trait not clearly seen in Elijah is that prophets hate their own sin and thus consider it an act of love when others point out their sins. The only problem is that prophets also think they are doing others a favor when they point out their sins. Most people do not receive the prophet's rebuke in the attitude that it is given.

Many people see prophets as being rude and inappropriate when they bring correction and often will reject them, leaving the prophets stunned. For the prophet, the correction is meant to be a message of love, and the box of roses is returned unopened or worse yet, with a hostile note.

Not surprisingly, prophets often experience a keen sense of rejection which simply tends to isolate them even more, at times driving them back to the only safe place—God's arms. If the prophet gives in to the flesh, rejection will drive him into isolation and self pity.

- ## What are the positive outcomes from Elijah's life?

Elijah is such a great example of how the gifts work. We can go through the motions of our calling, getting many of the actions right. Or we can walk with God.

When we walk with God, we don't just do and say the right things, we manifest the character and nature of God. We do what God wants in partnership with Him, and it bears much fruit. The more we let the flesh creep in, the more we are setting ourselves up for an eventual fall. The flesh will bear fruit in our lives sooner or later if we don't allow God to fully prune us. Elijah had that opportunity at the cave. I don't think he took full advantage of it.

Even so, Elijah cannot have missed it too far. God comes and takes him up to heaven in a chariot of fire. This is the same person that I have been saying was walking in the flesh? God has designed each one of us with a purpose. Each design has a definite ability to slide off the edge, but even in our sliding, we often complete the will of God. Elijah certainly carried out his primary mission. And God was well able to cover him in his shortcomings.

The greatest challenges for the prophet are balance and timing. A prophet is going to be what a prophet is going to be, but he does need to learn an appreciation for the other types of people who are also serving God. His way is not always the only or the best way and he has to learn to back off and realize that there is a tomorrow. Sit down! In general, when a person becomes compulsive, he is probably walking in human strength and is not fully staying in touch with God.

The prophets are the eyes of the body *(Is. 29:10)*. They are able to create a vision. That vision then becomes a beacon of hope as we look to the future and a standard by which we can correct our course. They help keep us on course when they stay in touch with God and man. When they become the course, then trouble develops.

> **Prophets are the eyes of the body (Is. 29:10).**

More than anything, prophets value what they perceive to be "truth" or "right" and they value seeing what is right established. It is the core of their inner being. Prophets truly are a gift to the church, but they are a gift—one of the gifts. When a prophet recognizes this truth and walks in unity and cooperation with others, he is an incredible blessing. When he becomes stuck on his own ability to hear truth and see truth, he is beginning to lose the truth. Even if he is guarding the right words, no one fully manifests truth unless he is also manifesting the character of God. We cannot manifest His character unless we walk with Him and with others.

[handwritten: Manifesting the character of God comes by walking with God and that needs to be our aim not what our gifts and missions are because our fruit comes from being connected not by what we can perform.]

Thus a natural gift, a personality, becomes a spiritual gift. A valuing of truth becomes a gift to the body. It is one of seven God-created values that are meant to be mixed together to produce a beautiful harmony. Six are left to come. All are needed to fully manifest the character of Christ. When we realize this truth, we all feel a little bit better about ourselves and others. We are only one part of the picture. We don't have to carry the whole load. We don't have to be perfect. We just have to walk with God. What a relief! God is awesome!

Snapshot of the Prophet

Note: For the next seven chapters, the snapshots and the activities will help you better determine if you have the core value talked about in that chapter. Core values actually come from multiple sources, so it is possible that you may have some of a core value, but not be that gift. All of the gifts have some overlapping traits. If you only look at traits, it can be confusing. If you take a test that only asks about traits, you will be frustrated trying to pinpoint your gift. If, however, you look at the motivation behind the traits, the picture will become much clearer. One person shows mercy out of a need to nurture others. Another shows mercy through acts of kindness and yet another shows mercy through emotional support. In each of the next seven chapters, try to see the motivation behind the response for each of the seven categories. Once you see the motivations behind the traits, your primary character gift will be relatively obvious. Mark all traits that fit who you are. Your gift should have the most items marked on these snapshots.

Passion: Establishing truth, separating right from wrong, being right, living right, strength and authority manifested, and fervency.

Primary fears: Being wrong, being shown as weak, being disrespected, or being passionless.

Spiritual connection/voice of God: Hearing God is easy; it is almost like hearing another person speak, like hearing a voice; the spirit realm tends to be very real to them whether in visions or voices; they are much more likely to see demonic or angelic activity and are quick to discern the spirits of people; connecting with God is life.

Relationship characteristics: Tend to have only a few close friends; want them to be very loyal and close; must be able to "test" them without them getting offended; relationship to people is secondary to establishing right and wrong; tend to be more comfortable in vertical relationship settings (vertical meaning that there is a ranking of who is in charge and who is under that authority and how and when they are under authority).

Conflict: They value conflict as a means of testing what is real, right, and authoritative; they see conflict as a needed and useful tool; like to have others point out any flaws or weakness in them that need to be corrected.

Task orientation: If it is worth doing, it is worth doing right; they can pour themselves excessively into the task or they can just as likely be caught up more in the spirit realm and be almost oblivious to tasks that need to be done around them; task is important almost solely as it relates to the spirit realm or to pleasing God.

Possessions: As a power personality, possessions can be important as a status symbol (more in the immature or unhealthy prophets); but possessions often have little meaning to the prophet; again possessions take on very different meanings in different situations according to how it impacts the spiritual.

Activity for Understanding

Who do you know that seems to fit the picture described in the prophet gift?

What part of the picture of the prophet fits you well? (If it is only a few traits, check out other gifts that might have similar traits!)

What values of the prophet seemed uncomfortable to you as a value "created by God"?

Is that value uncomfortable to you because you are seeing the sinful side being expressed or because it is in contrast to what feels right to you?

Who do you know that you have "despised" or at least devalued that may actually be acting on an internal value created by God as seen in the prophet?

Have some close friends identify those parts of the prophet description that fit you well. List results:

The Servant: "Just Live It"

Chapter 5

- ## What are some basic differences between the prophet and the servant?

You've heard people say, "I want to show people Christ through my life." This is a core value for the servant. In the last chapter, we saw the core value of the prophet who desires to lay hold of God's truth and to proclaim it. In contrast, the servant desires to lay hold of God's lifestyle and live it. The prophet is verbal. The servant is non-verbal. The prophet is more than willing to stand up and fight for what is right. The servant avoids conflict like the plague.

Perhaps you can begin to see the different values systems that the different gifts bring to the body of Christ. Each value is needed at different times and in different situations. In the words of *Ecclesiastes*, there is:

> *A time to tear,*
> *And a time to sew;*
> *A time to keep silence,*
> *And a time to speak;*
> *A time to love,*
> *And a time to hate;*
> *A time of war,*
> *And a time of peace (Eccl. 3:7-8).*

The values system of the prophet and the servant are both in these verses, just at different times. A study of the gifts is about learning to honor others and encouraging them to step up in the appropriate time and appropriate way for the good of the body—stand up; sit down! The servant and the prophet are two gifts with very different values. Many times there is enough of a clash between the values of the gifts that one has to sit down when the other one stands up. Sometimes the clashing values can cooperate in a way that both values influence the choice of response.

Servants are a little harder to spot than the prophets but are an equally definite type. The clearest Biblical example of a servant is Moses. Again, we do need to remember that Moses has a prophetic/leadership calling. Accordingly, he exhibits some traits that are more leadership oriented that are not typical of a servant. But his servant character comes through loud and clear in the story of the exodus.

- ## How does Moses' life show a greater awareness of the physical realm?

The first picture we get of Moses' character comes in **Exodus 2:11** when it says that Moses **"went out to his brethren and looked at their burdens."** Servants are some of the best at bearing burdens themselves. They are the pack mules of the spiritual gifts, willing to take on the hard physical labor almost single handedly at times. Perhaps because they often end up carrying more than their share of the load, servants are especially sensitive when others have to bear a similar kind of load. They notice, and they don't like it.

The first thing Moses noticed was the level of burden being put upon his people. Having grown up in the palace, this might have been easy to ignore. But he couldn't! He was a servant. Family is more important to the servant than a palace life, and a burdened people will cause a burdened heart. Moses had no choice but to identify with his own people. When he saw them in pain, he could not deny his connection to them.

> **For the servant, seeing his people in a place of pain is very difficult.**

That was even before what came next. He saw an Egyptian beating one of his fellow Hebrews. In **Exodus 2:12** it says, **"So he looked this way and that way, and when he saw no one, he killed the Egyptian and hid him in the sand."** And this is the man of God that the Bible speaks of as being the meekest of all men upon the earth?

- ## Spiritual gifts are about learning to walk out our call in partnership with God. How does Moses' life illustrate running ahead of God?

Actually, this is a perfect example of a man trying to walk in his call in his own strength, in his own time, and in his own way. In the book of **Acts**, Stephen gives us some insight into this event:

> *And seeing one of them suffer wrong, he defended and avenged him who was oppressed, and struck down the Egyptian. For he supposed that his brethren would have understood that God would deliver them by his hand, but they did not understand (Acts 7:24-25).*

God took 80 yrs to prepare Moses

Moses had already received the call of God at the time he went out to observe his brethren. To him, it was a no-brainer that God had placed him in the palace for a purpose, to be a protector and champion for his people. In his mind, this was no murder but an avenging of wrong.

Unfortunately, neither the Egyptian courts, nor the Israelites themselves would look upon it in the same way. The next day, when two Israelites are fighting and Moses tries to intervene, they mock his authority and refer to the death from the previous day. Moses thought the Israelites would guard his secret and see him as their deliverer. Not so. His life was now in danger.

- ## What makes servants a good candidate for "escape"?

Not many people run from their call for forty years and still complete the call that God has for their life. Not many people could live with themselves for that long, but Moses was not a natural deliverer. He was a servant. Servants are natural escape artists. If they can plunge themselves into a serving task and stay totally focused on the job, the past can easily be forgotten. Servants are prone to be workaholics, especially if there is some kind of emotional or relational stress they are avoiding. Moses certainly had a negative memory in his past that he was running from.

- ## Can we ever really escape the inner values that God has put inside of us?

Ironically, the next scene we get is Moses again being a deliverer. This time, he has fled to the land of Midian and sees the daughters of Jethro being taken advantage of by the local shepherds. Once again the deliverer in Moses comes out as he drives the shepherds away and allows these women to water their flocks.

God has designed us so that we almost can't help but complete the call on our life in some way. Our call is who we are, who God created us to be. We may pervert the call, doing it in the wrong way or at the wrong time, but it is so much an intrinsic part of who we are that we are all but guaranteed to act it out in some way. It is our inner values system and we will be attracted to people and situations that give us the opportunity to express who God created us to be.

- ## How does God speak to the servant as compared to the prophet?

In the next view we get of Moses, he is out shepherding the flock near Mount Horeb when he has an encounter with God. This encounter between Moses and God gives us a great deal of insight into how God relates to the servant and to a degree the other character gifts also. God knows each of us as an individual, and He relates to each one of us in our own special language. He catches our attention with what we value.

When God spoke to Elijah, He spoke. The description given seems to be verbal. God speaking, Elijah listening. Simple and straightforward communication. When God shows up on the mountain, the first thing that happens is a sign—a burning bush that does not burn up. As a servant, Moses is attentive to physical things. He notices that something unusual is going on and he approaches the bush with a sense that this might be a God thing.

When God saw that He had Moses' attention, He spoke from the midst of the burning bush (**Ex. 3:4**). Why the supernatural sign? Servants tend to need tangible symbols to make their walk with God more concrete, more in the language and thinking of their created person. The prophet Elijah didn't need that. The verbal touch was more than enough. Occasionally, a sign of confirmation is sought by the prophet, but for them life consists of listening and then speaking.

For the servant, interacting with God is more accurately described as processing what is happening and then responding. Servants value a lifestyle lived. The voice needs to be tied to actions and objects to have significant meaning. Notice how God does that with Moses. He has him take off his sandals *(Ex. 3:5)*. Later on, when Moses is balking at going forward, God gives him a staff as a tangible object of authority *(Ex. 4:2)*. God also gives him a physical location, promising him that on this very mountain Moses and the people of Israel will one day return to worship God *(Ex. 3:12)*. For the servant, spirituality must be translated into a current physical reality.

• What pulls at the heart strings of the servant?

When God speaks, what does He say to Moses? Paraphrased, it is simply, "Your people are suffering under great bondage." Moses is 40 years removed from being the deliverer of Israel. In the natural, that dream is dead. His call is dead. But with a few words, God reawakens the call. Servants hate oppression. They feel for the underdog. God touches the soft part of Moses' heart. It is no coincidence that God speaks what He speaks to Moses.

God knows our hearts, and He knows how to get through to our hearts. His approach to the servant will be different from that of any other gift. Servants often feel like they don't hear from God at all. They hear the prophet describe "the voice of God" with a sense of sureness that they never have, and soon come to the conclusion that God never speaks to them.

> **God knows our hearts, and He knows how to get through to our hearts.**

Servants usually don't understand that God speaks differently to them. *To the servant, God will come with a nudging toward a life response.* That is how servants hear and how they think. Moses is given an action. Elijah is given a word to deliver. God showed Moses the oppression of His people. God showed Elijah the sins and the compromises of His people. Moses was moved and so was Elijah.

Communication is a two-way street. We must connect with the values of another person to truly interact with him in a more intimate way. God wants intimacy with us. He meets us at our level, respecting who we are, speaking to us in a way that we can hear. For the servant, that must include the non-verbal and must be life response oriented.

• What is it like for a servant to be in leadership?

In *Exodus 11:2*, we see another trait of the servant: they are generally reluctant to lead. Servants tend to prefer to do jobs on their own. They don't like to bother other people and they definitely don't want to have to boss others around. This is not too hard to imagine when we understand that they are not particularly verbal and that they hate confrontation.

A servant like Moses, who has a calling that requires him to lead, will have a struggle within himself. Often, there is an interface within a person between the person's calling and his character. Moses is called to lead and wants to lead, but is naturally reluctant to get up and speak in front of others. Couple that with the failure the first time he tried to play deliverer and Moses is doubly reluctant to take on the task God is putting in front of him.

Even so, God knows how to get to Moses' heart. By showing Moses the oppression of his people, he has captured Moses' heart. Now all God has to do is instill confidence back into Moses that the job can be done.

- ## What is an almost universal way that we miss God?

We all try to jump out ahead of God in an attempt to complete the call of God in our own strength!

Every single person has to learn the lesson Moses is learning. Not everyone spends 40 years in training. We all jump out ahead of God in an attempt to complete the call of God in our own strength. Usually, instead of recognizing our presumptive behavior, we get mad and blame God or we turn our backs on the call. Life has to be lived in God's way and God's time. That is one of the hardest lessons to learn.

- ## What kinds of ways does God help Moses get over his reluctance to return to the call of being the deliverer of Israel?

When Moses balks at the call to return to Egypt to be the deliverer, God promises to go with him, to do signs through him, and even sends Aaron, his brother, to be a helper in the process. Servants need things they can get their hands on—like a staff. They need a genuine assurance that they are not going to be left hung out to dry. Because they struggle verbally, servants do not have confidence in their ability to deal with relationship issues and need extra levels of commitment from those around them. And tangible manifestations of the power of God don't hurt their confidence level!

For those who are questioning that Moses is truly a servant, what is the title that Moses is frequently given? Moses, servant of the Lord. Not only that, notice what God says in **Exodus 2:12**. He says that after the people have come out of Egypt, they will *"serve God on this mountain."* He doesn't say worship. He doesn't say learn of Me. He says *"serve"* and that they will serve in a tangible place and time. Moses can relate to that. God knows that He is speaking to a servant, and His language reflects that fact.

I also find it interesting the reward that God promises to the Israelites. After the plagues, He promises that the Israelites will "plunder" the Egyptians. How do they plunder the Egyptians? There is no major conflict. They simply ask them for gold and silver and the tangible goods that have been withheld from them during their years of slavery. Because the plagues have done their work, the Egyptians gladly hand over the goods to the Israelites and encourage them to leave quickly.

• How is being "grounded" a true benefit for the body of Christ?

Servants value living in the natural realm. That does not make them carnal. Just as I said about the prophet, God made them that way. There are those who try to make this life completely spiritual. That is not how God made us. In fact, in **Matthew 18:18**, it is the things on earth that actually bind and control what happens in heaven. God has ordained that what comes through the body is the final determiner that shapes all spiritual activity.

The fact that servants value the things of the natural realm of this life is just as much a gift to the body of Christ as the prophet's desire for truth is a gift to the body. Servants instinctively recognize the value of things, especially noting that things are important to people, and that when we mess with a person's stuff, we are messing with the person.

God has said, **"Thou shalt not steal" (Ex. 20:15, KJV)**. Property is an extension of a person. It has spiritual significance. Servants recognize that. This recognition can be taken too far to a point of carnally seeking after stuff. But in the flow of God's Spirit, it is a gift to the body. To a servant, proper respect for things is an important part of the Christian lifestyle.

• How does the servant's strength of valuing things get turned into a weakness?

Again, our greatest strength is usually also our greatest weakness. Because of the value that servants have for things and because the relationship part of life can be a struggle, they do have a tendency to let their lives get caught up in things. They can easily become gadget persons, or they can be on an endless search for the next best tool. In general, a lusting after the things of this world is a perversion that almost feels normal and right to a servant. It allows them to live in the world of their own values system, but it is not what God wants for their lives.

• Where do servants have the hardest time obeying God?

One of the least understood Scriptures in the Bible comes in **Exodus 4:24**. Moses is on the way to Egypt to be the deliverer of Israel, just as God has asked, and the Scriptures say, **"that the LORD met him and sought to kill him."** Here Moses is, doing the will of God, and God is about to kill Him? Where does this come from?

It comes from Moses being a servant. Servants hate contention. They especially hate to confront or fight with family or those closest to them. It is much easier to go with the flow and put up with negative consequences. In **verses 25-26**, Zipporah circumcises her boys, takes the foreskins and throws them at the feet of Moses in a kind of temper tantrum.

Servants hate contention.

Reading between the lines, it is pretty obvious what has happened. Since Moses had not circumcised his boys during his 40 years in the desert, God had asked Moses to follow through with this sign of the covenant. With the level of leadership God would be asking of Moses, there was no room for disobedience in this matter. To God, it was a life and death issue. If Moses would not obey on something as elementary as this, God would have to find another deliverer.

There was one catch. Zipporah had resisted Moses, and Moses had given in to Zipporah. As a servant, one of his greatest anguishes would be to fight with his wife, so he chose not to challenge her on this issue. Unfortunately, God did not see it the same way. Death to self means different things for different people. When God is preparing us for leadership, He will ask us to sacrifice the one thing that is most dear to us. In this case, God wanted to know if peace with Zipporah was more important to Moses than serving Him.

Moses was not passing the test. God sought to kill him. Zipporah realized what was going on and completed the obedience, throwing the foreskins at the feet of Moses, saying, **"You are a husband of blood!" (Ex. 4:26)**. She didn't exactly do it with a good attitude, but that is one of the consistent lessons of the Old Testament. God grows us into maturity. We learn to walk in the Spirit one step at a time. Angry obedience is at least obedience. When we are just getting started, God accepts the attempts of the immature to follow Him. In this case, He even accepts the attitude-laced effort of Moses' wife on his behalf.

Angry obedience is at least obedience.

God helps Moses toward godly obedience, even through the reluctant behavior of an angry wife. Learning to walk in our spiritual gift is about learning to walk with God more than it is about expressing some incredible talent. As I read the Scriptures, it is amazing to me how much of the success actually depends on what God does in and around and through us. But we are required to cooperate with Him and to take the next step. In this case, Moses had to get his children circumcised. It was not done perfectly, but it was completed and God relented from killing Moses.

- **What response of the people around a servant is hard for them to handle? What is a special blessing for a servant to receive?**

We see other classic characteristics of the servant coming out in Moses' leadership of the people. Every gift has its flash point. There will be something that absolutely sets it off. For the servant, a major flash point is whining, complaining, and ungratefulness. What a challenge that was for Moses with the Israelites! The wilderness seemed to bring those qualities out in waves.

In **Exodus 16:6-8**, we get the response of Moses to the complaints of the Israelites:

> *Then Moses and Aaron said to all the children of Israel, "At evening you shall know that the LORD has brought you out of the land of Egypt. And in the morning you shall see the glory of the LORD; for He hears your complaints against the LORD. But what are we, that you complain against us?" Also Moses said, "This shall be seen when the LORD gives you meat to eat in the evening, and in the*

morning bread to the full; for the LORD hears your complaints which you make against Him. And what are we? Your complaints are not against us but against the LORD."

Notice how Moses almost seems to take these complaints personally. It is hard for a servant not to take them personally. Servants pride themselves in being able to bear the load and to do so without complaining. In fact, they often press too long and too hard. They ignore the warning signs their bodies give them and don't stop until there is a price to pay physically.

As do all the gifts, servants tend to think others should be like them. They think others should bear the load quietly. They do, however, want to be noticed and thanked for their sacrifice. They have a kind of natural insecurity because of their tendency to be isolated in their tasks. They feel much better about themselves if they can elicit some kind of appreciation for their work, but definitely would never ask for that appreciation. Thus they value appreciation and hate complaining.

If you want to bless a servant, thank him or her for a job well done. If you want to turn them off, complain. Imagine how hard it was for Moses to put up with the complaints of the people! Without Moses' daily trips to the tabernacle to dwell in the presence of God, I doubt that he would have made

If you want to bless a servant, thank him or her for a job well done.

it. Instead, incident after incident was an opportunity for Moses to grow in his character and in his leadership. He was dying to self with these daily tests—tests of the severest kind to the heart of a servant. But while dying to self, he was also drinking in the very character and nature of God.

- ## What does it mean to be a loadbearer? What causes servants to exhibit this trait?

Servants also have the tendency of trying to carry the load for others. Sooner or later, this becomes unbearable. In *Exodus 17:4b,* Moses is about to crack from the strain and says to God, *"What shall I do with this people? They are almost ready to stone me!"* God has to remind Moses that He is still the One in charge. He is still the One carrying the load. When we try to carry the load ourselves, we become loadbearers. We become cranky, compulsive, and generally hard to live with. God wants us to carry the load *with* His help. When we do that, we are true servants.

If a job needs to be done, a servant wouldn't think of asking someone else to do the job; he simply does it himself. This is evident to Jethro who counsels Moses to change his ways. Moses had been out judging the people from sun up to sun down. This is not good for Moses. It is not good for the people. Moses can't do it all alone, but he definitely tried.

Servants are prone to spiritual pride in the task area. Because they are especially good at task, they often feel like no one else can do a job as well as they can and that "if you want a job done right, you have to do it yourself." For them, this is often true because they don't fully communicate instructions or desires. Rather than working through the difficulty of communication, they choose to retreat and do it "by myself."

Again, this is a fleshly tendency. God wants to bring us together as a body. Anyone who isolates himself, seeks his own desire *(Prov. 18:10)*. Isolation is selfishness. Spiritual gifts are not given to help us become more selfish! We must learn to depend on God and to walk with Him—which often means depending on others instead of doing the job by yourself.

• What are the outcomes of continually stuffing things?

Servants have a tremendous need to feel appreciated. As such, they will often go above and beyond the call of duty. If that appreciation is never felt, sooner or later an explosion of bitterness will come as it did for Moses in **Numbers 20:10**. In this passage Moses strikes the rock even though he has been told by God to speak to the rock. His anger spills over to the point where he disobeys God, and because of this disobedience, Moses is not allowed to go into the Promised Land.

Because servants hate contention, they will tend to stuff things inside for as long as they can. In this instance, Moses had dealt with the lack of appreciation of the people over and over again. He had absolutely taken all he could stand, and he exploded.

Explosions of the servant tend to come in the private world of family and close friends.

This is very typical of a servant. They tend to be the "meekest man in all the earth" day after day. They are the model citizens of the relationship world, always being polite and never creating conflict. Most of the time, the explosions of the servant tend to come in the private world of family and close friends. Thus, it is a total shock and generally unbelievable to the general public that the servant could actually ever explode. But it happens.

In fact, it is almost inevitable. Frequently, the servant will direct the explosion at an object and not at the source of frustration. Moses does this by striking the rock. But the impact on those around is no different than if the explosion had been right at the people. In fact, because the explosion is so unexpected, it tends to be traumatic for those who observe it.

After the explosion, servants usually try to go on as if it never happened. Moses repeatedly approaches God to get the judgment of not going into the Promised Land overturned. Because the explosion is for such a brief moment in time, servants seem to feel that it should be disregarded as being a moment "out of character." What those around them know is that the stuffing process has already begun again, and that the next explosion is inevitable.

• What does the servant need to do to stay healthy?

The only solution for the servant to change this pattern of build up, blow up, and then try to go on as if it never happened is to truly become relational. In other words, they need to talk about their frustrations—something which they hate to do. They need someone who is more communicative and confrontational to help them move to the more balanced lifestyle of a walk with God.

When servants get a chance to shine for a time with some good work, they tend to overdo until bitterness sets in from the heaviness of the load. Because they are not verbal and because they hate open contention, it is not unusual for servants to still be holding a grudge from as many as 50 years earlier.

The combination of the physical effects of bitterness and the carrying of extreme loads that they should not be carrying makes them prone to prolonged and often painful illnesses. This is even made worse since they usually suffer in silence for as long as they possibly can take it, which for the servant is a long, long time. Ironically, the servant who most quickly feels the pain of others, is the worst about admitting his own.

The servant needs to learn to interact with the other gifts, freely expressing what is going on inside. Actually, servants often seem to be great communicators because they are so good at talking about the "normal" things of life. They can go on for hours about the intricate details of jobs and the practical stuff of life. On the other hand, if you ask them to talk about feelings and the more intimate emotions of relationship, they suddenly become tongue-tied. Unless they press through the discomfort to communicate what is on the inside, the stuffing process is happening despite the many words they are speaking.

> **Servants often seem to be great communicators.**

Some servants actually adopt frequent explosions as a manner of expressing what is happening inside. Of course this is unhealthy and results in family relationships that resemble the remains left after a raging fire. For the servant, these outbursts are embarrassing and feel very out of character. They always regret them, are uncomfortable processing them, and seldom are willing to talk about the outbursts or the cause of the outbursts. They just want to go on with life as if it had never happened. Moses tried that approach, but God did not let him off the hook. Servants hope to forget contention points as quickly as possible, which means not talking about it. Of course, not talking about it only means it will be repeated even sooner.

The key, then, is for servants to freely express what is going on inside them in a kind of "safe" zone, where a level of agitation is tolerated and even encouraged by those around them. If expressed in a "safe" zone with those they love, it can be fully released and never needs to get to the point of explosion. If stuffed, it becomes dangerous.

Moses had a safe zone with God in his daily trips to the tabernacle. He also could have had a safe zone with Aaron or others around him. When servants learn to share the more intimate things with others, they usually learn that they really are appreciated after all and that others are also willing to help out if they know there is a need. Others just couldn't see the need until the servant already had the job done.

Servants bring to the body the challenge to live the Christian lifestyle. For servants, one of the greater difficulties is connecting with God and others, but when they do, the results are incredible. Just look at Moses as an example. Moses, servant of the Lord. When we walk with God, great things happen.

Snapshot of the Servant

Remember: Core values actually come from multiple sources, so it is possible that you may have some of a core value but not fully line up with that gift. The gifts in this character category also have overlapping traits with other gifts. Look for the basic motivation behind character traits to see if your deepest core value lines up with this gift. Mark any items that fit who you are. Your gift should have the most items marked on these snapshots.

Passion: Living life to meet needs; working in this life to produce and to bless others; greatly value appreciation.

Primary fears: Not being capable to handle life and relationship situations; they fear conflict or tension in relationships; can struggle with a sense of inadequacy in communication and relationship.

Spiritual connection/voice of God: Hearing God is difficult especially in any verbal sense; God's voice is more of an inspiration for better real time living; it is an encouraging presence; there is a sense of being connected with God but is hard to describe or put into words; they often attach God's moving to tangible activities or things (i.e. Moses' rod).

Relationship characteristics: They greatly value the "family" which can consist of true family and close friends but generally struggle with any situation where emotions are being expressed; they want emotions to be intuitively understood and not spoken about; prefer to live more in the world of appreciation; in a way, they like everyone to be more equal in status (horizontal relationships) but actually are more vertical as they like to know their place in the order of things; the fact that they place a high value on respect puts them more in the vertical relationship category—but not too vertical or it becomes uncomfortable for them.

Conflict: They despise conflict; they will devise entire systems to minimize and structure all conflict so that any outward display of emotions can be minimized.

Task orientation: They prefer to work alone; hate to ask others to do anything thinking it will bother them; feel almost a sense of superiority in terms of being able to handle great tasks alone and as such will often go the extra mile but not always in a way that is good.

Possessions: Tend to be very important to them both in terms of efficiency—tools to do the job, and status—a sign of having been productive and thus successful in life; the physical realm actually takes on a spiritual importance to servants.

Activity for Understanding

Who do you know that seems to fit the picture described in the servant gift?

Self, Mother

What part of the picture of the servant gift fits you well? (If it is only a few traits, check out other gifts that might have similar traits!) *All 7 fit*

What values of the servant seemed uncomfortable to you as a value "created by God"?

① Sense of inedquacy   ③ Hate asking for help
② Hearing God is difficult

Is that value uncomfortable to you because you are seeing the sinful side being expressed or because it is in contrast to what feels right to you?

Seing sinful

Who do you know that you have "despised" or at least devalued that may actually be acting on an internal value created by God as seen in the servant?

Self

Have some close friends identify those parts of the servant description that fit you well. List results:

The Teacher: "Get Understanding!"

Chapter 6

Proverbs 16:16

How much better to get wisdom than gold!
And to get understanding is to be chosen rather than silver.

- ## How would different values lead to a different approach on a church work day?

The core value for the teacher is understanding. The contrast with the servant's core value is striking. The servant is ready to move beyond the time of instructing to the things that really matter—getting the job done. Instruction is what matters to the teacher. It is more important than gold or silver. It is to be sought after more than any prized possession. It is the beginning of everything that matters.

Perhaps by now, you can see the potential clashes just waiting to happen. On a church work day, the teacher would think it proper to start the day with a time of devotions. The servant would want to get to work. The teacher would want to step back and assess the situation to better understand all that needed to happen and then go about the job in a systematic way. The servant would want to find that part of the job that he or she was capable of handling and get after it.

> **We all have our own way of doing things. One is not necessarily superior to another—though in a given situation, one may be more effective than another.**

Different styles. Different values. Potential clashes—unless we understand and appreciate the core values of each of the gifts. We all have our own way of doing things. One is not necessarily superior to another—though in a given situation, one may be more effective than another. On the work day, taking a step back and making sure that you are doing the job right is often helpful. Taking too many looks can keep the job from getting done at all.

Each gift has its time and its place. Each gift is meant to spur others on to love and good works. The teacher is a gift to the body to encourage all of us to value the understanding that we can gain through the Word. The servant challenges us to put feet to that understanding. The prophet challenges us to seek the presence of God and to hear the voice of God. All three gifts need each other to complete the call. One is not better than the other. One is not complete without the other.

• What is the relationship between natural talents and spiritual gifts?

There is perhaps no better gift to demonstrate the correlation between the natural and the spiritual than the gift of the teacher. Some people are more dominated by emotion, some by intellect, and some by will. Others are a relatively balanced mixture of the three or maybe of two of the three.

So does that mean that every person who is dominated by intellect is a teacher? The answer is "No." There is not a one to one relationship between the natural ability to think and the gift of being a teacher. Not all people with higher levels of intelligence are teachers and not all teachers have a higher level of intelligence. However, there is a correlation!

Having the spiritual gift of a teacher is not a question of intellectual ability so much as it is a core value. Teachers value understanding. Accordingly, they will put time and effort into understanding which means that in most cases they will come off as being intelligent in an area. Whatever talent a person uses, he will grow in that talent. If he exercises his intellect, it will grow. If he exercises his practical skills, those too will grow.

• As we study the gifts, where should our emphasis be?

The key to the body of Christ functioning in unity is for each of the gifts to value the other gifts in the body. When this happens, each of the gifts will learn and grow from the strengths of the other gifts. By giving proper value to other gifts, each gift will moderate itself so that it comes forth much more in the timing and the manner that God intended. The teachers will grow in the practical, and the servants will grow in devotional life and understanding.

It is not talent that typically puts a lid on where we can go so much as it is value. If we value something, we focus on it. If we focus on an area, we will grow in that area. We must each learn to value all of the gifts that God has created!

Too often, a study of the gifts promotes just the opposite of learning to value the gifts of others. We read about the gifts to find out who we are, and then we focus totally upon that area. While it is good for us to grow in our own area of gifting, it is better for us to learn to value the other gift areas and to develop a more multi-faceted personality. It is good to enjoy your own value area. It is better to see the whole picture and value and celebrate the body of Christ as a whole.

• If the Holy Spirit is doing the speaking, why do each of the Biblical authors demonstrate their own unique personality?

Ezra, in the Old Testament, and Luke, in the New Testament, are both clear examples of teachers. In *Ezra chapters 1-2*, we get an immediate feel for the writing of a teacher. These chapters are loaded with factual details and rather lacking in emotions. This too brings up an interesting point. We believe that the Bible was written through inspiration. God guided the writers to pen His thoughts for us in the Word of God. Even so, we clearly see the personalities of the writers of the Old and New Testament come out in the writing. How can this be? If the writing is inspired, why do we see the personality of the writer?

The Holy Spirit never replaces the spirit of the individual. He illuminates the spirit of the individual. **Romans 8:16** implies a coming alongside, a bearing witness. One of the names for the Holy Spirit is paraclete or one who comes alongside. The Holy Spirit guides, energizes, and gives some shape to an individual, but He does not dominate nor replace the individual.

Thus, a teacher still looks like a teacher, and it is a unique representation of an aspect of the character of God. A servant looks like a servant and that too is in the image of God, even as two siblings can both look very different from each other and yet both look very much like their parents. This is the miracle of God manifesting Himself through many different children, each unique and yet each one completely in His image.

- ### How does Ezra's writing demonstrate that words matter to the teacher?

Teachers want to know everything about everything. They value understanding and have a great capacity to gather and remember information. Details, details, and more details are the hallmark of a teacher in any area that they consider important. No fact or idea is too small or too unimportant to be included.

As such, they often fit the absent minded professor type. They begin with a wonderful sense of organization, but soon losing the feel of being organized in an overwhelming sea of detail. They really are very logical people, though sometimes they are hard to follow as they work from general to specific much the way an outline would. The only problem is one good detail leads to another and soon the pattern of logic is overridden by the concentration on interesting facts and figures.

Words are the pathway to understanding and are to be taken very seriously.

In the book of **Ezra**, the feel of the teacher begins almost immediately. Teachers value the Word of God, and Ezra begins by referencing the prophet Jeremiah who prophesied the return of the captives to Jerusalem after 70 years of captivity. Words and decrees matter to the teacher. Words are the pathway to understanding and are to be taken very seriously. Even the words of the pagan king are serious to the teacher as Ezra quotes the decree of Cyrus. Words that are written down seem to take on an even greater significance.

Then it begins. Details. Ezra lists how many platters, basins, and knives were being returned to Jerusalem. He lists all of the people who were returning by family with a specific count of how many there were. He also listed those who were returning but who could not verify their Jewish heritage through the registry that existed at the time, noting that, **"These sought their listing among those who were registered by genealogy, but they were not found; therefore they were excluded from the priesthood as defiled. And the** *governor said to them that they should not eat of the most holy things till a priest could consult with the Urim and Thummim" (Ezra 2:62-63).*

In the passage above, we see Ezra first consulting the registry of the genealogy. If a family could not prove its heritage in writing, it was not acceptable to simply take the word of the family's oral tradition. Everything was put on hold for these families until the priest could be consulted with the casting of lots. God had given the Israelites the Urim and the Thummim as a means of deciding any conflicts in a "Yes" or "No" manner. Where the written word was not clear, Ezra sought out an authoritative source.

• How do teachers respond to authority figures?

Teachers very much respond to authority. If we picture a teacher in a classroom, there is a definite sense of a person who understands the need for vertical relationships. The teacher teaches. The students listen. The teacher is informed. The students are not. There is need for the teacher to be held in esteem by the students. Therefore, the teacher and the student cannot be on a level playing field.

Because of this fact, teachers somewhat instinctively fit into either the role of the teacher or the role of the student. Often, those around a teacher will feel like they are being treated like a child. They see the teacher as being intellectual, aloof, and thinking that he is better than everyone else. The teacher does not actually think of himself as being better than others but does place a high priority on the one with the better information. And if he happens to be the one with the better information, he is the one who should control the flow of the situation. If not, he is quite at ease to sit in the seat of the learner.

Often, those around a teacher will feel like they are being treated like a child.

Those who are more relational, especially those who want to have more horizontal relationships (everyone equal and on a level playing field), can easily be offended by the teacher. Again, the teacher means nothing demeaning by his more vertical approach to relationships. In fact, the teacher is generally oblivious to any slights because relationship is low on his values scale as compared to information and understanding. A teacher's closest friends tend to be those who place a high value on a quality exchange of ideas.

• What appears to be arrogance in the teacher? Why does it come across this way?

The seeming arrogance of the teacher is not really arrogance so much as it is simply living in a completely different world. In fact, one of the few times Ezra ever shows a sense of emotion is toward "the children":

> *Then I proclaimed a fast there at the river of Ahava, that we might humble ourselves before our God, to seek from Him the right way for us and our little ones and all our possessions (Ezra 8:21).*

Notice the term *"little ones."* This is a term of endearment. While it is not unusual for teachers to come off with a kind of vertical feel, the teacher also feels almost a parent-like sense of responsibility toward those he is teaching. Along with this sense is a very real emotional attachment, even if it does tend to be expressed with the more functional feel of information exchanges most of the time.

In the mind of the teacher, he is just doing what comes natural. He is teaching students. For many people, being treated like a student feels like they are being treated like a child. They feel like they are being talked down to. What the teacher means to be a positive message of "you are one of my students" is taken as if it were belittling.

- **What does humility look like in a teacher? How does that way of thinking come across to others?**

As vertical people, teachers often see themselves as a tiny speck on the evolutionary scale of knowledge. They are not vertical toward their students to make them feel small, but they see themselves as being a tiny dot in the writings of history. It is the way they think. Again, some take this more vertical feel of the teacher as if they were being personally insulted. Those who do are completely missing the heart of the teacher.

The vertical feel of teacher is frequently not arrogance so much as it is perspective. The teacher understands his "small" place in the scheme of things and he thinks it only normal and right that others should also understand their place in things. The teacher is responding to that internal value of being a keeper of knowledge. Teachers feel a sense of worth when they step into that role of being the guardian of a very important treasure.

- **When does the message of the teacher actually become arrogant?**

In *1 Corinthians 8:1b*, it says, ***"We know that we all have knowledge. Knowledge puffs up, but love edifies."*** In the middle of that verse is the simple statement, ***"Knowledge puffs up."*** There is not much room for exception in that statement. Those who gain knowledge will struggle with pride. Teachers struggle with pride. When a teacher is walking in pride because he has a sense of having better information, the message he sends to others will carry the spiritual feel of arrogance with his words. Sometimes it just feels like arrogance. Sometimes it actually is arrogance.

For the teacher to send a message of humility, there has to be a proper understanding of God's role in his life. Solomon was the wisest man perhaps in all of history (aside from Jesus!). Even so, what was the end result of having all that wisdom? It was turned to futility and foolishness. From the moment that he made covenants with foreign kings for peace and married foreign wives, his downfall was set in motion. When he stopped obeying God and built temples for idols in order to satisfy the foreign wives, his insights became corrupted. He still appeared to have unbelievable wisdom, but godly wisdom is much better than worldly wisdom.

Obedience comes before true godly wisdom. There is a kind of "this world" information that is practical that can be effective … but that wisdom builds arrogance. There is a kind of wisdom that knows it must stay connected to God to stay in a place of being accurate. That kind of wisdom sends a message of humility with its words.

In **Psalm 119:100**, the psalmist says, ***"I understand more than the ancients, because I keep Your precepts."*** Since the fall of man, the ego of man tends to color his thinking. Those who obey God find it much easier to think His thoughts, to fully get what He is saying. Notice, I said "what He is saying." Teachers can easily get caught up in the flow of their own thoughts. Our greatest strength is our greatest weakness. We are most tempted to depend on self in the place of our greatest strength. The teacher easily believes he doesn't need to hear the voice of God to know truth. He can figure it out on His own. Arrogance.

In **Isaiah 55:9**, God declares that ***"So are My ways higher than your ways, and My thoughts than your thoughts."*** When the teacher loses his awareness that he needs God to guide his thoughts, the end result will be arrogance. Period. It happens. The teacher's mind will run from one thought to the next, with little or no guidance from God. A blind spot soon develops because the teacher is thinking his thoughts and is not being guided by God.

> **When the teacher loses his awareness that he needs God to guide his thoughts, the end result will be arrogance.**

It is hard for a teacher to see when he has left God behind because his mind works so quickly. When his mind takes off in this way, his spirit will start to radiate arrogance. Because teachers are not overly relational, the teacher often doesn't notice when others have started responding to the arrogance of his message. He won't see it but others will feel it in his message.

- ## How do logic and authority work together in the mind of a teacher?

For the teacher, the written word is the ultimate authority. They have an instinctive connection to the eternal and unchangeable law of God, because that is how they think and who they are. They are wired for the more fixed logic of absolute truth. That same logical nature also causes them to relate well to the idea of civil law. In **Ezra 4**, Ezra is not willing to see the building of the temple stop until he gets written word from King Artaxerxes. Oral threats had little impact on him. A written command brought the building to a halt.

Teachers seem to instinctively know that knowledge without application is futile, but the application that they hope for is a universal and fair application of truth to all. Thus, even the decrees of a king that seem to go against the decrees of God have to be taken seriously. There must be a more universal application of the law. Knowledge must be intertwined with authority.

In the mind of a teacher, the order that comes from law is one of the greatest hopes for society. Where there is law, there can be a Golden Rule type of fairness that is our best chance of showing mercy toward all men. Otherwise, people do as they wish, and the world is plunged into chaos. As you might guess, the teacher's idea of mercy is very different from a true mercy person. For the teacher, mercy comes through the law, not apart from it.

- ## How does a teacher build confidence in an interpretation of the Word of God?

Because of the important place the teachers give to knowledge, they will spend extended amounts of time researching the thoughts of the masters of the ages. Extra biblical sources are likely to be more important to teachers, because they have the ability to read and comprehend so much more data than most. They desire to get the best interpretation of God's Word and seek out any input that might help guide them toward that goal.

In the same way, the traditions of the fathers tend to be honored by teachers unless there is some definitive statement in the written Word to challenge that tradition. The Pharisees were likely dominated by those with a teaching gift. Traditions, even down to the minute detail, had become the hallmark of the Pharisees. They had the application of the law down to a rigorous and detailed science.

The fathers of the faith had decided how far a person could walk, what he could carry, and even when spitting was considered working on the Sabbath.

One of the best examples of this is in how they taught we were to observe the Sabbath. The fathers of the faith had decided how far a person could walk, what he could carry, and even when spitting was considered working on the Sabbath. Jesus mocked their interpretations with many of His miracles, showing that they had gone beyond the intent of the law. The greatest strength of a gift becomes its greatest weakness.

Every gift is prone to go too far in its own gifting. We see our talents and we choose to depend on our talents instead of depending on and following God Himself. The Pharisees had done that. They had become the epitome of the gift of the teacher gone bad. The traditions of the fathers had become more important than the Word itself. This led them into legalism and then blindness toward God.

In the very same way, all of the gifts when left to themselves, will run into all kinds of grievous error. I believe that the greatest errors committed in the body of Christ are when people run too far with their area of gifting. By comparison, the number and type of mistakes we make in our areas of weakness are minimal. We need to learn to value gifts other than our own to help keep us from this error of becoming extreme in our own gift area. We need each other to walk in truth, to walk in the image of Christ.

- ## What does it look like when teachers are responding emotionally?

Even how teachers describe things can be unique:

> *Though fear had come upon them because of the people of those countries, they set the altar on its bases; and they offered burnt*

offerings on it to the LORD, both the morning and evening burnt offerings (Ezra 3:2-3).

Most of the time, when people talk about fear, there is a strong sense of emotion in the way the wording is phrased. Instead, the tone here is very matter of fact. Fear is just a detail to be included but is not worthy of any more focus than any other point of information. If a teacher is a male, and his wife is a person who values emotions and needs emotional nurture, this kind of matter of fact tone can get him in trouble in a hurry!

> **Fear is just a detail to be included but is not worthy of any more focus than any other point of information.**

Teachers have a hard time dealing with emotional situations. It just doesn't feel right to them. In their world, emotions should be given a lower place. The higher value is understanding. Emotions can get in the way of this value. Listen as Ezra describes a very emotional scene:

> *But many of the priests and Levites and heads of the fathers' houses, old men who had seen the first temple, wept with a loud voice when the foundation of this temple was laid before their eyes. Yet many shouted aloud for joy, so that the people could not discern the noise of the shout of joy from the noise of the weeping of the people, for the people shouted with a loud shout, and the sound was heard afar off (Ezra 3:12-13).*

Emotional reactions are simply recorded as if they were the facts of the situation. They are merely one element of information that might need to be taken into consideration. For those who value emotions, this approach often seems dead and lifeless. At best it is uninspiring, and at worst it is harmful.

Teachers don't mean to be distant, cool, or cruel. However, for the teacher to begin to value the more emotional areas, it very well may have to come through the intellectual lobe of their brains first. They may have to factually see the need to function more on an emotional level before they begin to develop the value. Once the logical need is seen, it is much easier for a teacher to choose to increase his level of function in the area of emotions. The teacher does not lack emotions but typically will suppress them because he thinks intellectual function is living in a manner that is expressing a higher values system.

We do see Ezra react with a high level of emotion in *Ezra 9*. It happened when Ezra found out that the people of the land had taken wives outside of the Jewish nation—wives who were not believers in the most High God. This behavior was very serious as it had been a major part of Israel being sent into captivity just a few years earlier. Listen to Ezra's response:

> *So when I heard this thing, I tore my garment and my robe, and plucked out some of the hair of my head and beard, and sat down astonished. Then everyone who trembled at the words of the God of Israel assembled to me, because of the transgression of those who had been carried away captive, and I sat astonished until the evening sacrifice (Ezra 9:3-4).*

When the law is directly broken, it is almost as if the teacher feels the whole world is going through an implosion. For the teacher, this is the kind of event that sparks emotions. He sat down, *"astonished until the evening sacrifice."*

Our character gift is a kind of internal valuing mechanism that goes off according to how it is designed. The teacher has emotions. He just has them at different times and in different ways than the other gifts. The teacher is wary of anyone being led by emotions, but will embrace those emotions when they are in response to a clear breaking of the written Word. Each of the gifts thinks differently, feels differently, and chooses differently.

- **How does the "hearing" of God for the teacher differ from other gifts?**

Teachers hear differently too. God approached Moses, the servant, with tangible objects and symbols to better communicate with him. God just spoke to Elijah. With Ezra, there is only the written word. In *Ezra 7:10*, it tells us: *"For Ezra had prepared his heart to seek the Law of the LORD, and to do it, and to teach statutes and ordinances in Israel."* Teachers hear best by reading, studying, coming to a sense of what fits the total picture, and then resting in the "voice of the Lord."

When I ask teachers about their ability to "hear" God, it can be a touchy subject. They almost bristle because the written Word must be supreme over any subjectively heard "word from God." But they also bristle because the "voice" is usually so tied up with their own logical flow that they feel a bit unsure of themselves in "hearing" God.

- **Though administration is not a core part of the teacher, in what way do they seem to be administrators?**

In *chapter 10*, we get a picture of the administrative side of the teacher. Even though Ezra was highly incensed over what had happened, he was willing to take months to get it sorted out if that is what it took to handle the situation fairly and down to the last detail.

Because they look at relationships from a vertical perspective, they do have administrative ability. However, their need to be very precise in all things will drive a true administrator nuts because it is so inefficient. The teacher's version of administration is far too detailed for the true administrator.

- **When are teachers especially hard on sin? When do they respond in a way that "gives others a break"?**

The verse in *Ezra 7:10* is worth repeating because it gives us the classic picture of a teacher: *"For Ezra had prepared his heart to seek the Law of the LORD, and to do it, and to teach statutes and ordinances in Israel."* Ezra prepared his heart to "seek the Law of the Lord." It was his value. He had a heart both to do and to teach the law, and he did so in a manner that many of us might find a bit meticulous. For the teacher, that is life. It is neither meticulous nor tiring but is fulfilling.

In *chapter 9:4*, Ezra joins with those who *"tremble"* at the law having been broken. That "trembling" can often cause them to team up with the prophets in challenging sin. However, there also can be an almost ironic trait in both prophets and teachers in the way they treat children. Though both are normally severe towards evil as they define it, both also seem to see young children as unable to live up to the standard. As a result, they see the child as not being fully responsible for his own actions.

I've seen some normally strict people be totally excusing of incredible things, especially in their own children. Then at some magical age, the axe falls. The child is now old enough and suddenly is held to absolute responsibility. The sudden change often breeds rebellion in the child because of the sudden change. A more healthy approach holds children accountable for whatever is appropriate at each particular age and stage.

• What helps teachers stay in a healthy place?

Teachers need to learn the need for individual variation and for various applications of a single principle. Teachers often want a universal application of the law even as the Pharisees did. While the principle of honoring the Sabbath needs to stand universally, the application of that law has to vary from one situation to the next. For a teacher, these variations as well as the contrasting ideas of the paradoxes of Scripture are difficult to leave untouched. They want to find a way to simplify them to one universally applied standard. At times, it cannot be done. Our God is too complex to be fully understood by logic.

Teachers need to allow these seeming contradictions to stand side by side. They are a reflection of the infinite God that we love and serve. Love and support of the individual must be a constant point of emphasis, lest the very ones they seek to help become the very ones they hurt. Otherwise, in their zeal to get understanding, they will lose the very thing they think they are finding. After all, understanding is only understanding when it reflects the heart of God, and our God is a God of love.

What seems like a contradiction can be a reflection of the infinite God that we love and serve.

By now, you should be better able to see the need for each of the gifts. We desperately need each other. We cannot just major on the gift that God has given us, but true understanding needs to see and honor others even more than we honor ourselves. When we do, we will learn to walk in His life. Logic will take its place. Hearing from God will have priority and so will living the life. The teacher values understanding, but when understanding becomes *the* value of life, it loses its way. May we all learn from the teacher, and may the teacher learn from all of us!

Snapshot of the Teacher

Remember: *Core values actually come from multiple sources, so it is possible that you may have some of a core value but not fully line up with that gift. The gifts in this character category also have overlapping traits with other gifts. Look for the basic motivation behind character traits to see if your deepest core value lines up with this gift. Mark any items that fit who you are. Your gift should have the most items marked on these snapshots.*

Passion: Getting understanding; seeing how things work; fair and equitable application of the written Word or a policy manual; training the "children" (not just physical children but spiritual children).

Primary fears: Making a mistake; not having a handle on a subject; not maintaining respect or control—especially in a teaching/learning environment; not doing things properly; emotionalism.

Spiritual connection/voice of God: The experiential sense of hearing God is more difficult for them; they tend to hear God as a result of a thorough study of God's Word with a right application that seems to "fit" the situation; it is this "fit" that becomes the subjective hearing for the teacher; they prefer order and right application as the voice of God.

Relationship characteristics: They have a deep sense of connectedness to the "little ones" or ones who need to be taught or nurtured; tend to be on a more practical, non-emotional basis with those who are horizontal in relationship; prefer to be either the teacher or the learner; like a clear ordering of who is in charge; they have deep emotions but find it hard to express them or to even admit them with anyone other than an inner circle.

Conflict: Conflict is almost irrelevant or not noticed by the teacher; it is viewed as either an obstacle to or a vehicle to understanding; if it is an obstacle, it is an enemy to be dealt with; if it is a vehicle, it is embraced as a way to bring growth.

Task orientation: Doing the job the right way *after* it is fully researched is the mode of operation for the teacher; they can be slow to get to practical tasks but usually are thorough, almost bordering on perfectionists once they do get to the task; they can bog down in the middle of their tasks, needing to be rescued by a less detailed/more efficient person.

Possessions: Because ideas are most important, some of the most important possessions for teachers are their books; where teachers see practical value, possessions can be important but usually are not overly significant in their lives.

Activity for Understanding

Who do you know that seems to fit the picture described in the teacher gift?

What part of the picture of the teacher gift fits you well? (If it is only a few traits, check out other gifts that might have similar traits!)

What values of the teacher seemed uncomfortable to you as a value "created by God"?

Is that value uncomfortable to you because you are seeing the sinful side being expressed or because it is in contrast to what feels right to you?

Who do you know that you have "despised" or at least devalued that may actually be acting on an internal value created by God as seen in the teacher?

Have some close friends identify those parts of the teacher description that fit you well. List results:

The Exhorter: Taking on the Challenge

Chapter 7

- **How does the idea of "all things to all people" explain the heart of an exhorter?**

So far, we have been studying character gifts that are relatively clear types. A prophet is a prophet. A servant is a servant. A teacher is a teacher. But an exhorter is ... "who knows?" That is because the value of the exhorter is to exhort, to come alongside another and to encourage. One who is really good at coming along side will largely lose himself in order to connect with another person. The end result is that the exhorter is all over the map, depending on who he is with at any given moment.

I'm not sure if Paul was an exhorter, but Paul's statement of **"I have become all things to all men" (1 Cor. 9:22)** typifies the heart of an exhorter. Without a doubt, Paul had some of the teaching gift, but it is almost impossible to tell whether Paul's teaching gift was a character gift or a calling.

The **"I have become all things to all men"** statement makes me think that he was an exhorter in character with a calling as a teacher. As we will see through this study, exhorters (and givers) are very hard to pin down. Just when you think you have them figured out, something comes along that seems to totally contradict everything you were thinking. That is part of why I think Paul may be an exhorter. You never know quite what to expect with Paul.

The biblical example that we will use to learn more about exhorters is David. He is a classic exhorter, from being a "man after God's own heart," to being a passionate worshiper, to taking on the impossible challenges. Exhorters are people of passion ... but in a way having no passion at all. *PASSIONATE ONE MOMENT UN PASSIONATE THE NEXT*

> **Exhorters often find themselves lacking in direction for their own lives.**

Exhorters often find themselves lacking in direction for their own lives and wondering just where God is leading them. Because of this, there are times when they don't seeming to have an identifiable passion. Again, it is important to remember that they tend to live their lives through others. In the modern world, they are coaches, whether athletic or personal who try to bring out the best in others.

- ## What is it that gets an exhorter excited about life?

In *1 Samuel 17*, we see David gearing up for a challenge with Goliath. He's just a kid comparatively, but that doesn't stop him. He's not a trained soldier, but that is no obstacle. Exhorters are visionaries. They love a challenge. They thrive when overcoming problems or taking on the impossible. It takes vision to take on the impossible. Normal, everyday life takes little vision and is ho hum for the exhorter. The impossible … now that is fun.

Once a challenge appears, and an exhorter gets pulled into the challenge, it is almost impossible to get him to back off. David brushes off the ridicule of his brothers and keeps on going:

> *Now Eliab his oldest brother heard when he spoke to the men; and Eliab's anger was aroused against David, and he said, "Why did you come down here? And with whom have you left those few sheep in the wilderness? I know your pride and the insolence of your heart, for you have come down to see the battle."* **MIS UNDERSTOOD SLANDERED**
>
> *And David said, "What have I done now? Is there not a cause?"* **OTHERS BEFORE SELF**
> *Then he turned from him toward another and said the same thing; and these people answered him as the first ones did (1 Sam. 17:28-30).*

Normally, exhorters are very sensitive to what others are thinking or saying. Most of the time, they live to please others. In the midst of an "impossible" challenge, that is all brushed aside.

- ## How do exhorters go about decision making?

Listening to these verses, it would seem like David was a very single-minded, knows-where-he-is-going kind of person. Actually, nine times the Scriptures record the phrase "David inquired of the Lord." On the one hand, that would seem to be a very noble trait for David in that he was very dependent on God. While exhorters can seem to be dependent personalities, the more accurate picture is that they put off the decision until the last possible moment, waiting for the last little bit of information to come in before they make up their minds.

However, when chasing the impossible, all of that changes. Exhorters suddenly morph into a single-focused person, often coming across as a very proud, insolent, or stubborn person as they refuse to take no for an answer. The exhorter typically would be bouncing from one thing to the next, totally open to input and always ready to change course. But when taking on a tough challenge, all of that changes. They become focused for a time even to the point of turning people off. When King Saul questions him, he doesn't show even the slightest bit of doubt:

But David said to Saul, "Your servant used to keep his father's sheep, and when a lion or a bear came and took a lamb out of the flock, I went out after it and struck it, and delivered the lamb from its mouth; and when it arose against me, I caught it by its beard, and struck and killed it. Your servant has killed both lion and bear; and this uncircumcised Philistine will be like one of them, seeing he has defied the armies of the living God." Moreover David said,"The LORD, who delivered me from the paw of the lion and from the paw of the bear, He will deliver me from the hand of this Philistine" (1 Sam 17:34-37a).

David doesn't show even the slightest bit of self doubt. He is totally focused, rehearsing the victories that God has given him from the past. His brothers are certainly turned off by this about-face they are seeing from him, but King Saul is not. In fact, he puts the future of the nation in David's hands with his simple response to David of **"Go, and the LORD be with you!" (v. 37)**.

• What makes the exhorter persuasive to others?

This passage also illustrates the ability of exhorters to win others over. Imagine David, only a young boy, being able to convince the King to put the fate of the nation in his hands. Goliath had proposed to the Israelites that if he won the battle with whomever the Israelites sent, the Israelites would agree to be subject to the Philistines.

What king in his right mind would have ever given David a chance to take on Goliath under those circumstances? But David's description of having killed the lion and the bear, along with his faith in God to bring deliverance, convinces Saul to put the fate of the nation in his hands.

Because they are motivators, exhorters are instinctively control persons. In the Goliath situation, David moves the heart of the king. Later on, when Saul wants David to wear his own coat of mail to face Goliath, David again takes charge saying, **"I cannot walk with these, for I have not tested them" (1 Sam. 17:39)**. Think of it. The kid tells the king how it is going to be, and the king goes along with it!

Exhorters generally are very subtle in the way they influence others.   When running for his life, David is quick to make up a story for Ahimelech about being on the king's business *(1 Sam. 21:2)*. When not walking with God, the ability an exhorter has to influence others very easily turns to manipulation.

> **When not walking with God, the ability the exhorter has to influence others very easily turns to manipulation.**

With King Saul, David was not subtle. An impossible challenge was before him, and he was very open and forward in his influencing style. In *1 Samuel 21*, David is much more crafty, hiding the fact that he was running from King Saul. He presents an image that is a lie in order to get what he wants. Later on, David would berate himself for what he had done.

• How do exhorters relate to authority figures? What do they look like as leaders?

Teachers and prophets influence others through a more vertical approach. They appeal to a sense of authority that is instinctive to them and which they think should be instinctive to others. Several of the gifts are more horizontal. They want all people to be treated as equals and the idea of one bringing influence from an over the top kind of position is instinctively offensive to them.

The exhorter is instinctively a more horizontal person. Most of the time, he will approach persons in a way that the person hardly knows that a request has even happened. The exhorter frequently makes the other person think that it has been his idea. In these instances, the exhorter could be described as being less than horizontal. He is invisible.

However, once again the "all things to all people" can easily take over. Just as David was very forward with Saul and then very subtle with Ahimelech, exhorters instinctively change to meet the values system of the person they are with. With a vertical person, they become vertical. With a horizontal person, they become horizontal. When they are with one of each, they become a bit schizophrenic!

Though natural leaders, the exhorter does not necessarily like the limelight. As is typical for the exhorter, this one can easily go either way. Perhaps more than any other gift, the exhorter is significantly shaped by the callings that we will discuss in the next section of the book. If an exhorter has a calling as a prophet, he becomes very verbal and very vertical very quickly. If an exhorter has a calling as a servant, he tends to be very quiet and behind the scenes. In other words, the exhorter part of the person often becomes quite invisible as it "comes alongside" the calling gift.

• What does the leadership/friendship of the exhorter look like?

Exhorters are leaders in that they love to influence others but not necessarily in a classic "leading" sense. Often, they blend in, almost to the point of not being noticed, but still are often subtly influencing the person or the situation. They virtually can't keep themselves from being an influencer, whether that influence takes on the role of servant or of leader. We see both of these in extreme with David and Saul. At times, David is excessively subservient. At other times, he virtually tells Saul what to do.

> **Exhorters virtually can't keep themselves from being an influencer, whether that influence takes on the role of servant or leader.**

That desire to be in control also tends to make them somewhat one way in their relationships. They are very much a people person and will do almost anything for others. But what they do for others, they often refuse to let others do for them. As such they remain somewhat aloof, distant, given to no one, but prefer to be equally distributed among all.

Again, this is a bit ironic. Because they are so totally given to relationships in general, others often feel very much loved by them. The friends of the exhorter often feel as if the exhorter is their absolute best friend. While exhorters do have close friends, they have an instinctive need to equally distribute their love to all who come near. As such, the idea of a "best" friend is difficult for them. They are great at giving to others in ways that make them feel very special, but they will try to do the same for everyone that they come in contact with. To the exhorter, that is just what you do. It is not necessarily meant as a sign of a special relationship.

In *1 Samuel 18*, we are told that Jonathan passionately loved David and entered into a covenant with him. The son of the King entered into a covenant with a peasant. Jonathan had everything to lose and very little to gain … but he loved David. I find it interesting that the Scriptures never say the reverse. It never talks about David's love for Jonathan. Even in David's lament for Jonathan, he says of Jonathan, ***"Your love to me was wonderful" (2 Sam. 1:26)***. Notice the direction.

It is very difficult for an exhorter to completely let go of the reins and just love another person. It is so ingrained in them to be the motivator and visionary that it is difficult for them to just let down and receive from others. Again, the contradiction. The one who is arguably (A) one of the best at relationship, in some ways could be the worst at developing close friends. The one who is the most open to all is, in a way, open to no one. (B)

• How does vision shape the exhorter's actions?

Exhorters also tend to turn their vision skills very much inward. They are excellent at visualizing all kinds of different approaches to situations, and the possible outcomes to those approaches. When David is thinking about challenging Goliath, he begins to focus on possible outcomes. David's reaction is described in *1 Samuel 17:26, "Then David spoke to the men who stood by him, saying, 'What shall be done for the man who kills this Philistine and takes away the reproach from Israel? For who is this uncircumcised Philistine, that he should defy the armies of the living God?'"*

While everyone else is intimidated by the size and ferocity of Goliath, David is already thinking about what would happen if he were somehow able to defeat the giant. When David is questioned by Saul, he talks about times when he had defeated a lion and a bear. He is already making a visual transfer from those events to seeing Goliath defeated. It is all about vision for an exhorter, and having seen a potential positive outcome, it is almost as good as done.

Those vision skills come in handy both in problem solving and in motivating others.

Exhorters have to hear themselves (or others) say something out loud before they can fully think it through and make a decision.

Exhorters are able to use imagination to preview hundreds of possibilities. Because they are flexible and able to see things from all points of view, they make great brainstormers. Not only that, they tend to be auditory external processors. In other words, they have to hear themselves (or others) say something out loud before they can fully think it through and make a decision. They love to take ideas and float them with a group of people to watch for reactions—they are very reactionary people. Life is about coming alongside others. It is about motivating others

Because they are visionaries, and because they tend to think of things they have visualized as already being done, they are easily misunderstood. What they put out as an idea to process together with a group, often is taken as a statement of fact by others. Typically, the exhorter is floating an idea and watching for reactions. To an exhorter, an idea is only as good as the reaction that it produces.

If a person is more vertical in the way he thinks, he will take the statement by the exhorter as an order from a superior and will then give appropriately respectful feedback, which in turn might be misinterpreted by the exhorter as support for the idea. Subordinates of an exhorter often run with ideas that are just tests and then are hurt when they find out that they are doing something meaningless to the exhorter. The misunderstanding that can come out of the exhorter's tendency to process out loud is huge!

- **What are some of the strengths and weaknesses of processing out loud?**

The Psalms are the product of the heart of an exhorter who is processing life experiences "out loud" before God and man. Often, we see David begin at a point of confusion or even fear or bitterness, and then we get the opportunity to "hear" him verbally process through to a surrender to God.

The vision of the exhorter may be internal, but working out of those visions almost has to be external. They have to hear themselves say it out loud to others and then watch and listen to the reactions of others to get to a point of peace.

Exhorters also use the outward verbal as a way to build their own courage to go forward. David appeared confident in the passage where he was convincing Saul of his ability to fight through the illustrations of him killing the lion and the bear. Actually, I think he needed to rehearse that information as much for himself as he did for Saul.

> **Exhorters also use the outward verbal as a way to build their own courage to go forward.**

Wanting to please all, an exhorter can easily be paralyzed at a point of inaction. As external processors, sometimes they need to hear themselves say things just to build their own courage. To others, the exhorter seems confident. Within themselves, it often is all they can do to stand against what they perceive to be the potential hostile reactions of others.

After all, they are visionaries. Visionaries can visualize positive outcomes and become very bold and decisive, or they can visualize very negative outcomes and shrink back and withdraw. The difference for an exhorter often lies in their ability to float ideas around others and to be able to see a positive response on the faces of those who are listening to them.

Exhorters do tend to study faces as a means of determining the "truth" of a situation. How can "truth" be based on faces? Because of the core value of an exhorter, reality is defined by people and their reactions. This would never make sense to a prophet or a teacher, but it makes perfect sense to an exhorter.

- ## How does the ongoing visualizing affect the way exhorters live?

Exhorters like to be original, like to do things in a way that they have worked out. David refuses the conventional body armor but chooses a stone and a sling for weapons. Exhorters like to be creative, to try new things even if it doesn't work out. That is part of the joy of learning how to more successfully take on problems. They have the ability to see failure as a stepping stone to future success and thus continue to look for new and better ways to move forward.

As mentioned before, these external processing skills and the zest for new things make them quite at home with a brainstorming session. These sessions simply allow them to do with others on a more grand scale what is regularly happening in their brain. Their minds tend to never stop, continually doing role plays with situations, continually working toward problem solving.

Because they love the impossible and problem solving situations, exhorters greatly value

Exhorters seek practical application of information toward problem solving.

knowledge, but it is a different kind of knowledge than the teacher would seek. Teachers love information for the sake of understanding. Exhorters seek practical application of information toward problem solving. If information is not readily usable, the exhorter is not overly interested, whereas the teacher values understanding no matter what a current situation might call for in a practical application.

When an event does finally play out, odds are good that the outcome has been anticipated by the exhorter in at least one of the internal scenarios that he has pictured. If the situation does not play out well, the exhorter usually has pictured that outcome as a possibility and then tends to be very hard on himself for not having adjusted his reaction sooner in order to get a different outcome.

- ## What does the perfectionism of an exhorter look like?

Simply put, exhorters are perfectionists. They are not perfectionist the way a servant would be a perfectionist. A servant will get it right down to the last detail in physical things. The car will be shining. The house will be immaculate. The meal exquisite. The value of the servant tends to be more in the area of physical things, and thus his perfectionism is in that area. The teacher is a perfectionist in information, the prophet in right and wrong, and the exhorter in relationships. He demands of himself that every word, every facial expression, even the innuendos be perfect. It is his value to be the perfect influencer, the perfect coach. When the response falls short, he will be very, very hard on himself.

We get a clear picture of this kind of reaction in *1 Samuel 22:22*. As described above, David had misled Ahimelech in order to get bread and to get the sword and spear of Goliath. David led Ahimelech to believe that he was serving Saul when he was actually running from him. When Saul found out that Ahimelech had helped David, he commissioned Doeg to kill all of the priests and the people at Nob.

In *1 Samuel 22:22*, Abiathar, the son of Ahimelech has escaped from this murderous scene and has come to tell David that only he had escaped. David's response is classic exhorter, *"I knew that day, when Doeg the Edomite was there, that he would surely tell Saul. I have caused the death of all the persons of your father's house."* If David had truly "known," he would have likely done something about it. As an exhorter, he saw the possibility, and might have even flirted with a response. When it truly did come to pass, he came down on himself as having *"caused the death"* of all of these priests.

WEIGHT OF RESPONSIBILITY

- **What are some good and bad outcomes of the exhorter's ability to visualize?**

Exhorters are excellent at visualizing. As described in the last paragraph, this ability can easily lead to significant levels of perfectionism and then self condemnation. This same skill of visualizing can take them into "foreseeing" all kinds of negative things, resulting in a stronghold of fear. When dominated by a strong fear base, many turn to manipulation and control of people and situations to try to better manage the fear that can so easily become overwhelming.

The gifts that God has given us are not necessarily positive or negative. They are potential. An exhorter can use the ability God has given Him unto the glory of God, or he can be used up by it. Because of the ability to visualize, it is easy for an exhorter to begin to play God, owning guilt for all kinds of situations. Or he can step back, learn to wait and depend on God, and allow others to be responsible for their own actions. If he doesn't, his gift can become an incredible cross to bear.

Because of this ability to visualize, exhorters do have a tendency to "land on their feet" even when the situations looks bleak. In *1 Samuel 18*, even as a young man David behaves "wisely" and gains favor because of his military leadership. With Aschish, he fools him to make him think he is a mad man one time *(1 Samuel 21)* and convinces him that he is a competent leader at another time *(1 Samuel 28, 30).*

Exhorters learn to be all things to all people in any kind of situation and frequently are able to make the adjustment needed to turn the impossible into a scene of triumph. The irony is that having brought the deliverance once, they tend to take on the role of being the person who should be able to do it over and over again. There is that tendency to play God … to carry the weight of the world. Call it perfectionism. Call it loadbearing. Call it what you want. It is an exhorter trying to do what he does best—to do what he was created to do, but not realizing that apart from God, he can do nothing.

- **What does it look like when David steps into depending on self?**

Unfortunately, exhorters tend to depend on their ability to adjust and to "make it work" more than they depend on God. When sold out, as David is, they become a "man after God's own

when unchecked and unaccountable we can become dependent on self very quickly

heart." Yet, even David, who is passionate for God, stoops to incredible levels of manipulation in the Bathsheba incident. In this incident, David's naturally passionate personality leads him into sexual sin. David demonstrates both the ability to depend on God and the ability to depend on self.

When the challenge of beating the odds is in play, even the normal perfectionism of the exhorter gets overruled.

The Bathsheba incident also demonstrates the ability of the exhorter to step over into an ongoing game of deceit in the name of winning a game of intrigue. Again, when the challenge of beating the odds is in play, even the normal perfectionism of the exhorter gets overruled. Because he is able to see things from multiple directions, he can send Uriah (Bathsheba's husband) into battle in a location that he will be killed, and for a season, feel OK about it.

Living in a world of constantly seeing things from many perspectives, it is easy for the exhorter to "spin" things a bit until he has gone too far. Motivation becomes manipulation. Setting forth things with a positive tint becomes outright lies.

There is a strong parallel between the exhorter character gift and the calling gift of sharing the "good news." The exhorter likes to put a positive face on all things—even murder (in the case of Uriah). If there is a way to be positive, he will find it—at least in the public eye. When alone with himself, that is when the doubts and the second guessing of self begins to rage on the inside. That is when the fear base begins to take over if he is not submitted to God. When in front of people, he has a job to do—to be the best influence that he can be.

- **What difficulties does the exhorter face because of his changeable nature?**
....

The exhorter is very much affected by the faces of people. He has a natural fear of man, which is part of the motivation for studying faces. He studies them to know how to react to each different person. Most people end up feeling like they have been perfectly understood by the exhorter, but this puts the exhorter in a real bind when he is in the company of two very contrasting people. He is suddenly pulled to respond in two very different ways.

Accordingly, they prefer one on one situations or at least controlled situations with compatible people. Probably the exhorter's greatest struggle is to come to an identity of his own since he is so wrapped up in others. Certain absolutes must be established in his life. He cannot continue to flow forever with the wind. Also, he must guard against getting out of balance on either the self condemning or the self congratulating side.

Exhorters tend to hear God in a problem-solution format. David never questioned if he would win, but focused on how he should go about it. In *1 Samuel 30*, David's followers have had enough and are thinking about stoning him. In *verse 6* it says, *"But David strengthened himself in the LORD his God."*

In typical exhorter fashion, David calls for Abiathar and begins walking out a solution one step at a time. He refuses to be negative and turns to the only One he can trust. His verbal

Key

processing before the priest and before God get him back to a place of feeling encouraged and then he is able to take what he has received from God to challenge the people to go forward.

- ## What problems come out of the "take one step at a time" approach? What is the strength of that approach?

Again, it is as if exhorters have to have a positive orientation. They have to be able to see some kind of positive next step. Even when his own people want to stone him, David turns to God and manages to pull something positive out of it. Exhorters thrive as counselors because they usually can see the next practical step needed in some of the most difficult of situations. The next step brings hope for people. And exhorters love to give hope to others.

While they can see a long-term vision, they are like the teacher who often struggles because of wanting to push too far in the area of information. The teacher gets bogged down in factual detail. The exhorter gets bogged down in vision. He hits an overload point of "this could happen … or this could happen… or maybe this…". With so many possibilities out there, he struggles taking more than one step at a time, lest he close off some incredible path for the future. He wants to keep his options open.

With this kind of orientation, they tend to drive others crazy because of an erratic lifestyle. They can go from one end of the spectrum to the other in moment's notice, and those who don't understand the exhorter are often miffed by the change. They see it as hypocrisy or deceit or any of many other negative traits, when the reality is that an exhorter is likely just responding to people in his vision format.

Developing consistency is a great need for the exhorter. The exhorter needs to look beyond just the next step, working to establish a process and a manner of doing things. He needs accountability and structure, though those are things that will not come easy for him.

Actually, that is a principle for all of the gifts. In most cases, the thing that is most difficult for them is the very thing they most need to bring balance to their lives. That is why finding your gift and "going for it" can actually be dangerous. In many cases, finding your gift and "moderating it" is a better solution.

Finding your gift and "going for it" can actually be dangerous!

The best solution for all of the gifts is to simply walk with God. Until the exhorter learns that his gift of encouragement has a tendency to degenerate into manipulation, he is not likely to depend on God in an encouragement situation. Until he learns to depend on God, it is very doubtful that there will be any eternal fruit.

Do you want your life to count for something for eternity? Once again the exhorter shows us that for us to count for eternity, we must learn to walk with God … in the places that are hard for us. We must die to self for our gift to truly bring life to others. That is God's way. Until we die to self, He cannot shine through our gift area. After all, He is the One who is to receive the glory … not us.

Snapshot of the Exhorter

Remember: *Core values actually come from multiple sources, so it is possible that you may have some of a core value but not fully line up with that gift. The gifts in this character category also have overlapping traits with other gifts. Look for the basic motivation behind character traits to see if your deepest core value lines up with this gift. Mark any items that fit who you are. Your gift should have the most items marked on these snapshots.*

Passion: Vision; seeing a preferred future come to pass; coming alongside others to see them reach their potential; taking on any challenges that would stand in the way of this maximized potential.

Primary fears: Missing the moment; exhorters want to make the most of every opportunity and desire to live life to its fullest; they hate missing anything that would have made for a better life for them or for those they are trying to influence; they fear not being who they need to be to make things happen.

Spiritual connection/voice of God: Like so many things in life, the voice of God is hard to pin down for them; they are constantly sensing, but always wanting more information and input to be sure of themselves as having heard from God; they tend to "sense" and not hear; they are passionate worshipers.

Relationship characteristics: They are extremely horizontal in relationship; they want all people on a level playing field and only bow to the need for vertical relationships when it is absolutely needed for function; are friends with all people but find it difficult to build the closer, more intimate relationships because it is hard for them to pin down exactly who they are on the inside; they are always changing according to who they are with.

Conflict: They typically hate and avoid conflict unless they can clearly see that it is a means to some kind of positive future; in that case, conflict is of secondary importance as the goal is pursued; they want to be able to get along with all people all the time.

Task orientation: Task is seen in light of maximizing people's futures; relationship is typically preferred over task, but where task has a clear practical value, the exhorter can and will plunge headlong into it; they seldom do anything halfway; once into the task, they tend to go to excess until it is completed; tend to have one focus at a time and if it is task, it is task.

Possessions: Possessions are of minimal value to an exhorter; they are a means to an end; if practical—great; if not—forget them; there is usually minimal attachment to them.

All 7 describe me to a tee

Activity for Understanding

Who do you know that seems to fit the picture described in the exhorter gift?

Self, parents, pastor James,

What part of the picture of the exhorter gift fits you well? (If it is only a few traits, check out other gifts that might have similar traits!) *It fits to the exact measure*

What values of the exhorter seemed uncomfortable to you as a value "created by God"?

They all felt uncomfortable because the picture of me has been made so much clearer.

Is that value uncomfortable to you because you are seeing the sinful side being expressed or because it is in contrast to what feels right to you? *Realizing all those values I see how easy it is for me to try and control, manipulate, "TRY HARDER"*

Who do you know that you have "despised" or at least devalued that may actually be acting on an internal value created by God as seen in the exhorter? *SELF*

Have some close friends identify those parts of the exhorter description that fit you well. List results: ▰▰▰▰▰▰▰▰▰ *identify the negative characteristics. Alot of people good but what sticks out the most is when people Especially those I looked up to for love, acceptance, attention from Casey, God, family ➜ Most ▰▰ times they saw my change in attitude and plans and they saw it as a character flaw rather than an unidentify, unchecked, unaccountable gift trying to come forth but due to an unsubmitted spirit it came across as arrogant, prideful, hypocritical, unstable.*

The Giver: Creating and Nurturing Value

Chapter 8

- **What are some of the different descriptions that help us better define the giver?**

Most of the time, when I teach about the character gifts, I am cruising right along with the first three: prophet, servant, and teacher. All three of these are clear types and I find people nodding their heads in agreement, thinking about people that they know who fit each of the types. Then comes the exhorter. Most exhorters will complain saying, "I am some of all of them." Or they will challenge the validity of the whole system.

The giver is equally challenging. It too is a hard gift to define. Even the name for the gift, "giver," does not capture the essence of the gift as well. Some better descriptive names for the giver would be nurturer, caregiver, or provider. Actually, the best description is just "mom" or "dad."

Obviously, this does not refer to a physical mom or dad. Givers seem to adopt others into a kind of extended family that has nothing to do with blood lines. If older, the givers are often the church grandmother or grandfather. They just seem to naturally fit into that nurturer, caregiver role. However, having a natural family is also very important to them. Abraham was a giver, and it is quite obvious how important having a natural child was to him.

Givers are often the church grandmother or grandfather.

As the name "giver" implies, givers do like to give things to others or more accurately to provide for them. Most of their giving is done inside the context of relationship. In order to give things away, the giver has to have something to give. Accordingly, they tend to be very frugal people, but they have a very generous heart when the right chord is struck. This contrast of frugal to generosity is one that is repeated in many areas of their personality. Like the prophet, they tend to swing from one end of the spectrum to the other very quickly.

- **Why is it so important to a giver that others trust them and are loyal to them?**

Givers tend to live for other people and very much want to be able to trust others. Because of the very nature of their gift, people often try to take advantage of them. The result is that they usually categorize people as being either "in" or "out" of their good graces. Those who are "in" become "family" for them. Those who are "out" do not qualify for time or attention or help. The Scriptures admonish the giver to ignore those things that cause them to shut down their hearts toward others and to continue to give with liberality. Elisha of the Old Testament provides us with a clear example of a giver.

The core value for the giver is somewhere between family and loyalty. The mom and dad theme will come through many times as we discuss this gift. There is a family code of loyalty, of sticking together no matter what. This trait shows up early with Elisha. In *1 Kings 19:20*, it says, **"And he left the oxen and ran after Elijah, and said, 'Please let me kiss my father and my mother, and then I will follow you.'"** When the call of God came, Elisha saw it in terms of a new loyalty. He would have to transfer from family to Elijah, but that could not be done without paying proper respect to father and mother. Givers think in terms of loyalty.

- ## How does the giver respond according to the picture of either a parent or a child?

The name giver implies a strong connection to money, and frugality is important to a giver. Because they want to provide for "the family" (which can be much larger than a flesh and blood family!), they are very industrious people and frequently are the entrepreneurs of the group. Yet, one of the things that makes them successful in business is simply loyalty. They desire, yes, demand loyalty. It is one of the most significant building blocks for a successful enterprise.

We see this quality come through Elisha when his master, Elijah, is about to be taken up into heaven. Elisha refuses to be left along the way but continues to stay by the side of Elijah. Elijah, being the clear prophet type, even tries to ditch Elisha. Elijah would just as soon spend his final moments on earth alone. For Elisha, it is all about loyalty, and he is not about to be separated from Elijah by anything less than the angel of God. Three different times, Elijah entreats Elisha to stay at a place along the way. Three different times, Elisha says, **"As the LORD lives, and as your soul lives, I will not leave you!"**

> **For Elisha, it is all about loyalty.**

It is also interesting to watch the interplay between the prophets and Elisha. The prophets know that Elijah is about to be taken up into heaven. When they approach Elisha with this news in *2 Kings 2*, he says two different times, **"Yes, I know; keep silent!"** You can almost hear a parent speaking to a child in this terse statement. The giver frequently comes across in both a vertical and a sharp manner that many will say is "prophetic" in its feel.

However, it is not prophetic because the core value motivating the statement is completely different. It is a tense moment for Elisha because he is about to lose one that he has been serving. He is not about to dishonor his master by messing up in any way at this point. For Elisha, it is a very emotional day. He is about to lose the prototype of his parent. Though he is the "child" in this relationship, Elisha tries to respond with strength at this emotional moment. The giver has a natural sense of needing to be the parent, and typically is determined to be strong in any situation.

- ## What are some ways the reactions of the giver seem to go through some radical swings?

Givers are like that. They want to put on a good face for others. Mom and dad need to be strong for the kids' sake. Elisha needs to be strong in front of the other prophets. In order to do that amidst all the emotions swirling inside, he answers them in very short, terse statements.

Elisha is being stretched to the ultimate degree, and he doesn't need or want any distractions. Elijah has already messed with him by trying to leave him along the way. He doesn't need anyone else to complicate the process.

In many ways, the giver is like the exhorter in that he plays off from other people, and thus can be very different from one relationship to the next. Both gifts are nurturers. Both live for others and adjust to others. But there is one huge difference between the two. The exhorter is horizontal in relationship; the giver is vertical.

The giver approaches others more as either a parent or a child.

The exhorter approaches others as if he were just one of the guys. He tends to blend in and frequently brings his influence in such a subtle way that the person hardly notices that he is being influenced. The giver approaches others more as either a parent or a child. He is more vertical. If he comes as a "parent," the approach will have almost a prophetic, "Take it or leave it" kind of feel.

We get a sense of this in the way he talks to the other prophets. If he comes as a child, the approach will feel extremely submissive, with a "whatever you say" kind of feel. Elisha responds to Elijah more in this manner.

Obviously, these two approaches are radically different. As a pastor, I have worked with many people who started out within the church and then were promoted into some kind of leadership position. Occasionally, a person seems to radically morph when given a leadership position. They go from being very quiet and servant-like to being very inquisitive and authoritative. That kind of change is likely to happen with the more vertical gifts, especially the giver. The giver goes from being a child to being a parent, and the disparity is huge.

With Elijah, Elisha stays connected and stays subservient. When Elijah asks Elisha what he wants from him, Elisha answers that he wants a double portion of Elijah's spirit. It is almost a perfect parallel of the Hebrew tradition that the oldest son would get a double portion of the inheritance.

When Elijah is actually taken up in *2 Kings 2:12*, Elisha cries out, *"My father, my father, the chariot of Israel and its horsemen!"* Elisha even calls him "My father." The whole idea of nurturing and being nurtured is instinctive to the giver. Life happens inside of that picture.

• What is almost a kind of trauma for the giver?

It is also important to note that Elisha is not afraid to ask for a significant gift from Elijah. On the one hand, this is a bit strange for a giver, because they like to be in the giving role and not the receiving role.

One of the greatest traumas to a giver is not being able to pay a debt that is owed. They not only want to be able to pay any debts, but want to pay them quickly. They hate to owe anyone anything for any amount of time. It is almost funny to watch a giver who has had a good deed done on his behalf. It is like he can't wait to return the favor, even if he has to artificially contrive some excuse to do a good deed back.

Givers prefer to be in the parent role and be the provider not the receiver. In *2 Kings 4*, a Shunammite woman provides lodging for Elisha, even going to the effort of preparing a room in the house for him to stay whenever he is in the area. Elisha cannot let this go unrewarded. He calls his servant and persists until he finds a way to give back to her. He prays for her to have a son and she has a son. This is consistent with givers need to feel like the accounts are settled.

• How does the "provider" side of the giver translate into having a good business mindset?

However, Elisha does ask for a double portion. When it comes to "industry," givers are big time investors. They are entrepreneurs. The gift Elisha was asking for was the capital of his industry. The anointing of the Holy Spirit was what it would take for him to continue in the "business" of the prophet.

Givers understand business and the need to manage money for the good of the whole. In this case, receiving is not a selfish thing but instead is the basis of providing for others. Having the heart of an entrepreneur puts them in the position to be able to give. They generally hate to borrow unless it is to invest in some sort of enterprise. Enterprise is how you provide for others, and providing is a worthy cause even if borrowing is necessary.

Givers will almost never ask for something for themselves, to be spent on themselves. If a gift is needed for the sake of another person or group, they will ask, but they typically like to be the initiators. They want to be the one doing the asking, not the one being asked. They like to be in the parent role.

> **Givers will almost never ask for something for themselves, to be spent on themselves.**

Givers are usually some of the first ones in the church to complain that the preacher is "always asking for money." Especially if they feel like the money is being used unwisely or on selfish needs, the giver will balk at such requests. Givers don't mind initiating an appeal on behalf of someone oppressed, but they will be much more cooperative with the raising of money if it is their idea. If it is someone else's idea, they tend to feel pressed. It feels more like the child is demanding action from a parent. If so, the "right" thing to do is for the parent to resist the request of the "child." Again, a very subtle shift in circumstances can trigger some very different reactions. Those who don't understand the giver get quite confused by them and tend to see them as being "all over the place."

• How do givers "use" people in a way that is good for them?

After Elijah is taken up, Elisha takes the mantle of Elijah that has fallen from the chariot and picks it up. He is about to test the "double portion" anointing:

> *Then he took the mantle of Elijah that had fallen from him, and struck the water, and said, "Where is the LORD God of Elijah?" And when he also had struck the water, it was divided this way and that; and Elisha crossed over (2 Kings 2:14).*

Because givers are generous with people, they tend to get used. I don't know if it is because of this, or just because it is a part of their nature, but givers tend to test things, people, and situations. Here, Elisha is testing the mantle. Will it have the same power for him that it had for Elijah? Will it have a double portion? The waters parted, so it definitely passes the first test. The anointing is now resting on him, given to him in the symbolic form of the mantle of Elijah.

Like the servant, givers do have a sense of attachment to tangible objects. The mantle is significant to Elisha. When Elisha does miracles, he almost always starts with some kind of tangible object. When Elijah did his miracles, he mostly just spoke, and it happened. He

Elisha always has the person he is working with participate in a tangible way.

demonstrates the more verbal tendencies of the prophet. Elisha asks for a stick, some salt, for oil, or flour. He always has the person he is working with participate in a tangible way. He seems to understand that miracles are not just about demonstrating the power of God, but about changing the lives of men.

When we involve people in something, they are much more likely to get heart change. Elisha understands the need for people to cooperate in their own miracle. Besides, asking for involvement is a kind of test to see if they are willing to do what they need to do to get better. Elisha tells the widow to gather jars. In the miraculous supply of oil, the oil keeps flowing until all the vessels are full. The widow's faith in gathering jars sets the amount of oil she would receive (*2 Kings 4*).

Givers love to take something insignificant and turn it into something of great value. He takes a little bit of oil and turns it into enough oil to support a widow and her sons for an extended season. He takes salt and pours it in the waters to heal the water. He tells the men to dig ditches in a barren place and the next day, the ditches are filled with water.

Elisha uses objects and efforts that have seemingly no value, and with the blessing of the Lord, turns them into something of great value. Givers don't just nurture people. They also "nurture" business-type efforts to create the provision needed so that they can effectively nurture people.

- **How does the giver respond to people in a way that resembles a parent-child relationship?**

The parent to child theme continues in the exchange between Elisha and the prophets after Elijah is taken up:

> *Now when the sons of the prophets who were from Jericho saw him, they said, "The spirit of Elijah rests on Elisha." And they came to meet him, and bowed to the ground before him. Then they said to him, "Look now, there are fifty strong men with your servants. Please let them go and search for your master, lest perhaps the Spirit of the LORD has taken him up and cast him upon some mountain or into some valley."*
>
> *And he said, "You shall not send anyone."*
>
> *But when they urged him till he was ashamed, he said, "Send them!" Therefore they sent fifty men, and they searched for three days but did not find him. And when they came back to him, for he had stayed in Jericho, he said to them, "Did I not say to you, 'Do not go'?" (2 Kings 2:15-18).*

This passage is a classic picture of a child begging a parent. Initially, the parent says "No." He knows better. When the child persists, he gives in. Why? He knows that the only way to teach the child a lesson is to prove to the child that he knows what he is talking about. When the child returns empty handed, he answers with his version of "I told you so!"

The more non-vertical gifts are frustrated by the "I told you so." To them, this kind of answer is insensitive and unnecessary. To the more vertical gifts, and especially to the parental giver, it is simply a matter of reminding the "child" of the authority structure. It validates the authority of the parent. It is a kind of plea to "Please listen to me next time. I won't speak with conviction unless I know I am right. You need to trust me when I speak."

For the giver, it is a question of honor and respect. The giver does not like being dishonored, but being dishonored is not seen as a personal slight to them. It is not an ego thing. It is like right and wrong for the prophet. It is a core value of the universe, and they have a sense that if honor is not being shown, the world will begin to unravel. It is disorganization to an organized (administrative) person. It is a world of pain and torment for a mercy person. Every single gift has its ultimate ten, its most important core value. When that value gets violated, the world is not right!

- **How does the sense of "family" shape the response of the giver?**

Another aspect of this exchange is simply the timing. Givers are intensely relational persons, though the vertical way they approach people can at times seem a little standoffish. One of the reasons Elisha reacts a bit curtly to the prophets is because he is still intensely feeling the separation from Elijah. He has lost his "father." It has been a traumatic event. The giver "adopts" people into his family and they are family to him. When something happens in his "family," when one of the relationships is suffering or a person "leaves the fold" by death or by choice, it is a great trauma.

However, like a good parent, Elisha tries to be strong for the "children." Elisha doesn't dump his emotional world on the prophets—at least not openly. Givers tend to be very private in their expression of emotions. As can be seen here in his response to the prophets, it is almost impossible for them to hide the evidence that they are struggling emotionally. But Elisha doesn't lay it out on the table. He plays more of the strong, silent type who simply minimizes his communication during times of struggle.

• Why is guarding of reputation a high value for the giver?

Another trait of the giver that can be seen in this passage is that givers know there is a need to maintain a reputation. If a person is not recognized as being competent, he won't be consulted. He won't have the opportunity to use his competence. When facing criticism for not searching for Elijah, Elisha relents and tells the prophets to go search for him. He knows they will find nothing, but if he says, "No," he potentially looks bad. If he looks bad, he loses the respect that he needs to be the functioning "parent."

Another related trait is that givers like to put their best foot forwards. They don't like to air

Givers like to put their best foot forward.

their dirty laundry. They are private with grief and intense emotions, and they are private with their struggles. Our ministry frequently needs to get people to open up in order to resolve issues from the past. Givers struggle mightily with this. First, they don't want to openly admit that there are issues. Second, to expose those issues usually makes someone they love look bad ... maybe a mom or a dad or a sibling. To make someone they love look bad is breaking the code. It is dishonoring. It goes against the core value of the giver.

• When should the giver make a special effort to be open with people?

I have been in relationship with givers for years before they are able to open up and deal with past hurts. The first person the giver has to be honest with is himself. In many cases, he has not even allowed himself to think about life situations honestly because it felt disloyal. The next difficult step for a giver is for him to open up and trust another person with that same information. To the giver, that feels like dishonoring, which goes completely against the grain.

Yet, **Psalms 32** is very clear. When we cover a matter, it will become rottenness to our bones. We will groan and travail. Yes **Proverbs 17:9** does say that there is a time when concealing a matter is honoring to a friend and will establish a quality relationship. But I believe that verse is dealing with a resolved issue. God wants unresolved issues brought out into the open—first before Him and then before others. This kind of openness is difficult for a giver. If done at all, it will likely need to be done with a close and trusted circle of respected friends, or even better, if it can be with someone who is seen as a "parent" to the giver.

• **What are some other high passion areas for the giver?**

In *2 Kings 2*, we see another image of the giver consistent with this picture. They hate to be insulted and can have a very severe anger when disrespected. ***Verse 23*** describes the offense to Elisha: ***"Then he went up from there to Bethel; and as he was going up the road, some youths came from the city and mocked him, and said to him, 'Go up, you baldhead! Go up, you baldhead!'"*** In response, Elisha turns, pronounces a curse on them and two female bears show up and maul these young people. To the giver, disrespect cannot be tolerated. It is worthy of a significant response.

In *2 Kings 3*, we see another aspect of the giver. They hate mixed messages. They want things more black and white. In this chapter, the godly king, Jehoshaphat has allied himself with the ungodly king, Jehoram. In *2 Kings 3:14-15* we get Elisha's response to Jehoram:

> *And Elisha said, "As the LORD of hosts lives, before whom I stand, surely were it not that I regard the presence of Jehoshaphat king of Judah, I would not look at you, nor see you. But now bring me a musician."*

Out of loyalty to Jehoshaphat, Elisha does agree to seek the Lord for a word, but he does so begrudgingly. Elisha is in a place that he doesn't like. He hates the mixture of good and evil.

• **On a practical level, how do givers respond to life situations?**

Because of this, Elisha is struggling to make contact with God and he calls for a musician. Again, I compare with Elijah. You never see Elijah call for a musician. Elijah just hears from God. Givers are different. They involve people in their hearing. They love music, and it is very much a part of their ability to connect with God. Connecting with God is much more of a life process for them and is not necessarily quite so immediate.

Givers are different. They involve people in their hearing.

They also tend to be answered more in pictures. Both Joseph and Daniel demonstrate a number of the characteristics of a giver, and both had dreams and interpreted dreams. Givers seem to live in a more visual world and tend to be at home in the creative world of both music and imagination. Perhaps that is what makes them great entrepreneurs. They are able to "see" some kind of finished product while it is nothing more than a mere stick or an almost empty jar of oil. Givers think differently and see the world in a way that others do not.

Because givers are more vertical, they tend to think more in terms of management of others. They are not true administrators, because their values are not the same as those of the administrators. But they often end up doing some of the same things.

We see this with the way Elisha handles the other prophets. He is not at all afraid to parcel out the job to a number of different individuals, but he does so as much to grow the

The giver sees tasks given to others as a way to grow individuals.

individual as to complete the task. With Gehazi, we see Elisha sending his servant on various errands. Again, we see great differences between the gifts. Moses, a servant, had Joshua right there, ready to wait upon him. Yet we never see him giving Joshua missions to carry out. Joshua is never seen doing much of anything until Moses is out of the picture. The servant tends to do things by himself. The giver sees tasks given to others as a way to grow individuals.

Givers also have a desire to be independent of others. In *2 Kings 5,* when Naaman came to him as high dignitary of the Syrians, he did not even bother to come out to greet him. Instead, he sent a messenger with a simple directive (to go wash in the river). Naaman, of course, is furious at being slighted in this way, but Elisha is not the least bit moved. He is a servant of the Most High God; no servant of God needs to grovel before any human authority. Elisha stands up in the same way to the kings of Israel and to others. If honor is due, Elisha is more than willing to give it, but honor is due to the righteous and not those who think themselves to be something special.

True to their name, givers are money conscious. This is more easily seen in some other Old Testament examples of givers. Joseph is the best illustration in the way that he handled Pharaoh's kingdom during the famine. By the time the famine was over, Pharaoh literally owned not only the entire country but the people as well. Givers know a bargain when they see it and are very good at pressing for a "deal." It doesn't necessarily have to be on a grandiose scale like it was with Joseph. A bargain is a bargain, and many deals add up to a great profit!

- **Why do givers have the tendency to become rescuers, and what can they do to avoid that trap?**

Because of his soft heart, the giver can easily fall into the trap of becoming a rescuer. A rescuer is someone who goes the extra mile to help another person, even at times and in ways that may not be good. Once a giver begins to help someone, he usually adopts him into his "family." Once that happens, it is almost like the person can do no wrong for a time. If the person does something stupid, he is just "a child in need." A rescuer sees the need and draws a sense of self importance from helping out with that need.

A healthy giver will know the difference between helping with a need and truly helping a person. Sometimes, helping with a need actually cripples a person; sometimes it sets them free. The giver needs to stay away from the trap of being a mom or dad that gets used by the other person. Sometimes, the only way a giver can keep away from being used is to become closed or hard.

There is a better way. If the giver is truly drawing his sense of meaning and purpose from God, he will not "need" to help others but will "get" to help others. When a person "gets" to help others, he is at a place where he can hear the voice of God and accurately know when to help and when not to help.

When the giver "needs" to help, the compulsion inside will mess up his spiritual hearing, and he will get burned over and over again. When that happens, he will become hard and closed to any kind of appeal. Some of the angriest people at offering time are givers. And some of the happiest people at offering time are givers. Guess what makes the difference?

- **What is the most important principle for the giver to be healthy in life?**

When a giver walks with God, he is a nurturer and a lover of people. He is also a very resourceful and creative person with a great ability to imagine and to flow artistically—whether in music or in art.

As a business person, givers are not happy with simple management but love to create, and expand, and to grow the possibilities for the business and for its people. Or they can become very bitter, judgmental, and closed individuals. Especially for the giver, the difference is simply "Are they walking with God?"

There are people who don't walk with God and yet seem to be soft and loving. Some of these just seem to be naturally drawn to biblical heart attitudes. Some of them started out with a great advantage due to saved parents or grandparents or possibly drawing from mentors or friends.

However, the Bible is very clear that every good thing does come from God *(James 1:17)*, whether directly or indirectly. Those who do not connect with God can achieve some level of goodness, but it will be a goodness that is more "rescuing," more caught up in its need to be needed and helpful. Givers are instinctively like that. They want to be helpers of others.

When a giver is not connected to God, his help will typically be very vertical. Elisha demonstrates that feel when he communicates with the other prophets. Most of the time, he speaks to them in very black and white tones. Because of this, the one being helped can easily feel like he is being done a favor and give the glory to the one giving the help. When that happens, an unhealthy dependency is created. Good is being done, but it is being done in a way that cripples both the giver and the receiver. It has the appearance of being a good thing, but it is not helping either of them to grow. The giver is not being a true nurturer through the giving process.

When the giver is not connected to God, his help will typically be very vertical.

When a giver is connected to God, he is more able to give out of obedience to God with no strings attached. It has a more horizontal feel, and the one receiving the gift is more likely to give praise to God and not to the person. In this case, both the giver and the receiver are being challenged to grow in God. It is a much healthier situation.

For the giver, this is a crucial point in understanding. In all life activities, a person is either becoming more God-like, is stagnating, or is closing down. The giver needs to interact with others in a way that cooperates with God to bring growth and not just to help out a need.

Often, givers do see the need for growth and try to help out the process. With their more vertical nature, they instinctively move into areas of control, and the gifts they give come with strings attached. Again, all this does is move the giver more into the place of God and creates an unhealthy dependency. All true growth in God comes because of the free will choice of the person. Manipulated growth is never permanent growth. Only when others get pointed to God are we truly walking in spiritual gifts.

- **What are ways the giver can limit his tendency to step into a place of control?**

Givers generally like to stay out of the spotlight and often try to do any giving anonymously. While there are times that anonymous giving is helpful, there are many times when it makes little difference. The greatest difference is made because a person is truly walking in humility, not taking any glory to himself. When a person gives with this kind of heart, the gift is usually received more as if it were coming from God.

It is the attitude of the giver that makes the most difference, not the level of public awareness.

If instead, the giver sees himself as more competent and successful than others, and as being in a position to help others, he will draw the glory to himself. It is the attitude of the giver that makes the most difference, not the level of public awareness. Givers need to see themselves as just one part in God's nurturing of an individual.

All of the gifts are needed in some way to bring about the healthy nurturing of those in the body of Christ. Teaching is needed and so is service. We need motivators and those who connect us with the voice of God. We need comforters and organizers. Even though the giver feels the need to nurture more keenly than some of the other gifts, the giver is not preeminent in the nurturing process. He is called to challenge the other gifts to walk in this value of nurturing others, but the task can only be done with a balanced and complete participation of all of the gifts.

When the giver gets a sense that he is preeminent, it is likely that he is already out of step with God. Every gift has a tendency to feel preeminent when a need is triggered in its value area, but for the giver, the pull to go vertical is a huge temptation. Because they are typically very competent people, it is hard not to have a sense of being a cut above others. As an antidote for this tendency, a great verse for the giver is *1 Corinthians 4:7: "For who makes you differ from another? And what do you have that you did not receive? Now if you did indeed receive it, why do you boast as if you had not received it?"*

The giver is a high achiever, but if that achieving does not bring God glory, what good is it? The giver needs to remember that it is not about the gift but the growth and the glory. Growth only comes when God is glorified. Givers can easily become very class conscious, hypocritically judging others according to achievement or of wealth accumulated. When they do this, they are saying that their ability in the achievement area is more important than the values the other gifts bring to the table. When they get too stuck on what they have achieved or on what God is doing through them, it is not pretty. When they humble themselves as one essential part of the body, it is very good.

Givers do tend to live in the extreme. When they see their own judgments of others, they will judge themselves as the "worst of all sinners." That too is a mistake. Humility sees the whole body. It sees the value of each part. It even sees the value of self, but sees it relative to the whole. That is true humility. False humility devalues self. Devaluing of self is nothing but spiritual pride in a negative form.

When walking with God, the judgments of others and the tendency toward "in my family" and "out of my family" will fade. The giver's tendency to set a value on men according to what they have accomplished needs to give way to the value that the Creator has given all men. The giver must recognize his need for others as much or more than he recognizes the need of others for him. The giver learns to receive ... as well as to give. That is a lesson we all need to learn! What have we given to others that has not been first given to us?

Snapshot of the Giver

Remember: *Core values actually come from multiple sources, so it is possible that you may have some of a core value but not fully line up with that gift. The gifts in this character category also have overlapping traits with other gifts. Look for the basic motivation behind character traits to see if your deepest core value lines up with this gift. Mark any items that fit who you are. Your gift should have the most items marked on these snapshots.*

Passion: Nurturing life; creating something out of nothing or bringing value out of something that had no value; being efficient; finding and giving value; influencing.

Primary fears: Being inadequate as a nurturer/caregiver/provider; losing the respect of others; losing a child (whether to death or to walking away from the relationship and whether an actual child or one in the care of the giver).

Spiritual connection/voice of God: Tend to be very visual in their relationship with God; frequently see in pictures and music often is very important in their ability to connect with God; dreams and visions are not unusual; tend to be more sure of their hearing/seeing much as the prophet is sure; there is a very black and white sense of being connected or disconnected with God; not much gray area in terms of what is right or of God.

Relationship characteristics: "Family"—whether actual family or whether those adopted to come under the care of the giver are very significant to the giver; to the giver a person is either in the "family" and is a priority or is out of the family and mostly important according to the practical value of the relationship; they like the parent role and are more comfortable where relationships are vertical; where appropriate, they can play the child role.

Conflict: Conflict is seen in light of the need for nurturing; where necessary for the "parent" to raise up the child, it is of little consequence; in situations where it might bring a loss of face or would be debilitating to role as nurturer, it becomes significant.

Task orientation: As entrepreneurs, they tend to be excellent at managing task; they like to involve others in task for their growth and for the sake of making a profit; they seldom work alone on a task unless it is during the visioning phase; task holds a relatively high value but not above primary relationships unless things are out of order.

Possessions: Things can be a status symbol for the giver, both as a sign of having accomplished something and for the value they assign to the things themselves; they are a means to an end but an important means.

Activity for Understanding

Who do you know that seems to fit the picture described in the giver gift?

Joe N   Gary
Dad

What part of the picture of the giver gift fits you well? (If it is only a few traits, check out other gifts that might have similar traits!)

What values of the giver seemed uncomfortable to you as a value "created by God"?

Is that value uncomfortable to you because you are seeing the sinful side being expressed or because it is in contrast to what feels right to you?

Who do you know that you have "despised" or at least devalued that may actually be acting on an internal value created by God as seen in the giver?

Have some close friends identify those parts of the giver description that fit you well. List results:

The Administrator: Completing the Job Efficiently

Chapter 9

- **We hear according to our hearts. What does Nehemiah hear in the report about Jerusalem, and what does that tell us about his heart?**

With the administrator, we get back to a character type that is not so easily influenced by people and situations. Several translations of **Romans 12:8** refer to administrators as "he who leads." Other translations refer to this gift as a ruler. Yet, even as the name giver doesn't capture the core value of that gift, neither does leader, ruler, or even administrator fully capture the core value of the administrator.

Administrators love to use all resources in an organized manner to complete the job efficiently. Fairness is also a core value to administrators, a value that gets about equal time with the need to finish the job. James is a New Testament example of an administrator, and in the Old Testament, we can see the heart of an administrator as we watch Nehemiah interact with life events.

The core value of Nehemiah surfaces almost immediately in the book of Nehemiah. Nehemiah is brought news of a two-fold woe concerning Jerusalem as the book opens: ***"The survivors who are left from the captivity in the province are there in great distress and reproach. The wall of Jerusalem is also broken down, and its gates are burned with fire" (Neh. 1:3b)***. Yet, in **Nehemiah 2:3**, when the King asks Nehemiah why his countenance is downcast, he answers, ***"May the king live forever! Why should my face not be sad, when the city, the place of my fathers' tombs, lies waste, and its gates are burned with fire?"***

Nehemiah is told of the "distress and reproach" of the people.

When God wanted to get Moses' attention, He showed up in a burning bush. Servants are attentive to physical things. When he wanted to pull on Moses' heart strings, He told him of the suffering of the people. In this account in **Nehemiah**, Nehemiah is told of the ***"distress and reproach"*** of the people, but it is as if all he hears is that the ***"gates are burned with fire."*** The heart of the administrator is one that values order, structure, and the ability to fairly enforce that order and structure. When the walls and gates of a city are not in place, there is no way to set things in order and to guard against intrusion.

Much of Nehemiah's mission seems to be about restoring the walls and gates, though as we read the book, it is much more. It is about restoring order. Nehemiah calls the family heads to restore order in their parts of the world. He calls the government leaders to task. He calls the people to join together to build in an orderly fashion. It is not that Nehemiah doesn't see the groaning of his people. It is merely that for Nehemiah, the only way to help the pain is by restoring the physical walls and gates along with family and governmental walls and gates.

- **How does Nehemiah demonstrate his heart for those who are hurting?**

Because of the focus on order and structure, administrators can seem to be oblivious to the cries of the people. Sometimes they are oblivious to such cries. In Nehemiah's case, I do believe that he was very aware of the cries of the people. He personally sacrificed, not taking his due as governor in order for there to be more for the people. In fact, he provided for the needy out of his portion *(Neh. 5:14-19)*.

One of the most passionate points in the book for Nehemiah was when he realized that the rich were charging their Hebrew brothers interest, eventually taking them to a point of slavery *(Neh. 5:1-13)*. Nehemiah explodes when he finds this out. There is no way to see Nehemiah as not having a heart for the needy.

Yet, Nehemiah's energy is almost always directed into systems, not people. When he sees a needy person, the answer he sees is not just to help the person directly. He targets the system that is creating the need. Yes, Nehemiah clearly does help people out of his own resources, but he doesn't stop there. Where there is a need, the administrative mind sees a new order that must be established.

> **Nehemiah's energy is almost always directed into systems, not people.**

- **How does the way the administrator responds emotionally differ from some of the other gifts?**

The emotional side of the administrator is an interesting study. As a systems person, the emotions do seem to be more muted, but they are still very present with the right kind of provocation. It is just that administrators react most strongly in their core value area. Moses responded to suffering. Ezra responded to injustice and to a lifestyle that was not built around the law. Nehemiah responds to the breakdown of proper order and structure.

In the very first chapter of the book, Nehemiah is overcome with emotion at the thought of the physical destruction of the Holy City. This normally calm, calculating man is in tears over something that some of the other gifts would hardly notice. In **chapter four**, Nehemiah again is very passionate when Sanballat and Tobiah are discouraging the people from completing the work. Nehemiah prays a scorching prayer—what could even be called a curse over these two, and then leads the charge to continue building.

Because of their core values, administrators do tend to be very much in control of their emotions. In **chapter two**, the King notes that Nehemiah had *"never been sad"* in his presence before. It does not say that Nehemiah was buoyant or joyful, but that he had *"never been sad."* Certainly part of the reason for Nehemiah being so self controlled around that King was that to be sad around the King might have resulted in death. But it is also likely that as an administrator, emotions were simply secondary to functional need.

That is, they were secondary till his heart strings were touched … by the walls and gates that had been destroyed or by the work being stopped or by the unfair treatment of the Jews against their brethren. The emotions of the administrator do come through, but they come through in times and ways that can be odd to other people.

Most people look for emotions to surface in key relational moments. When the administrators are more even keeled during those times, they can be seen as lacking in compassion or caring. They do care. They just manifest the care in a very different way … a way that will likely show up on their planner for the days or weeks to come.

- **What does the prayer life of Nehemiah look like? How is it shaped by his core value? List prayer traits in the margins.**

Even the prayer life of the administrator is impacted by his core value. In the **first chapter** of **Nehemiah**, we see Nehemiah start off his prayer as follows:

> *"I pray, LORD God of heaven, O great and awesome God, You who keep Your covenant and mercy with those who love You and observe Your commandments, please let Your ear be attentive and Your eyes open, that You may hear the prayer of Your servant which I pray before You now, day and night, for the children of Israel." (Neh. 1:5-6).*

Nehemiah is instinctively drawn towards honoring the greatness of God.

Nehemiah starts the prayer, almost as if he was approaching the king, whom he is serving as a cupbearer. It is like he is approaching some kind of dignitary, more than he is approaching a close friend. Phrases like *"God of heaven"* and *"great and awesome God"* and asking God to be *"attentive"* give the sense that Nehemiah is instinctively drawn towards honoring the greatness of God. While this is somewhat typical for Old Testament prayers, it is especially typical for those who are of a spiritual gift that is instinctively vertical.

What are vertical gifts? Gifts that are more vertical instinctively understand the need for a hierarchy, and they are very comfortable with a system that assigns a chain of command. Those that are more horizontal instinctively struggle with a hierarchical system, feeling like it undercuts the dignity of the individual. The more horizontal gifts want both consultation and consensus in decision making. The vertical gifts tend to be frustrated by the extra time it takes and the general inefficiency of the horizontal approach.

VERTICAL VS HORIZONTAL

Nehemiah begins his prayer with a very strong sense of honoring God vertically. God is high; He is sovereign. Certainly this sense of awe for God is strengthened by the fact that Israel has been in captivity in Babylon under the judgment of God. God is not someone to be messed with even as the king that Nehemiah serves is not someone to be messed with. Both Nehemiah's natural experiences and his spiritual gift have heightened his sense of the vertical, and this comes out in a very formal, almost legal sounding prayer.

Nehemiah appeals to the character of God as a basis for his approach when he says, **"You who keep Your covenant and mercy with those who love You and observe Your commandments."** In this same phrase, notice the responsibility that he puts on the servants to follow through in obedience. God will have mercy on those who **"observe Your commandments."**

The administrator believes in getting the job done. He is not going to ask for mercy unless he is sure that there will be some follow through. Others ask for mercy just because God is merciful, but Nehemiah is willing to stake his prayer on his own obedience and the obedience of those that he will soon begin to lead.

Nehemiah is willing to stake his prayer on his own obedience!

The prayer continues with a confession of sin and then a quoting of God's own words that He would scatter the people for their sins but that He would also return them to the land of Israel. Nehemiah's prayer reminds me of Daniel's prayer over the people in **Daniel 9**. The two prayers are almost identical in structure and feel. What is interesting is that both the giver (Daniel) and the administrator (Nehemiah) are vertical gifts.

The formality of the prayers is striking. The legal approach is very clear. All of it is based on law and order and an approach that is totally based on wooing the favor of a high and mighty God. I'm sure that the common experiential influence of serving under a great king helped shape the prayers of these two, but there does seem to be a consistent difference between the prayers of the more vertical gifts from those of the more horizontal gifts. We will see that difference again as we study the mercy gift.

Another phrase that Nehemiah prays is for God to **"be attentive to my prayer."** Again, this is so core to an administrator's mind. The administrator is a big picture person. He knows that the leader has many important things to take care of. Not everything is worthy of his attention. But Nehemiah, on the basis of a promise from God and on the basis of a person who is willing to repent and help set a new direction, appeals for the attention of God.

It is as if Nehemiah is saying, "Here is something worth paying attention to." This **"attentive"** phrase is actually used twice in this prayer, and a similar idea of **"remember me"** or **"be attentive to my efforts"** is prayed throughout the book of Nehemiah. Nehemiah wants to be found worthy of getting God's attention. In his mind, he does that by actually completing God's commands.

Nehemiah wants to be found worthy of getting God's attention.

In **chapter two** of **Nehemiah**, we see the phrase **"So I prayed to the God of heaven"** **(v. 4)** tucked right into the middle of a conversation with the king. Again, administrators are extremely practical. He had been in prayer. He had prayed the longer, more orderly prayer in his private time with God. Now, at the point of need it was time for one of those more brief, "God help me" kind of prayers. He recognized his need for God's favor. He quickly prayed and went on with his request to the king. Administrators tend to be very practical in their prayer lives and often tie their prayers to needed outcomes.

As such, they will often be the ones who develop prayer lists, thoroughly covering all of the different areas that need prayer. Frequently, they will take the additional step of tracking the answers to prayer. While administrators are not the only ones who pray this way, most of the time a person has to have some administrative influence to feel more alive spiritually because of this kind of praying. The character gift of the giver also has a strong administrative feel to it, and it too will draw a sense of life from a more structured style of prayer.

GIVER CHARACTER (DAD) ADMINISTRATOR GIFT

- **How do administrators hear the voice of God?**

From the different quotes about Nehemiah's prayers, we can also infer some things about how administrators hear the voice of God. Everything in the book of **Nehemiah** about prayer seems to be one way. It is an appeal to the "great King." It has a tone of respect and comes across as almost not needing to be answered. **"Remember me, my God"** in **5:19** is one example of this.

God tends to speak to people through their core value and administrators are no exception. God got Nehemiah's attention through the report about the city being in ruins. Nehemiah prayed and then formulated a response. It is more like God comes alongside and guides administrators through practical life situations than it is Him "speaking" in a clear voice.

When administrators see the whole picture, have a good sense of the task at hand, and understand how to go about the task, they have a sense that they have heard from God. There is a sense of order in their world, and order is from God. Not surprisingly, they tend to be uncomfortable when there are conversations about "hearing" from God as if they were supposed to hear God's voice in a speaking format.

- **What do you see in Nehemiah's approach to life?**

Nehemiah's conversation with the king is a great place to see another trait of the administrator, especially in contrast to the teacher. When the king asks Nehemiah what he wants, Nehemiah is ready down to the last detail. He knows supplies, men, and costs. He knows the approximate amount of time the job will take. He is ready from A to Z. In **Nehemiah 2:9**, it indicates that the King had even sent guards with Nehemiah to help him complete his task.

The comparison with Ezra is striking. Ezra's approach to the king had been on the basis that God was supreme and would reward the king if he honored Israel. Ezra concluded that he could not ask for guards **(Ezra 8:22)** when he had made his request based upon the sovereign nature of His God. The administrator saw God as working through a request that was

ADMINISTRATOR VS TEACHER

organized down to the last detail. The teacher had laid out a logical construct and depended on God to move on the king in whatever way the king responded. We are all so different in the way we think and the way we approach things!

For Nehemiah, receiving the king's guard was a way of working within the established authority structure. When Nehemiah first arrives, he checks in with the governors of the area and documents his authority from the king to do the work in Jerusalem *(Neh. 2:9-10)*. He spends the next three days presumably with the local officials, given that when he formulates his plan for the wall, he includes all the key leaders of the community.

Administrators seem to instinctively realize that working with the social structures can help pave the way to getting the job done, though they are not particularly impressed by persons with social status. Sanballat and Tobiah were two people who were respected by the people, and who carried clout in the social status. When these two stood in the way of progress, Nehemiah openly opposed them repeatedly.

When the nobles of the land did not do their fair share of the work, they too are singled out for criticism *(Neh. 3:5)*. To the administrator, social structure is functional, not to be bowed down to regardless of healthiness. It is about getting the job done, and it is about everyone carrying a functional and fair part of the load. Leaders are needed, but leaders should put their hands to the task.

> **Social structure is about getting the job done!**

When Nehemiah arrives in the land, the first thing he does is to survey the situation by night. A good administrator is willing to burn the midnight oil, when necessary, to be ready to lay out the plan for those he is directing. Nehemiah takes only a few people with him, and he tells no one what is in his heart to do.

Again, this demonstrates the vertical feel of the administrator. As a leader, part of his work is to lead. It is to go before the people and set a plan. To do that, he has to accurately survey the situation. He doesn't want to hear the negativity of the people, but wants to be able to formulate a strategy with no distractions.

Sometimes it is helpful for an administrator to build a team and to gather information to formulate the plan. In this case, the people were so demoralized that he had to set the tone by himself. It was like he was storing up for one great big cannon shot of hope to stir the people into action.

Nehemiah's plan is simple. Each family group takes responsibility for the area of the wall that is near their homes. Fairness. It is a core value to the administrator. Spread the load and it makes for light work. If each one does his part, the job will be done with ease and simplicity. It just makes sense … to the administrator. His mind is into order, structure, and function. Others are more preoccupied with relationship. The potential clash of the two is quite easy to imagine.

> **If each one does his part, the job will be done with ease and simplicity.**

Administrators are often early risers. They like to get the jump on others and be on top of the situation. They tend to be well organized, using some sort of planner with a scheduling of completion of tasks being a priority. The more relationship oriented gifts might also use a planner, but guess what takes priority for them? Appointments with people are the primary thing listed on their planners, with tasks taking a back seat. For the administrator, appointments with people might take a front seat … if it is a key to completing a task. For the administrator, so much of the motivation centers around getting the job done.

• How does responding well to people help get the job done?

Sometimes, completing the job efficiently means a significant amount of supervision time. If an administrator becomes overly in love with this part of his gift, he actually can develop an attitude of not wanting to put his own hands to the work load. Because of what he is able to accomplish through others as compared to what gets done through the labor of his own hands, he easily feels more efficient by "wisely" using his time on management and thus refraining from any common labor. When this happens, the administrator sends a message to the people that he is "too good" to do common labor.

In contrast, Nehemiah sets a clear example of sacrifice, both in terms of work and of finances. He does not use his entire allotment as a governor for himself but uses it to feed the poorer workers. He works night and day, hardly even stopping for a bath. He not only does the work of supervision, but he pulls guard duty and manages to put in long enough hours to get in his fair share of the manual labor as well *(Neh. 4:21-23)*. Even in Nehemiah's prayer, this value for sacrifice and example comes through: *"Remember me, my God, for good, according to all that I have done for this people" (Neh. 5:19)*.

The core value of the administrator is clearly getting the job done efficiently. They tend to be good motivators in the area of task. They are able to organize jobs in a way that is manageable. The task of rebuilding the wall, a task thought to be totally impossible, is actually completed in 52 days. This "miracle" is completed because every single person is given a part of the job and is expected to follow through in his area. Completing the task is the heart of the administrator. He loves those who respond to the call to work. He chastises those who don't.

Completing the task is the heart of the administrator. He loves those who respond to the call to work.

It is not hard to imagine that an administrator might clash with some of the other gifts in choosing staff for a church. The administrator is going to put the primary value on ability to complete the work load. The prophet is going to be much more concerned with the life of the person. Is he walking in holiness? The teacher would be asking about his knowledge of the Word and his study habits. An administrator who is hearing from God, and who is valuing the other gifts, will see the relevance of these questions. An administrator who is living in his own administrative world, might be willing to compromise, using even a very immoral person in inappropriate ways if it will get the job done.

Because the administrator is so focused on task, he can set a pace that is too demanding for others. In **Nehemiah 4**, Nehemiah has to respond to the complaints of the people and adjust the work load. This same focus on task comes through when the enemies of the Jews threaten attack and call for a meeting with Nehemiah. He refuses to be deterred, having the workers post guards and keep working. He refuses to take the time to meet with the enemies. He has more important things to do.

- ## In the mind of the administrator, how should money be used?

The number of times that Nehemiah talks about financial sacrifice also illustrates the heart of the administrator. Money is to be used for the sake of progress and not on self. Administrators tend to be efficient managers of money, though money is not the core value.

Money is a tool—just as social structure can be a tool, but neither of these is a core value. Several times in the book of Nehemiah, he is aggravated with the people over how they are taking advantage of others and wrongly using money. Fairness is a core value to the administrator, which includes how people are treated financially. Equal pay for equal work is an instinctive value.

That certainly doesn't mean that an ungodly administrator will always treat people fairly. Like all human beings, administrators are able to rationalize that the work of leadership is so much more significant than that of the laborer, and that they are justified in taking a significantly greater wage. Almost every gift is vulnerable in the area that they are most gifted. Administrators, though efficient when they are walking with God, can become some of the most self indulgent of leaders if they stray from God.

- ## How do administrators respond in a church setting?

In a worship setting, administrators love a sense of order and structure and often are drawn toward a more formal type of worship service. Spontaneity is low on administrators value scale, but the need for worship to relate to practical life is high. If a concept does not play out in real life, it has little interest to them. They like teachings that are specific, having little ambiguity. Life is about efficiency after all!

Because of a task focus, administrators are sometimes willing to use people and to love things. The order is obviously backwards. Once a task becomes too central to them, healthy life fades. Administrators, once on the trail of a task, freely ignore even blatant sin if it will help complete the "God-appointed task." Administrators must maintain a constant people awareness of how a task is impacting the people if they are going to be effective.

> **Once a task becomes too central for the administrator, healthy life fades.**

Administrators can make poor followers, especially if the leader they need to be following is inefficient or disorganized. When that happens, an administrator can fall into an "It is either my way or I won't help" attitude. They must learn to be servants first, staying within their own limitations.

It is ironic that one of the most efficient of the gifts is one of the more difficult to describe, but even so the administrator is a relatively clear type. He is who he is. No apologies. No games. Let's get after it and get it done … decently and in order. If it is God's order that he is pursuing and not his own, it is very good order.

Snapshot of the Administrator

Remember: *Core values actually come from multiple sources, so it is possible that you may have some of a core value but not fully line up with that gift. The gifts in this character category also have overlapping traits with other gifts. Look for the basic motivation behind character traits to see if your deepest core value lines up with this gift. Mark any items that fit who you are. Your gift should have the most items marked on these snapshots.*

Passion: Getting the job done efficiently; seeing goals reached; maximizing potential in accomplishment; value order and structure.

Primary fears: Being inefficient and ineffective; chaos; emotionalism; waste.

Spiritual connection/voice of God: Tend to see God and hear from God in the big picture of things; they like to see and understand all the pieces and when things "come together," it is God; they don't want to be pressured into a tight time or space of hearing but like to be able to manage their walk with God in an orderly way; God is in it when things are working out; minimal emphasis on the "experiential" side of hearing God.

Relationship characteristics: Relationships fit more into a practical model of life; they are to be functional and fair; vertical is comfortable to them because it is practical and effective; family is significant in that they have a greater authority and responsibility in those relationships but strong emotionalism is not real comfortable.

Conflict: Conflict happens and should be managed toward the best end.

Task orientation: Effective completion of task is life; it provides the basis for people to come together and to create something that is greater than any one individual; it is the natural outworking of all the good that God would accomplish on the earth.

Possessions: Possessions are tools; they can be symbols of success and thus held more closely; mostly they are something that is used to get to God's desired end.

Activity for Understanding

Who do you know that seems to fit the picture described in the administrator gift?

What part of the picture of the administrator gift fits you well? (If it is only a few traits, check out other gifts that might have similar traits!)

What values of the administrator seemed uncomfortable to you as a value "created by God"?

Is that value uncomfortable to you because you are seeing the sinful side being expressed or because it is in contrast to what feels right to you?

Who do you know that you have "despised" or at least devalued that may actually be acting on an internal value created by God as seen in the administrator?

Have some close friends identify those parts of the administrator description that fit you well. List results:

Mercy: To Be and To Be With

Chapter 10

- ## What is a basic description of a mercy person?

The last of the character gifts is that of mercy. The mercy gift is one where the name pretty much says it all. A mercy person is … merciful. Just as the intellect tends to be stronger and more valued in the teacher, the emotional component tends to be much stronger and more valued in the mercy person. In **Romans 12:8**, the admonition to the mercy person is that **"he who shows mercy,"** should do it with cheerfulness. A few verses later, **Romans 12:15** gives another directive which also captures the calling of a mercy person: **"Rejoice with those who rejoice, and weep with those who weep."**

Even as the exhorter is called to come alongside a person as more of a coach or motivator, so the mercy person is called to come alongside others emotionally. There is something therapeutic about having another person to rejoice with you or to weep with you—especially if that person knows how to "just be there for you" and to be with you. It is validating for another person to say by his presence that "You are worth my time and attention."

[handwritten margin note: MOTIVATES/COACHES — Exhorter vs Mercy — ENCOURAGES EMOTIONALLY]

Jeremiah is known as a weeping prophet and for good reason. Though having a calling as a prophet, his consistently merciful inner man shines through. I'm sure the kings being rebuked by Jeremiah saw and heard more of the prophetic ministry gift coming through Jeremiah. It is typical for the infrequent observer of a person to pick up more on the calling of the person than the character of a person. But the mark of the mercy person is unmistakable in the words of Jeremiah.

[handwritten note: CALLING → PROPHET / CHARACTER → MERCY]

- ## Mercy persons like to do life at an intuitive level. What does this look like in their relationship with God and with people?

Mercy persons are very intuitive in their relationship with God. It is almost as if they come alongside God in the same way that they are called to come alongside people. As such, it is not uncommon for them to have a kind of unexplainable connection with God from an early age. In Jeremiah, this early connection of the mercy person is coupled with a prophetic calling when he begins to hear from God at an early age:

> **Then the word of the LORD came to me, saying:**
> **"Before I formed you in the womb I knew you;**

Before you were born I sanctified you;
I ordained you a prophet to the nations."

Then said I:
"Ah, Lord GOD!
Behold, I cannot speak, for I am a youth" (Jer. 1:4-6).

Jeremiah's response is classic for a mercy person. The mercy person is into being, not doing. He is into coming alongside. He is not into speaking, and he is definitely not into speaking anything confrontational or challenging to others. In this instance, Jeremiah may be giving the excuse of being young. Over and over again in the book of **Jeremiah**, Jeremiah repeats the theme of "Do I have to speak up again?"

- **What are some of the internal conflicts that can happen because of the clash between character and calling gifts? Can you see and describe the clash that is happening inside of you?**

The calling of a person and the character gift of that same person will frequently have a point of interface where there is a clash. As a mercy-prophet Jeremiah had a point of interface in the area of speaking up and even more in speaking up confrontationally. The mercy person does not like to speak up in any public setting, and he hates to speak confrontationally in any setting. The prophet thrives in the midst of a confrontational setting, and a core part of his ministry is speaking. Can there be a much greater point of clash?

CLASH WITHIN

Most people are some kind of combination of gifts, even as Jeremiah is a combination. Accordingly, almost all people have a similar point of interface. A servant-exhorter would have an extreme clash in the area of "do it by myself" vs. "come along side others to motivate." A teacher-administrator would have a huge clash in the area of getting a detailed understanding vs. staying focused on those things that move a project forward.

SELF (JOSH)?
12/16/19

DAD?

- **Where do the character and calling gifts of Jeremiah actually work with each other?**

Any combination of gifts will have both an interface point where there is conflict between inner values. There will also be a point of symmetry where the values of the gifts line up and thus produce a kind of double strength character trait. For Jeremiah, the point of symmetry between the prophet and the mercy person is not real obvious. One such place is the heart for the child or the underdog. The prophet tends to be the champion for the hurting or the oppressed. The mercy person also is a mother-like protector for the young and vulnerable. This double strength trait is part of what drives Jeremiah to overcome the natural reluctance to speak up, especially in the confrontational ministry of the prophet. Jeremiah sees the oppression, and he is moved to speak.

Another trait that acts as a double strength trait for Jeremiah is in the way he hears God. Prophets are very verbal in their relationship with God, and they "just hear." They typically have a hard time understanding that other people don't "just hear." It comes so naturally for them. The mercy person "just knows." A mercy person usually can't explain how he knows or even has a hard time putting into words what he knows, but there is just a kind of knowing that happens. When someone else gives voice to something that he "knows," he will be able to say, "Yeah, that's it!" It is almost like even his hearing has to come alongside someone else to take a tangible shape.

A mercy-prophet combination actually is a kind of double strength trait in the area of hearing. For both of them, it just kind of happens. There is no figuring it out. There are no steps along the way. A word from God just appears. It is and that's the way it is. Most of the other gifts are far less intuitive in their hearing. The teacher needs to check out anything intuitive with Scripture. The exhorter tests it out against practical reality, one step at a time. The servant needs to be able to apply it to a real life response. The giver often receives his guidance in more intuitive visual form but also checks it out with a practical application.

HEARING GOD

For Jeremiah, the connection with God just is.

For Jeremiah, the connection with God just is. *Jeremiah 1:5* speaks of him being called from his mother's womb. While this verse is much more about God having His hand on Jeremiah than it is about Jeremiah having his hand on God, it seems clear that Jeremiah was connected to God from a very early age. He was still a youth when the prophetic call came, and it was likely that the walk with God had begun much earlier. Samuel is another example of a man that was called at a very young age; Samuel too exhibits traits that seem to line up with this same mercy-prophet combination. For a mercy person, the intuition generally starts at a very young age.

• How can instinct or intuition lead a person in the wrong direction?

However, it is important to realize that intuition is intuition. It is a sensing. The person whose intuition is off will struggle greatly. A teacher who starts his point of reasoning from a wrong premise can use great logic but come to a wrong conclusion. In the same way, intuition is a sensing that comes out of coming alongside. In other words, the intuitive person is usually drawing from someone or something else. When he is drawing from an ungodly source, he too will end up at the wrong place.

The mercy person is one of the greatest at connecting but needs to be careful with the connections that he has. Those connections can easily guide him to the wrong conclusions. Jeremiah had a two-fold connection. One was with God. The other was with the people. The connection with God was obviously leading him in the right direction. The connection with the people was, at one point, leading him down a wrong path.

In *Jeremiah 11:14*, God gives Jeremiah a very strange command: ***"So do not pray for this people, or lift up a cry or prayer for them; for I will not hear them in the time that they cry out to Me because of their trouble."*** As a mercy person, everything within Jeremiah wanted to cry out for mercy for his people. He was connected to them, and his "heart" told him that mercy was a right prayer for the people. The voice of God told him differently.

God knew the hearts of the people. God knew that only His judgment would bring the kind of breaking that would cause them to return to Him. Jeremiah's only consistent prayer was for mercy for the people. Mercy was not the solution. God's solution? He told Jeremiah to stop praying for this people!

Until Jeremiah was ready to pray the prayers God wanted him to pray, God told Jeremiah to stop praying. God does this not once, but three times *(Jer. 7:16, 11:14, 14:11)*. Intuitive persons don't process as much as they connect. If the connections are wrong, the intuition will be wrong. A mercy person must carefully guard his core relationships. If he doesn't, it is only a matter of time until he "just knows" that something is right when it is actually wrong in God's eyes. His intuition can be completely turned on its head by wrong connections.

- ## How does what is happening inside of us determine our spiritual connections?

What flow are you connected to? 12/16/19

A mercy person who is struggling with bitterness or fear is in for a long fight because of this incredible ability to connect. The heart of a man connects spiritually with what is being activated in it. If bitterness is activated and stirred within the heart, the heart of that person will connect with and be energized by the demonic. (*Matthew 16:19 and 18:18* declare that what is *"on earth"*—the heart, determines the spiritual connection—*"in heaven."*) If the mercy person activates humility, the Spirit of God will be right there to connect with him.

Once he starts down a road of fear or bitterness, a mercy person's connectivity and intuition actually work against him. When he is connected to the negative flow, it is like there is a voice that says, "This is right. Stay here." For a mercy person, the connections tend to determine what feels right and thus the direction that he or she will take. Observing this, some of the other spiritual gifts often wrongly identify the mercy person as being carried away by emotionalism. To guard against that, they put up a shield against getting caught up in a similar flow of emotions.

> **For the mercy person, the connections tend to determine what feels right and thus the direction that he or she will take.**

The reality is that it has very little to do with what we would typically think of as emotionalism. Truly, a person who is connected to a fear flow may be overcome by emotions, but what is the root cause? Is it the emotions that carry the person away, or being connected with the wrong spiritual flow that creates the problem?

The strong emotional response is just that. It is a response. It is produced by a connection and a spiritual flow of fear or bitterness or other negative flows moving through the heart. Because it feels right to the person, the flow can actually be cultivated until it reaches a point of hysteria. Most of the time, when it becomes excessive, even the mercy person will realize that the emotional tidal wave is unhealthy. But he will likely have a hard time comprehending that it is originating from a wrong source.

• What power do connections hold in the life of the mercy person?

As we look at Jeremiah, we see evidences of this kind of function. Being trapped between the world of the heart of God and the evil hearts of the people, he was in a quandary. Should he speak? Should he be quiet? Should he cry out for mercy? Should he cry out for judgment?

It is this same kind of conflict that is described in *Jeremiah 20:9*:

> *Then I said, "I will not make mention of Him,*
> *Nor speak anymore in His name."*
> *But His word was in my heart like a burning fire*
> *Shut up in my bones;*
> *I was weary of holding it back,*
> *And I could not.*

BATTLE WITHIN · *WHO DO YOU LET WIN?* · *12/16/19*

Jeremiah was connected to God, but he also had a heart for the people. He had both the prophet and mercy influence crying out inside. He was "Yes" and then "No," but then "Yes" finally broke forth.

This is a picture of the battle a mercy person can face if he gets connected in the wrong way. Mercy persons are especially vulnerable to love relationships with unbelievers. They allow their merciful heart to reach out and connect with a hurting individual. Before long, their intuition is telling them that it is right and that they must go forward.

His discernment will tend to be shaped by those around him.

The mercy person must pay attention to his connections. His discernment will tend to be shaped by those around him which means that his inner circle must be godly. This is a huge issue for the mercy person. Some of the other gifts can show a little less caution in this area but not the mercy person.

CONNECTIONS MATTER!

The key to winning a battle with fear or bitterness for the mercy person is at the point of connection. If he is already negatively connected, he will likely need to connect with another person who has God's presence to break free. Some will be able to connect with God in a way to throw off things like fear or bitterness, but most will need help from another person. By turning to a loved one for help, overcoming becomes relatively simple.

• How does the value of love and acceptance shape the life of the mercy person?

The mercy person is created to come alongside emotionally. They are to **"rejoice with those who rejoice, and weep with those who weep" (Rom. 12:15)**. They give a sense of value and validation to others. They enjoy being with people. They accept them for who they are. Right now. The way they are now. That is such a great picture of the unconditional love of the Father, especially as we see it in the story of the prodigal son. That kind of love is powerful and is an incredible force for good. But it is much more powerful when it is aware of its connections and manages to maintain a flow with God and His will for a situation, rather than getting sucked into the darkness.

We see this same battle continually throughout the book of *Jeremiah*. He connects with the people and loves on them, and then he hears from God and is given the task of rebuking them. He gets caught up with the people again until they turn on him. Once again, he is shaken back to reality. It is impossible to connect with an evil people and not get burned. The pain of life is a reality check and should be a wakeup call that causes us to keep our primary connectedness with God.

- **How does a person's mercy heart shape his view of who God is and how He responds to us?**

What is also evident through Jeremiah is that love and marriage become a lens through which all of life is seen. Sin is commonly pictured through the metaphor of a harlot who has departed from her husband. When we sin against God, we jilt our greatest lover. Jeremiah makes numerous appeals for the people to restore the love relationship with their God.

The mercy person also has a hard time seeing God as the disciplinarian or judge but rather pictures judgment as a person receiving the fruit of his own ways:

> *Your own wickedness will correct you,*
> *And your backslidings will rebuke you.*
> *Know therefore and see that it is an evil and bitter thing*
> *That you have forsaken the LORD your God,*
> *And the fear of Me is not in you,"*
> *Says the Lord GOD of hosts (Jer. 2:19).*

Again, notice that sin is pictured as having **"forsaken"** God. The heart of the mercy person sees differently. He thinks differently. **"Your own wickedness will correct you."** God is put in almost a passive position in terms of judgment. The judgment may come and may have to happen, but it is difficult for the mercy person to think of it as actively coming from God.

Most of the time, when I hear someone saying some version of "My God would never judge," it is a person with some kind of strong mercy gifting or mercy influence. Some people do wrongly accuse God for the sinful things that man does. But it is impossible to worship a God who is sovereign and not recognize that He is at least "allowing" things that are judgments to go forth. The mercy person would rather see it as the **"backslidings"** rebuking the person, rather than God actively judging the person.

The mercy person generally struggles with this concept of a God who allows "bad things to happen to good people." The only way for them to reconcile it is that God allows us the fruit of our own doings.

> **The mercy person generally struggles with this concept of a God who allows "bad things to happen to good people."**

Even that is not enough for some, and they get fixated on a tragic event and turn against God and become dark and moody. Some of the most dark, hostile persons can be mercy persons, because the connections almost always determine the outcome in the mercy person. It doesn't seem to make sense, but the person that is designed to be a soft, loving, and accepting person becomes hard, bitter, and hostile. A mercy person who has fixated on some kind of woundedness will be like this.

• Why is taking up an offense on behalf of another such a great danger for the mercy person?

I believe that is part of why God commanded Jeremiah not to marry *(Jer. 16:2)*. The mercy person can usually endure hurt and insult toward himself, but he goes ballistic when those he loves are being treated in a hurtful way. Imagine what it would have been like for Jeremiah to have watched the evil people of the land torment his family! He would have been beside himself and likely would not have been able to complete the mission that God had given him.

Because of their great love for people, mercy persons do have to guard against taking up offenses on behalf of other persons. God's grace is adequate for every single person who gets wounded. If a person is wounded, God will help that person through that wounding, but if someone takes up an offense on behalf of another person, there is no grace to help that person until he lays down the offense. God can't connect with an offended person.

If a mercy person allows himself to collect offenses on behalf of others, he is on his way to the fixation that is described in previous paragraphs. Darkness will set in, and mercy will turn to hardness.

The mercy person can help people through things. He can't keep them from things.

The only solution is for the mercy person to remember that it is his job to value and to validate, but he can't play God in a way that protects others from wounding. The mercy person can help people through things. He can't keep them from things. When we take up an offense, we are playing God. We are in sin. We are taking a place that is not ours to take.

The mercy heart is tempted to go there. It wants to protect those in its care. It cannot. The mercy person needs to humble himself and accept the role that God has given him, not putting God in a box. He must allow Him to move in His sovereign ways, even if that means judgment. That is tough for a mercy person, but it is also liberating.

• How do the different gifts respond to the poor and hurting?

The mercy person does hold a special place in his heart for the poor, the widow, and the fatherless. It is interesting to contrast mercy, giver, and servant in these areas. All three of these gifts are especially drawn to the down and out. The mercy person will be especially drawn to the emotional trauma but will not necessarily be greatly impacted by the physical. A mercy person is often unfazed by a surgery situation, especially after the person is sedated. The emotional trauma is now gone. The physical is of lesser impact on him.

In contrast, the servant is drawn much more to the physical needs of the widow, the orphan, or the poor. He will want to see that they have a place to stay, fix them a meal, or be drawn toward some other practical intervention. The giver is a bit more of a "father" or "mother" figure and looks at the situation in a more long-term, nurturing picture. They don't just want to meet immediate needs but try to focus more on the big picture of how to turn the situation around.

Each gift has its own core values that will drive its response. The mercy person is a connector. He values loyal and lifelong connections. He tends to be more of a follower than a leader, more of a responder than an initiator, unless of course the one in need is a child or someone that the mercy person sees as a natural place to nurture—i.e. the poor, the hurting, the widow, or the orphan. In those kinds of situations, the mercy person will be bolder and will initiate more.

> **The mercy person is a connector. He or she values life long and loyal connections.**

Mercy persons are also more susceptible to be taken in by a hurting person even when the hurt is simply the result of self inflicted pain: In *Jeremiah 8:21-22*, it says:

> *For the hurt of the daughter of my people I am hurt.*
> *I am mourning;*
> *Astonishment has taken hold of me.*
> *Is there no balm in Gilead,*
> *Is there no physician there?*
> *Why then is there no recovery*
> *For the health of the daughter of my people?*

When a person is hurting, the mercy person is drawn to them, to their excuses, and to their cause. In general, the mercy person is more easily taken in by people than some of the other gifts because they do care so much. A mercy person needs to learn to exercise that caring without necessarily turning caring into approval.

- **How does the imagination of the mercy person work for both good and evil?**

The mercy person typically has a great ability to visualize and to use imagination. It is interesting that *Jeremiah 9:14* rebukes the people for walking according to the **"dictates of their own heart."** Jeremiah understands what can spring forth from the heart and how quickly it can overtake a person.

When life gets too tough for a mercy person, it is not uncommon for him to check out from the pain in some form of escape. Because they have active imaginations, it is not hard for them to get lost in a book or a television show. Sometimes sleep is a good escape but so can alcohol or drugs be a form of escape.

When submitted to the Lord, their imaginations can see God's intended future, and they pray with the fervent heart of an intercessor. Without His touch on their imaginations, fear tends to take over, and the negative anticipation of dark things for the future causes them to check out of reality.

• What does the discernment of the mercy person look like?

The mercy person does tend to be much more discerning towards sins of pride and rebellion. The intuitive nature of the mercy person senses the hardness of those sins, and he will tend to pull away from connection. In *Jeremiah 13:9-10*, we see Jeremiah chastising these kinds of sins:

> *Thus says the LORD: 'In this manner I will ruin the pride of Judah and the great pride of Jerusalem. This evil people, who refuse to hear My words, who follow the dictates of their hearts, and walk after other gods to serve them and worship them, shall be just like this sash which is profitable for nothing.'*

If there is a temporary brokenness, the walls of the mercy person drop and connection with a "hard" person can develop quickly. The mercy person is totally turned off by the heart of the oppressor, but the love and acceptance tendency can overtake his "discernment of evil" if the "hard" person can work the relationship angle.

Like the servant, the mercy person hates contention and strife. In *Jeremiah 15:10*, Jeremiah is on the verge of depression in a strong lament over the fact that God has used him to press against the evil nation, and they have rewarded him with strife. The prophet would see value in standing up to this kind of fight.

The mercy person sees little or no value in fighting. For Jeremiah, fighting is a waste. When God forces him to go there, it takes him to the point of struggling with self pity. Rather than fight, the mercy person will usually turn the arrows inward and shoot at himself, often in a way that is not justified. When that happens, he will struggle with either self hatred or self pity. There is a time to stand up for truth!

• How does the mercy person continue to "hold out hope"?

I don't think it is any coincidence that the famous passage of *"I search the heart" (Jer. 17:10)* comes out of *Jeremiah*. The mercy person is always looking for something good in another person's heart that he can connect to. He is always looking for a glimmer of hope.

This image is followed up in *Jeremiah 18* with the image of the potter and the clay. Even though the pot is marred, God will rework it into something beautiful and useful. Because they are more emotion based, mercy persons do go up and down with some significant swings, but their eyes are always searching and hoping for something at the heart level that will give them hope.

Again, a mercy person can be an awesome intercessor … or can just be taken in to connect with evil or hopelessness. They look upon the heart and hope. They need to look upon God's heart and believe. They need to pray and come alongside and love.

God will use them to mend and restore the broken pieces. They are often the first line ministers among the broken because they bring such a ministry of healing, but in most cases, they will need to pass the person on to others for the more confrontational aspects of ministry. A mercy person ministering by himself will tend to be too tolerant of sin as long as he is seeing some kind of glimmer of good in the heart.

The core value of the mercy person is enduring relationship. If he is not careful, he will allow continuing sin in order to maintain a relationship. Because they are not typically analytical people, they need to depend on someone that they intuitively trust to lay out truth for them. As such, they are quite vulnerable to someone whose heart is basically right but whose doctrine is a mess. The same is true of someone caught up in an improper lifestyle but who basically "means well." The mercy person often will be tempted to come alongside them and walk right into sin.

> **The mercy person is vulnerable to someone whose heart is basically right but whose doctrine is a mess.**

The mercy person is excellent in discernment of heart motives and usually tries to isolate himself from anyone he thinks might lead him astray. It works most of the time … until he gets taken in by the pain factor. It is very difficult for him to see pain and not run to it. If he runs in a time and in a way that God does not direct, his gift will become his curse.

Forgiveness is probably his greatest strength, but if he ever gets to the end of his natural man strength to forgive, unforgiveness can be an incredible stronghold to overcome. Some of the most bitter, hostile people I know are mercy persons who tried to forgive in their own strength. The mercy person must realize that the ability to forgive really is a gift of God and not of his own doing.

What a summary to all the gifts! We each have types and shadows in our personalities of the real gifts of the Holy Spirit which are distributed according to God's direction. When He empowers us, it is the real deal. When we live on the strength of our own personality, it is a weak shadow. In fact, it is likely to lead to a permanent stronghold when we try to live out the strengths of our personality apart from God.

In Christ, we each are capable of displaying strengths from other "gifts" which we might not normally possess. In Christ, we become more complete—more like Jesus. In self, we become more unbalanced and more perverse. In Christ, we can also demonstrate the strengths consistent with our own personalities but in a way that we know it is actually God's power working through us. As we study how the spiritual gifts work, we come to understand that it is not about talent. Truly, it is God working in us that is our "hope of glory."

Snapshot of the Mercy Person

Remember: *Core values actually come from multiple sources, so it is possible that you may have some of a core value but not fully line up with that gift. The gifts in this character category also have overlapping traits with other gifts. Look for the basic motivation behind character traits to see if your deepest core value lines up with this gift. Mark any items that fit who you are. Your gift should have the most items marked on these snapshots.*

Passion: Compassion; faithfulness; enduring relationships; being with others in a way that affirms and blesses them.

Primary fears: Broken relationship; any kind of harshness; not being able to comfort and make it right.

Spiritual connection/voice of God: Very intuitive in their relationship with God; often not able to explain what they are sensing but do have a sensing of His Spirit and have a basic sense of what He wants that comes out of that sensing.

Relationship characteristics: Having a sense of close, non-stressed relationship is everything to them; prefer a much more horizontal feel to relationships but are comfortable with a vertical relationship if that is what it takes to live without stress; if the relationship is vertical, they want to be under authority, not in authority; they too have a strong sense of family with key people being special and "in" the family.

Conflict: Absolutely dread conflict and will do everything they can to avoid or appease conflict.

Task orientation: Tend to live more in the world of emotions and thus often are not particularly disciplined toward task accomplishment; if it is important in the scheme of relationship, it becomes important to them; if not important for their relationships, task is of lesser consequence.

Possessions: Again, possessions that are reminders of relationship or tokens of affection are very important; others have a lesser value.

Activity for Understanding

Who do you know that seems to fit the picture described in the mercy person?

What part of the picture of the mercy person fits you well? (If it is only a few traits, check out other gifts that might have similar traits!)

What values of the mercy person seemed uncomfortable to you as a value "created by God"?

Is that value uncomfortable to you because you are seeing the sinful side being expressed or because it is in contrast to what feels right to you?

Who do you know that you have "despised" or at least devalued that may actually be acting on an internal value created by God as seen in the mercy person?

Have some close friends identify those parts of the mercy person description that fit you well. List results:

The Clash

Chapter 11

• Why is the calling gift the more visible gift?

Having studied the character gifts, some of you are probably still confused and struggling. You can identify with parts of what was presented, but other parts just didn't seem to fit. Or maybe you felt like you were a combination of several different gifts. That actually is very typical because we are very complex beings whose values come from several different sources.

A second source of values is our callings. Jeremiah was a mercy-prophet combination. He was mercy in character but a prophet in calling. The deeper picture throughout Jeremiah is that of a mercy person, but he also displays some of the traits of a prophet.

The character gifts will bring the deepest level of satisfaction.

The values of the character gifts are the deeper layer of values and will account for the deepest level of satisfaction for the individual when those values are being lived out. The callings also shape the values of the individual, but in a way that it is not quite as core to the person as the character gift. I am an exhorter-teacher. To everyone around me, I come off as a teacher. That is my ministry.

People see me teach everywhere and all the time. What satisfies me the most is not teaching. It is seeing people grow because of what I have taught. A teacher in character values gathering and dispersing knowledge. Dispersing knowledge is almost neutral for me unless I can see it begin to impact someone who is being taught. I value teaching, but my deeper value is encouraging others.

In the same way, Jeremiah is continually prophesying. He is bringing words of rebuke and correction to the people. That is his ministry. He is seen as a prophet and known as a prophet. But a closer reading of Jeremiah gives a clear picture of a mercy heart. Jeremiah is deeply caring for his people … and for his God. The two aren't getting along very well and it is breaking his heart.

Do we ever see Elijah with the same kind of soft, pleading heart that Jeremiah has? No way. Both have a prophetic ministry, but the character gifts animating the ministries are very different.

People tend to be known for their calling gift more than they are for their character gift even though the character gift is more core to what satisfies the individual. The character gift is the values engine. The calling gives that engine a direction, a path to move on. When a person moves on a track for a period of time, it does create a sense of value for that area. Anything we invest in over a period of time will become a value. Our callings do result in a value center, but that value is more developed than intrinsic. The value matters to us but not in the same way that our character value matters to us.

• What are the mix of factors that shape the values of a person?

A person's inner values system can also be radically shaped by the influence of parents and even extended family. The core values of the parents (partially coming from the character gift of each of them) are a huge shaping factor on the individual. There usually tends to be a dominant set of values in a family which helps shape the individual. These family values come from values emphasized over generations. Groups of families or even nations emphasize similar values creating another layer of influence.

This family influence is very core to the individual and actually forms a great deal of the conscience. A person will generally feel like he is doing the right thing when he upholds the family values and feel wrong when he violates them. Family values have significant influence on the choices of people but don't provide the level of fulfillment that a person gets when walking in his character values.

If you can see where I am going, a person's outward behavior may not be the best indicator of his spiritual gifts. Outward behavior tends to be dominated by family values and life experiences that somehow funnel through a calling. If these outward shapers of behavior are different from the God-given inner character values, a person can struggle expressing exactly who he is and what he thinks to the world.

• What kind of internal war of values go on inside an individual?

With the different pulls of family values, the calling, and the character of a person, it is common for a person to have a clash within himself over what is right and what is wrong. These three areas can easily clash, setting up a possible inner war where a person feels like he is wrong no matter what he does. For Jeremiah, the inner self was saying "Be quiet. You are hurting their feelings." The outer call was saying, "Speak up. You are a servant of the most High God. Honor Him by speaking." And the clash was on.

Most people have a consistent place inside of themselves where this war of values meets. This interface can easily become a point of self judgment or self hatred. God has created this point of clash for balance. Even as the spokes on a bicycle tire help keep the tire round despite pressure being applied to one side of the tire, so the Divine tension between the various values help hold the person more in the image of God.

> **Most people have a consistent place inside of themselves where this war of values meets.**

Stand up. Sit down. Even within ourselves, sometimes the values don't get along, and we have to choose one and tell the other one to be quiet. Each of the gifts (value systems), left to themselves will become distorted and no longer represent the image of God without this tension. We need God, we need each other, and we also need the tension of the various values systems God has placed within us to truly walk in His image.

We need to learn to embrace these points of internal conflict within ourselves. These are the points where God wants us to hear His voice and to give priority to what is needed at the moment. In some cases, knowledge is needed. At other times it will be mercy. Each of us should have a healthy respect for the competing values within, knowing that each value is created for a time and a purpose.

• How do we seek input from outside of ourselves to help solve the clash within?

Being attentive to our own tension points is not enough to keep us healthy. We also need a healthy respect for others in the body of Christ and what each person can bring to the table. Frequently, tension between individuals is also a clash of values. When there is a clash, God is calling us to be dependent on Him, to keep our spokes tied to Him as the center of the wheel. He wants us to pray and seek Him to find the right timing and manner to bring forth His life.

Too often, our conscience is shaped by family values in a way that one or two values dominate. Or worse yet, the inner conscience will be sold out to one value and hate another.

The human shaped conscience will generally be sold out to one of the values and will refuse to hear any other input.

If a person has a family value of productivity and has an inner character value of mercy, that person will continually struggle in the area of productivity vs. compassion. Because of the productivity conscience, he is likely to have a kind of self hatred over his lack of self discipline. In many cases, the lack of self discipline actually is a valid expression of compassion, but the human shaped conscience will generally be sold out to one of the values and will refuse to hear any other input.

The place of interface (whether within a person or between individuals!) truly needs to become a place of dependence on God. It also is a place of letting go of the self judgments. We need to be able to relax about ourselves (which will help us more easily connect with God) and know that it is not necessarily an either/or decision between values. It may be a divine tension of productivity held in check by compassion. Productivity out of control becomes idolatry. Compassion out of control becomes permissiveness. Divine tension is a gift from God to shape us more into His image.

Sometimes it is stand up or sometimes it is sit down. Productivity wins. Compassion wins. More of the time, we need to stop forcing the values to compete and find creative ways for them to cooperate. We only see a clear picture of the true love of God when all of the values are respected in a way that they get to add the tension of their spoke to the wheel. We need all the competing pieces of who we are. We need each other!

Not Work

Chapter 12

• How is our calling a gift from God and not a gift to God?

Many ignore the difference between character gifts and calling gifts. **First Corinthians 12:4** tells us, that there are different *kinds* of gifts. In chapters 4-10, I have written about the character gifts (or *energema* in Greek). A second kind of gift is the category of "ministries" or "callings" *(1 Cor. 12:5)*. Immediately the question comes to mind, "How can what I do in ministry be a gift from God?" We might even think our ministry should be described as our gift *to* God and not a gift *from* Him.

At the end of the day, many of the workers in **Matthew 20** were angry. The owner of the vineyard had paid those who worked only a few hours the same as those who had worked all day ... and those who did more work were demanding equal compensation! The landowner paid each of them a denarius, an amount generally regarded as the amount needed for a person to sustain himself.

The landowner was generous with those who were hired later—which certainly was his right. But those who worked the entire day wanted to be included in that generosity. No, they didn't just want to be included. They virtually demanded that they should be given much more than the denarius that they had agreed to because it was only "fair."

God promises to meet our basic needs if we will at least meet Him part way. That is the promise of the denarius. It often has to come in the form of a gift because we often do not truly earn our day's wage, but the Father is generous. Yet, earning a day's wage is not supposed to be the primary purpose for our work.

> **Earning a day's wage is not supposed to be the primary purpose for our work.**

Those who make spiritual gifts about recognition or monetary reward will be disappointed. The work of God is the reward—getting the chance to participate with Him in His work is a high honor! Those whose primary desire is to bless God and to build His Kingdom will feel rewarded by the work itself. They do not wait for the paycheck at the end of the day but when they see people blessed and God glorified.

Some people also see gifts in a competitive way of who gets the highest calling, much like who has the most wealth. A greater calling means a greater responsibility. God does not reward us for doing more but for doing more with what we have been given—doing what we have been called to do to the best of our ability in partnership with Him.

- **What benefits do we reap from walking in our calling? How is our calling also a promise from God?**

People grow by doing work in the way that God has called them to do their work. The very essence of a man's spirituality is formed by the way he goes about his day on a 24/7 basis. When we connect with God and His Holy Spirit flows through us, it changes us. The more we cooperate with Him, the more our character is transformed to look like Him. When we flow in our calling in partnership with Him, we grow to be more like Him.

In addition, Kingdom work carries with it God's promise that He will enable us to complete the ministry to which He calls us. A ministry gift is both a privileged calling and a promised enablement. He will be right there with us, walking us through each step of the way and providing what we need to succeed in what He has called us to do.

If we understand this fact, a calling from God cannot be a work we do for God because it is not a work that we do. He empowers us. It is a work that He does with us and through us. If a task is something that we can truly do for God without God's help, the task is likely one that has little or no Kingdom value. God's callings are those things that can only be accomplished with His help. There is a reason why a calling is called a "gift."

- **In what ways are the gifts truly given "for the good of all"?**

There is also a sense in *1 Corinthians 12:28* and *Ephesians 4:11-12* that not only is a calling a gift to the individual, but that the gift of the individual is a gift to the church. In *1 Corinthians 12:7*, Paul completes a list of some of the gifts of the Spirit saying, **"But the manifestation of the Spirit is given to each one for the profit of all."** A person is called to be an "apostle" which is a gift from God—a position of high honor for the individual. At the same time, it is also a gift or an enablement to the church. A teacher has a gift to work in a teaching ministry area, but that gift is also given for the good of others. Work is like that. It is meant to benefit the person doing the work, but it is also meant to benefit the good of all of the people.

Callings are things that people are created to do. I somehow doubt that the ministry callings are exhaustively described by a few lists in Scripture. In one sense, there are as many specific callings as there are people, since each one of us is a unique creation with a unique call. No general term will perfectly describe any person's call. The Bible gives us summary descriptions that give us direction. Each individual is unique. Each church is unique. Each culture is unique. What is needed to minister in one time or season will be different from the next.

Gifts are not meant to limit us, but to give us a sense of direction.

Because callings are a description of God's task for the moment, they can be more fluid than the character gifts. They change from time to time so that the person's calling will better fit the **"good of all."** That makes sense if the calling gifts are summary descriptions. They are not meant to limit us, but to give us a sense of direction. God's primary purpose is to build His Kingdom. The calling gifts are one of the ways that He does His work of building.

- **What does the call of God look like in daily life—outside of the church?**

A difficulty with the concept of "callings" is that we have applied this idea primarily to designated leaders in the church. The way we talk about these "called" leaders makes it seem as if no one else is called. Some do have a primary life work of leading the church and are given a title. Some are "called" to work within the church without a title and many are "called" to work outside of the church.

A person needs to know *what* he is called to do and *where* he is called to do it. To me, the "what I am supposed to do" is the more important issue. The "what" is likely to be somewhat stable throughout the person's life. The "where" may change many times.

We do need to recognize those called to leadership in a church for the church to function properly and to grow. But it is just as legitimate for a businessman to seek out those called to work with him. Even the unsaved have a calling, and many times a businessman who is attentive to what God is doing in a situation may be able to identify that call through seeing a person function in a "secular" setting.

> **Even the unsaved have a calling that can be seen even in a "secular" setting.**

We cannot deny who we are. Our character will come through. Our calling will squeeze out in the form of consistent behavior. A person with a calling to teach will handle a business position very different than a person called to be an organizer. A person doesn't have to be saved or even godly for his calling to impact the way he lives his life. The calling of a teacher can be seen whether the person approaches the job in a moral way or an immoral way. Even before being saved, the calling is often evident in a person's life.

Callings are that deep. They will be expressed in some form, whether good or bad, whether connected and empowered by God or done in human strength. Patterns of behavior help identify the call on a person. Generally, a person's language will also emphasize teaching, organizing, nurturing, or any of many other values. Many times, if we help give a person a sense of God's vision for his life, it will actually nurture a desire in him to walk with God.

Once we identify this basic call on a person's life, a completely different question is where and how that person is to complete that call. Some are called to work primarily in the church. Others may be called to the political realm or maybe to business. The key point is that each individual is created for a purpose and a place. Part of his calling will be stable (what he does), but the places he will work can have considerable variety. And each place God calls a person to work will likely be a point of growth for that individual. His calling is a gift, both for him and for others.

- **Does a calling mean that we should focus primarily on doing that gift? What is a healthy way to pursue our calling?**

To some degree, every person is asked to do every calling at one time or another. The term evangelist works well to illustrate this point. The Scriptures make very clear that every single person is to do the work of evangelism. Every one of us has a responsibility to share the gospel with others. Even so, there are some who are called to consistently minister in that calling. They function as evangelists almost instinctively, and even if they are not saved, they are the kind of person who flows in a "selling" mode. They want to share what they are excited about with others.

This "sharing" describes a person with the calling of an evangelist. It is the work or the function of an evangelist. We are all called to do this work in some degree, but God has created some to do it more instinctively. The same is true for the work of pastoring. All are called to mentor and nurture others in some way and at some time. Not everyone is consistently called to that work.

Every person will do every function listed as a calling, at least in a minor way at some time in his life. Every person will do every function listed as a calling, at least in a minor way at some time in his life. A calling doesn't mean a person is exclusively one thing, nor does it mean that he is not called to do other things. What a calling means is that he may approach the work of an evangelist from more of a teaching viewpoint or from a nurturing viewpoint. He needs to do the work of the evangelist, but it will have a different flavor according to the calling of the person.

• What is the purpose of the five-fold ministry leader in a church?

I believe that the "five-fold" ministry listed in **Ephesians 4** is actually describing leaders who are recognized in the church to help strengthen the church in an area. The passage talks about these ministry gifts as being a gift to the body. The evangelist helps strengthen others in evangelism. Again, not everyone is called to be an evangelist, but everyone is called to evangelism.

The evangelist helps strengthen the value of evangelism in his local body. He provides divine tension for that value, keeping everyone focused on outreach. If evangelism becomes everything in a body, we get people saved only to see them wither spiritually and drift completely away from what God wants for their lives. If a local body does no evangelistic outreach, it becomes ingrown, selfish, and is heading toward death as a local body. Divine tension. It is within a person; it is within the body of Christ.

Another important point is that a person may have the calling of an evangelist but may not be ready to be a leader in a local church body as an evangelist. Even the unsaved display some tendencies toward their calling. We obviously would not want an unsaved person leading the church in evangelism. A newly saved person also will begin to move in the area of his calling. Does that mean we want to install that newly saved person as a leader in the church? A person with a particular calling needs to walk in that calling over a period of time and establish credibility and integrity before being recognized as a leader in the church.

The five-fold ministry represents five value areas that are absolutely needed in a church. The evangelist pushes outreach, the teacher instills a desire to learn, the pastor wants all cared for, the apostle organizes and starts new ministry, and the prophet keeps us connected to and hearing from God. Each gift area is a needed emphasis for the body of Christ to be healthy!

- **What are some reasons why the church is struggling to find needed leadership to grow the body?**

Proverbs 18:16 tells us that *"A man's gift makes room for him, and brings him before great men."* Even so, as a person exercises his spiritual gift, he will grow in that gift and move toward leadership in that area. The parable of the talents gives us a vital insight into how the gifts should work. If we use the gifts God desires, we grow in our area of giftedness. If we bury them, we will lose them. If we use them well in a small corner of the world, God will give us a greater degree of leadership.

I believe that the lack of leadership in the church today is due to this very point. We have relegated the "ministry" to the professionals, who are overburdened. Meanwhile, the one and two talent laymen—those who seemingly start with less, are in the process of losing what little they do have. If only they were in the process of doubling their talents!

Churches should seek out individuals who are gifted in each of the functional areas of the five-fold ministry and designate them as leaders. When a church has each of these areas operating, there will be a proper divine tension, and there will be a completeness that helps it grow its people to maturity. However, it is equally important to realize that an evangelist is an evangelist whether he is ready to be recognized as a leader in a local body or not.

If we start recognizing gifts at an infancy level and let people understand that they need to grow in their area of gifting, we will once again restore the church to a place where someone other than the "professional" is doing the work of the ministry.

Leadership is also a separate calling of its own. Not all mature Christians are called to leadership and some less mature persons who are called to leadership may need to grow in that calling by leading. The leadership positions in a church are not necessarily an indication of the person who is the "most spiritual." They simply indicate who is called to do what at a particular time.

> **The leadership positions in a church are not necessarily an indication of the person who is the "most spiritual."**

Because we have focused totally on a few "ordained" or "office gift" persons, we have missed the fact that every single person is called and has a calling. It is important to recognize leaders in an area but not in a way that discourages others from seeking their call, even a call that leads them to something completely outside normal church activity.

No matter where a person is called, we need to remember that our calling is not a work but a gift done in partnership with God. An attempt to walk in a calling without the Spirit's help is a useless, vain enterprise. Many have to stumble and fall over and over again until they learn that "It is God!" We must be fully involved in our calling but in His way and in His time. Without God's involvement, it doesn't matter how fully involved we are. It will be futile. Though we are called to do the work, the ministry gifts are truly a gift to us and through us!

The Foundation: The Apostle and the Prophet

Chapter 13

- ## Which character gifts are parallel to which calling gifts?

After studying the character gifts, getting a grasp of the callings requires little more than a shift from something that is an inner drive to something that becomes a way of doing life. In some cases, the names are even the same. A person can be a teacher in character or a teacher in calling. One values knowledge internally, and the other tends to live in a manner that stores and dispenses knowledge. Because of the similarities, I will spend only a minimal amount of time on some of the callings that are repetitive.

A brief run-down of some ministry gifts is as follows:

Apostle–Foundation builder, starter, organizer, one sent out to start a work
Prophet–Visionary who sees and hears from God how things ought to be and proclaims it
Evangelist–Proclaims "good news" and sees the good in all
Pastor–The shepherd, the care-taker, nurturer
Teacher–Details and analyzes and seeks to understand life, teaches
Healer–Knows when and how to see God move
Helps–Understands importance of the physical and supports others in ministry
Administrations–Task oriented leadership
Workers of miracles–One given to continually look to the supernatural
Elder, Bishop–Spiritual heads of a given group of believers

I start this list with what is called the five-fold ministry from **Ephesians 4**. Each of the gifts in this list has a very close correlation with one of the character gifts. The prophet parallels the prophet character gift; the evangelist parallels the exhorter; the pastor the mercy person, and the teacher the teacher. In the same way, the apostolic gifting mostly parallels the administrator, but there are many traits of the giver which are also present in the apostle. Both the administrator and the giver demonstrate the organizational traits of the apostle, but the giver demonstrates the nurturing and the risk taking that is often needed for a person to be an apostle.

• What are the basic activities of the apostle?

The term apostle literally means "one sent out." We generally think of the 12 disciples as being the apostles, but the same title was given to Barnabas, Paul, and a number of others, ncluding lesser known names like Andronicus and Junia **(Rom. 16:7)**. When we studied Nehemiah as an administrator, Nehemiah very much fits the pattern of one sent out to take on a task. He went out at night to survey the situation and put together a plan to restore the wall. All of these are traits that are very much a part of the work of the apostle.

An apostle is not just someone who spent time with Jesus. If that were true, a number of the people listed in Scripture as apostles would not qualify. An apostle is someone who does a particular kind of work. That work is foundation building. It is starting of a ministry or an outreach. It is going out ahead of others to get something in motion. As I stated in the last chapter, there is both a function that is apostolic in nature, and there is the "office of the apostle."

In the early church, Jesus' twelve disciples were generally recognized as holding the office of the apostle. They were the recognized leaders and were given a title as were many others whom we often don't recognize today. The office of the apostle came to be equated with oversight, but that is not its primary function.

The office of the apostle came to be equated with oversight, but that is not its primary function.

The function of the apostle is to consistently do the work of starting and then organizing things. A person doing the work of an apostle may or may not be spiritually mature. He may or may not be working at a level that will get him recognized within a church as an "apostle." Most churches today do not recognize this calling because to them the apostles are the early believers who got it all started. But a person is still doing the function of an apostle whether he is recognized as an apostle or not.

• When and how could a missionary fit the calling of the apostle?

There are a handful of churches that push the five-fold ministry concept and thus try to identify apostles. In most modern churches, the only persons considered to be apostles are missionaries. Many times, churches define a person who goes to some distant location as a missionary. In many cases a missionary is doing the work of the apostle, but in some cases, a missionary is more of a pastor or a teacher or some other ministry gift. Most people identify a missionary by the location of where he is doing his work and not by what he is actually doing

While it is not wrong to define a missionary that way, the place of ministry should be secondary to the function of ministry. Most people have a consistent calling throughout our lives in function but not in place. For a while, God will use a person in one place and then he might shift him to a radically different place. While places can and do change easily, the function that a person performs will usually have a greater consistency.

Accordingly, I believe it is more important for a person to understand the general function of his call than it is for him to determine a location of ministry. Those with the ministry of the apostle have a calling to start things. There are people who make great church planters but not necessarily great pastors. The two are different skills. They are different callings.

• What are some specific traits of the "start up" person?

A person who has an apostolic calling can easily run others into the ground if he is not careful. They are usually hard workers, willing to work the hours needed to fight through the startup process. Paul was like that. He was a tentmaker, providing for his own finances with his own work and yet still finding time to turn the world upside down with what was left of his time. Those who try to keep pace with the apostle often struggle with burnout issues—unless they too have a similar calling. Incidentally, apostles often go the extra mile to pay their own way.

The startup person has to be able to work with some of the unpredictability that comes with a startup situation. He has to be focused enough to fight through these times and yet flexible enough to adjust to things on the fly. Doing things by the book doesn't work until there is a book established. If we compare this to the description of the administrator, it is certainly not a one to one comparison. In some ways, the exhorter or giver personality may be shining through in this startup person as much as the administrator.

Doing things by the book doesn't work until there is a book established.

The reality is that each of these callings is a kind of "job" with its own unique job description. Even as the people that respond to the callings are unique, so the specific call to a person doing a "startup" ministry will be unique. A few things like the going out, setting order, and going the extra mile will almost always be a part of the ministry. But more things will actually be varied.

The most important point of all is the "use it or lose it" idea. The one who exercises his gift will grow in his gift and may someday become a leader of the church in that area. If he does his job well, the apostle will be the one who establishes a value for starting new things in the church. Others will need to fill in the gaps. They will need to complete the picture with the values and the job descriptions that they bring. That is how God has designed it. We walk together in unity as we grow to appreciate one another.

• How is the prophetic gift more than a form of fortune telling?

The ministry of a prophet is often seen as primarily a ministry of prediction. While some predictions will typically show up in prophetic writings, these predictions are usually only a tiny part of the prophetic ministry. Most of the time it is merely a minor detail of a more central theme of what will happen if the people don't stop sinning.

Modern use of this gift would try to turn it into something similar to fortune telling. God is not in the business of fortune telling but of giving direction toward His intended purposes. There are times when God does use prophets to foretell events that will happen in the future, but even then most of those future events also have a current application where sin is being rebuked and a call to righteousness is going forth.

In **Isaiah 7:14**, Isaiah prophesies that a virgin will give birth to a child. He prophesies this detail about the coming Messiah right in the middle of a rebuke to King Ahaz who has refused to ask for a sign from God. What could the two possibly have in common? One day, there would be a hard-hearted group of people who would refuse to listen to any and all signs that Jesus was the Messiah. The spiritual condition of Ahaz matched the spiritual condition of a people (especially the Pharisees) who would be alive during Jesus' day. The rebuke to Ahaz fit perfectly into the prediction of days and times of the coming Messiah.

• What are the needed functions of the prophet?

A second way that the prophetic ministry has been typically seen is that it is a ministry of correction. Much of the ministry of the prophet does end up bringing a challenge to the body to live holy. However, the core of the prophetic ministry is not a focus on sin, nor on foretelling the future, but a focus on connecting with God and God's voice.

Those who have a prophetic ministry have a very vivid sense of seeing and hearing God. In a culture that is skeptical of such seeing, prophets often feel a bit isolated, out of step, and even psychotic. In biblical times, it was just the opposite. The oracle or seer was considered to be one of the most prestigious persons in the community. After all, what could be more important than hearing from God?

In our modern Christian culture, we have devalued this gift, saying in essence that everything that we need to hear from God is already in His Word. If that is the right approach, what do we do with the prophecies given to Paul about the dangers that awaited him when he got to Jerusalem **(Acts 21:10-11)**? Were they just a waste of his time? What about the prophecy of the coming famine and the subsequent preparations made by the church **(Acts 11:28)**? Was that sort of thing to be figured out by studying the Word of God?

Some say that prophecy was still needed at that time because the Word of God was not yet complete, but which of the things listed in the previous paragraph would have been impacted at all by not having a complete Word of God? No matter how complete the Word of God is in giving us principles to live by, there will always be a need for spiritual guidance that is more specific than we can get from applying the principles of the Word of God.

> **Some say prophecy was still needed at that time because the Word of God was not yet complete.**

That is where the ministry of the prophet comes in. Again, we have not really valued, nor developed this ministry and accordingly it tends to go to one of two extremes. It can be a runaway train, getting misused, or it often is non-existent in the church. Especially with this gift, there needs to be a season of developing the gift before it "goes public." By its very nature, we tend to either ignore this gift or we propel it to the level of "office gift" before the person is ready to have that level of respect.

• How do we grow the prophetic gift in people?

In the days of Elijah and Elisha, there was a school of the prophets. To most of us, that doesn't make sense. We see the prophetical as a magical gift that just happens, not one that needs to be trained. I believe that the reality is much different. There are three basic sources for spiritual communication: God, self, and the demonic. Even as a person's thoughts can get caught up in any one of these three flows, so a person's spiritual connection can get caught up in one of these three flows, and he can be mistaken as to the source.

I have seen many who believe themselves called to be a prophet, giving a word to others that was primarily something of self. How did I know it was self? I knew both of the people involved. The word applied to the prophet himself, and it did not apply to the person to whom he was speaking.

The prophetic gift is no different than any other gift. It needs to be developed. In the early stages, a person is likely to be fooled by a selfish flow or by an **"angel of light" (2 Cor. 11:14)**. An angel of light is a description of when a demon wraps itself in some form that seems to be good. It may even have a Scriptural sound to it. Satan did the same thing when he tempted Jesus. He quoted Scripture. He tried to make it sound like a God-thing that he was proposing. Of course, Satan's temptation didn't work with Jesus.

> **The prophetic gift is no different from any other gift. It needs to be developed.**

The Bible gives very severe warnings against a prophet who speaks in the name of God without actually having heard from God. To speak for God is an awesome thing and needs to be guarded. A prophet in training needs to have a place to try out his hearing, to test it with a group of people who will test him and his word.

We don't think of this being a part of the prophetic. In our minds, the prophetic is not supposed to need training like the other gifts do. It is supposed to emerge full-blown and ready to go. If that were true, why would the Bible tell us to test prophecies **(1 Cor. 14:29)**? I know, the answer could be that we need to judge who is a false prophet and who is a true prophet, but sometimes it is not a matter of a person being a false prophet, but a person who needs to grow out of his immaturity.

• How do we grow the value of hearing from God in a church body?

When prophecy is being used in a body, it often takes on a "magical" feel in another way. A person seeks a word from a prophet and then receives that as the final word from God. Again, this is not good. Every believer has the ability to hear from God.

A word from a prophet should not replace individual hearing. It should confirm something God has already spoken or give previous words a slightly different direction that still needs to be confirmed by God. Otherwise, there is no testing of the prophetic word and it degenerates into a place where a single person starts to talk on behalf of God. That is dangerous. Any person who takes on that kind of role in a body is likely to become full of self, which will in turn shut down his ability to hear from God. That is the runaway freight train of prophecy that I referred to earlier.

Prophecy and the ministry of the prophet are meant to be an influence. A divine tension. They bring the value to the body that we need to hear a current word from God. Just like any other ministry, if kept in its place, it is a powerful force for good. If it takes over in a church, it will take the church to places that are unhealthy.

The one with a prophetic ministry calling already has a tendency towards the extreme. That is because prophets tend to be very black and white. They naturally push to one extreme or the other. Compromise is one of the most hated words in the prophetic vocabulary, even if it is over which color to paint the bathroom. If an immature prophet thinks he has heard from God, he will split the church over a bathroom color.

If we allow the prophetic ministry to become the centerpiece of all divine guidance, we are headed toward some kind of extreme. Instead, a church should also be guided by solid teaching and by mature men and women who are daily seeking the voice of God. The prophetic voice becomes one voice among several influences that helps guide the church. Again, they are the divine tension calling all of us to actively seek the voice of God in whatever way we hear God best.

- ## When does the prophet need to stand alone? What should happen most of the time in the church?

In Old Testament times, the prophet shines when almost everyone has departed from God. Only the prophet is left to speak for God and he is as a *"voice of one crying in the wilderness" (Is. 40:3)*. Even in modern times, there could be a time when a whole church has departed from God, and the prophet has to stand up as a lone voice in the midst of evil and insanity. It could happen, but that should not be the norm.

The norm should be that all the various ministries are walking together, with the prophetic voice serving as a call to continually seek out what God is saying. Again, the ministry of the prophet is not as much about speaking for God as it is about raising awareness in the body of the need to seek His voice. Once the prophet speaks, all eyes should be turned toward what God is speaking, not to what the prophet has spoken. Others will confirm, add to, or possibly reshape what the prophet has brought to the body. The body collectively should hear from God, but the prophet should remind the body to seek out His voice.

Left to himself—or left to themselves, the prophets will move to an extreme and take a body where it should not go. Thus, one of the greatest needs for someone who has a calling as a prophet is to stay in fellowship with other godly people and to practice proper submission. Again, this doesn't seem to fit the *"voice of one crying in the wilderness"* image, but it is needful in most cases. Only when an entire body has departed from God is the more extreme side of the prophetic ministry needed where the prophet stands alone.

Left to themselves, the prophets will move to an extreme ...

Prophets can seem to march to the beat of a different drummer, especially in the Western world, because they see things that others don't see. They often see visual images or hear actual voices. Those who don't experience life this way can brand them as being psychotic. The experience of seeing and hearing is very real to prophets. The problem is not that they see or hear things, but the way our culture has taught them to think. We either call them psychotic or an oracle. There is little room for growth in the prophetic in our culture, not even in our Christian culture.

A person who sees and hears things has to learn to discern what he is seeing and hearing in the same way that a teacher has to learn to discern between thoughts that are true, false, or just useless. If a person is spiritually sensitive, he is spiritually sensitive. If he can see and hear God, he will also be able to see and hear the demonic. Because Satan does present himself as an angel of light, discerning between the two is not that easy.

If a prophet takes off after the demonic and believes he is following God, it is a major problem. The prophetic personality tends to dig in and feel vindicated in the face of opposition. Thus, when the prophet becomes the only voice left, he actually feels like he is connecting with God. The reality may be that he has truly gone "psychotic."

- **How does a prophet test the accuracy of his word? How does the rest of the body of Christ need to respond to the prophet?**

Some ways that a prophet can test himself are the fellowship, submission, and fruit tests. If there are any godly people left, the message of God should connect with the godly. Jeremiah had Baruch. Elijah had Elisha. The prophet and his message should be met with a true sense of fellowship with the godly. Where there are others who are godly, the prophet needs to value what they are sensing from God so that the fullness of what God wants to do can come forth.

All the gifts should be taken seriously to help discern the full picture of God's purpose.

I say "sensing," because few of the other gifts hear God with the clarity or have the sureness that the prophet typically does. Even though the hearing of other gifts seems to be more muted, their input should still be taken very seriously to help discern the full picture of God's purpose in a situation.

Those who are less sure of their ability to hear from God can feel threatened by the strength of the word that the prophet brings forth. Rather than be bold about their own "sensing," they often shrink back and let the prophet take over. When that happens, a part of the heart of God is being quenched … not by the prophet being bold but by the shrinking back of those who should also assume their place in God.

The opposite sometimes occurs as people will try to silence the voice of the prophet. The prophet cannot and should not be muzzled. He needs to be heard, but he must be willing to submit what he speaks to judgment, hopefully from others who are also hearing from God and seeking Him.

Finally, there is the fruit test. The number one thing I look for is humility. If a prophet has become hard and unyielding, he has likely lost his connection with God. If his heart is soft and has an intercessory feel to it, he is likely hearing from God and speaking for God. Jonah did deliver the message of God, but he missed the heart of God. It can happen that way. But most of the time, if a person has heard from God, he should have the heart of God. God's heart is best seen when the fullness of His character manifests along with the message. Even when God's judgment is hot, that judgment will still be interspersed with the self control and compassion that we know to be a part of His nature.

> **Jonah did deliver the message of God, but he missed the heart of God.**

Those with a prophetic calling need to remember that it is more important to call us all back to seeking the voice of God than it is to speak for God. That emphasis brings health to the body. When prophets see themselves as *the* voice, problems develop. Because of those problems, the modern church has largely written off the prophetic voice, much to our own hurt.

In the Western world, we are a people who know little of the active presence and voice of God. That is what the prophetic ministry should bring to this day and age. Instead, we have tried to make the prophet an astrologer, a predictor of the future. We need to return them to a place of setting the value for seeking the active voice of God.

Throughout this book, I have emphasized the idea of the empowerment of the Holy Spirit as being a significant part of the spiritual gifts. We have tended to see only a few gifts, like that of the prophet, as being empowered by the Holy Spirit. The prophet is no more empowered than any other gift. If we are not all hearing from God and following His voice, we are doing nothing more than a human endeavor. The prophet reminds us of that, but it is not his exclusive domain. The apostle, who is the starter of new things, needs to hear from God and so do all of the other callings that are yet to be discussed. We all need God and His voice to walk in our ministry calling.

Snapshot of the Apostle

Remember: (The calling gifts are a way we do life.) *Others will tend to see and identify our calling more than they will see and identify our character gift. However, our character gift does shape the way we approach our calling. Mark items that fit who you are.*

Core Activity: They like to start things; are vision people; constantly seeking new ways, new approaches, new things.

Skill Set: Good at "making it work;" sometimes that means plugging in people where they don't quite fit and training them; sometimes that means operating with little or no resources; sometimes that means creating approaches and methods needed to survive; they adapt.

How They Operate: With high intensity; tend to work longer hours than most; have the passion and drive needed for startup; can easily burn out those who try to keep pace.

Tendency: To get bored once something is running smoothly and in an orderly fashion; adapt to change easily and thrive in the rapidly changing environment of a startup; when the time is right, they are ready to hand off "their baby" to others; can go from deeply involved to minimal connection or a more distant watching of their startup.

Activity for Understanding

Some of the ways we approach life are programmed into us and some are more instinctive. Who do you know that more instinctively approaches life in the manner of the apostle? What traits do you see in that person that fit the approach of the apostle?

Are there ways that you instinctively approach life that fit the manner of an apostle? Are there ways that the apostolic approach has been programmed into you?

What are things that the apostle does in a life approach that definitely do not describe you?

Are there parts of the apostle that are uncomfortable or almost offensive to you? What are they? Are there others you have judged because they are living out their calling as an apostle?

Have some close friends identify the traits of the apostle that fit you well. List results:

Snapshot of the Prophet

Remember: *The calling gifts are a way we do life. Others will tend to see and identify our calling more than they will see and identify our character gift. However, our character gift does shape the way we approach our calling. Mark items that fit who you are.*

Core Activity: Seek the voice and presence of God; instinctively spiritual; are attracted to the supernatural.

Skill Set: Tend to have instinctive responses to life situations; they "know;" right is right and wrong is wrong; there is no gray area.

How They Operate: Live with passion; if it is worth doing, do it big! Life is all or nothing—live in extremes.

Tendency: Conflict is conflict, it is no big deal whether it happens or not; it is seen as a necessary thing to bring clarity to a situation.

Activity for Understanding

Some of the ways we approach life are programmed into us and some are more instinctive. Who do you know that more instinctively approaches life in the manner of the prophet? What traits do you see in that person that fit the approach of the prophet?

Are there ways that you instinctively approach life that fit the manner of a prophet? Are there ways that the prophetic approach has been programmed into you?

What are things that the prophet does in a life approach that definitely do not describe you?

Are there parts of the prophet that are uncomfortable or almost offensive to you? What are they? Are there others you have judged because they are living out their calling as a prophet?

Have some close friends identify the traits of the prophet that fit you well. List results:

The Evangelist, Pastor, and Teacher

Chapter 14

In the last chapter, I listed some of the primary ministry callings:

Apostle-Foundation builder, starter, organizer, one sent out to start a work
Prophet-Visionary who sees and hears from God how things ought to be and proclaims it
Evangelist-Proclaims "good news" and sees the good in all
Pastor-The shepherd, the care-taker, nurturer
Teacher-Details and analyzes and seeks to understand life, teaches
Healer-Knows when and how to see God move
Helps-Understands importance of the physical and supports others in ministry
Administrations-Task oriented leadership
Workers of miracles-One given to continually look to the supernatural
Elder, Bishop-Spiritual heads of a given group of believers

• What does the role of the evangelist look like in most churches?

The evangelist is the third of the five-fold gifts. It closely parallels the character gift of the exhorter. The word for evangelist literally means to preach the "good news." The exhorter tries to put a positive spin on difficult situations, taking them on as challenges. The evangelist tends to emphasize the positive side of the message of Christ.

In the modern church, we typically call anyone who travels from church to church to preach an evangelist. This traveling speaker usually preaches in some sort of revival meetings, which theoretically is a time for church members to bring friends and guests who need to be saved. When that happens in any kind of significant way, the term evangelist could be an accurate description, but an itinerating preacher is not necessarily an evangelist.

The work of the evangelist is to share the gospel with those who have not heard the gospel, or at least those who are not actively embracing the gospel. One of the great tendencies of the church is to become ingrown.

Somebody has to continually emphasize the value of reaching out to those who are not saved. If there is not a continual stirring of the need for outreach, the cry of the church will quickly become, "We need to take care of those who are in need in the church first." When that cry takes over, outreach seldom happens. The needs never go away.

- **How does the thirst for "new" people stay in a healthy range for the evangelist?**

The evangelist tends to thrive on new people, new situations, and new relationships. In a way, that fits the itinerating preacher, but a true evangelist should have a heart for the lost. Within a church, a person with the heart of an evangelist can be a good person to help newcomers get started in the church. The evangelist will quickly connect with the new person and is willing to carry on an intense relationship with the person ... but only for a season.

The heart of the evangelist is for new persons and new situations. His heart is to help the person get "plugged in." It is not to continue working with that person forever. To the evangelist, continuing to work with the same people is a heavy load that restricts him from doing what he does best ... moving on to a "new" person.

In contrast, the people in the church with a more pastoral heart value long term relationships. They want to grab hold of a person and hang on, and they think others should do the same. The evangelist grabs hold long enough to pass them on to someone else and then is off to someone new. Again, if the ministry of the evangelist is not understood, there can be a huge alienation between the evangelist and the more pastoral person, who thinks that the evangelist is not completing his job.

> **If the ministry of the evangelist is not understood, there can be a huge alienation between the evangelist and the more pastoral person.**

Some of the people being ministered to by the evangelist can feel jilted when he moves on to reach out to others. It is important for those with the heart of the evangelist to explain to the newcomer that they are there to help the person transition into a place of connectedness. By setting up realistic expectations for the newcomers, they avoid giving them false expectations of relationship.

- **What kind of outcomes happen in a church as a result of the ministry of the evangelist?**

If someone with the heart of an evangelist becomes the primary driving force in a church, it is not hard to imagine what the end result will be. There will be a continual reaching out to new people, but to put it in church terminology, "the back door will be wide open." There will be as many people walking out the back door to leave the church as are walking in the front door to join the church. The church will revolve around events to "get people in" and the people will tend to be more shallow in their walk with God.

Any church that camps around a single gift will soon end up in some kind of extreme that is unhealthy. Some of those extremes are more obvious than others, but the woundedness that can come out of the ministry of this "positive speaking" evangelist is every bit as real as any created by direct confrontation. When the people lack a deeper connection with one another, they start to feel like a number. That feeling is a slowly rising pain but a deep one.

The greater ministry for the evangelist is not within the walls of the church. It is out in the community. The evangelist has a heart especially for those who are not saved but also for those who are not walking with God. His vision will be outward. He will create relationships for the purpose of sharing Christ. He will be energized by doing events in the community that provide an opportunity to share the message of Christ.

He may or may not be a person who would ever consider preaching in a pulpit, but he will be the one who creates the divine tension in the body needed to say "Let's get our eyes off of ourselves. Let's take this gospel to those who have not yet heard." This is the work of the evangelist. A few who do this work may get recognized by the body as being what we officially call an "evangelist." Unfortunately, that term is usually given only to those who travel and speak.

- ## How does the biblical concept of pastor differ from our modern definition of pastor?

In the modern church, the term pastor has become a very common name for the one who is given primary leadership over a church. When I refer to the term pastor, it is not necessarily the "pastor" of the church. A pastoral person is anyone who is called into the pastoral or caregiver role. As I have been emphasizing, there is the function of ministry and there is an office of ministry. Function comes first. It needs to be exercised. Office may or may not come later.

Since the term pastor has been largely equated with a position in the church, it is hard to think of all caregivers as pastors, but I believe that is the biblical picture. A biblical word that is similar to pastor is shepherd. When the shepherd would come to the sheepfold, there would be many sheep inside. Only the few sheep that personally knew the voice of the shepherd would come when the shepherd would call.

In some of the large churches of today, there are many sheep in the sheepfold but very few personally know the leader who is called pastor. Yet it is important for each of the sheep to have a shepherd, someone who is their pastor who does know them by name and whose voice the sheep do recognize.

Modern church has emphasized teaching and training to the point that many are missing this

Many are missing this personal touch of the shepherd!

personal touch of the shepherd. Churches that promote small groups help address this need, but often the small group leaders see themselves as teachers or facilitators and certainly not as pastors. God has created a whole group of people who are nurturers or caregivers. Nurturers are not necessarily good leaders. Because they are driven by a softer side of connecting with needs, they often do not want to make the hard choices of leading a church or even of a small group. Sometimes the true pastors will be almost hidden in their roles.

The mercy character gift is a parallel gift to the pastoral calling. Does the typical mercy person feel comfortable in any kind of leadership role? No way. Yet the mercy person can be one of the better nurturers of the body of Christ. The giver and the exhorter also make good nurturers, and these two do have a greater leadership tendency. The point is simple. We tend to equate ministry with positions and only those willing to step into leadership can be ministers. While there is a place for "offices" of ministry that fit that description, if we leave all ministry to the office gifts, very little ministry will happen.

The pastoral ministry is the best example of this fact. Hundreds of pastors are needed in a larger church. Babies cannot take care of themselves. If the evangelists are doing their work, the pastors need to be right there, following along behind to take over the nurturing work.

This is hands on, high touch work. This is not the work of a teacher or preacher who addresses a crowd once or twice a week. This is human to human nurture. It is real life experience being passed in a personal way. The church of today is dying for a lack of pastors. More caregivers need to hear the call to ministry—but not necessarily a call to "the ministry" as we define it today.

• What are the results of the pastor gift in different settings?

It is not just in the church that a pastor might exercise his gift. A businessman who had a pastoral calling would build his business by taking good care of his key employees. He would continually sow into and invest in them in ways that would help make them more productive. Of course, a downfall in some business settings is that he might have a hard time making the tough decisions that need to be made, much as a mercy person would not want to make the tough calls. But the point is that a calling can easily be used in any kind of setting.

In a similar way, a person with a call to evangelism might use his gift in sales or some kind of public relations job. He is good at meeting new people. He can use that gift to quickly build relationships with people and to positively influence them. If he has a heart to build the Kingdom of God, he will not misuse his gift to manipulate people. Even in a secular setting, he will build people and where possible, share things that could bring spiritual growth.

Our culture has tended to segregate the "spiritual" work from the natural. When a person is walking in His gift, he will touch the hearts of people. When he does that in a way that others sense the God factor in the relationship, Kingdom work is happening whether or not the name of Jesus is mentioned. The life of God should be flowing through us everywhere and all the time, not just inside of the church.

> **When others sense the God factor, Kingdom work is being done whether or not the name of Jesus is mentioned.**

While in most churches, the pastoral ministry is largely missing, there are churches where it dominates, generally because the Pastor (with a capital "P"—the head of the church) is more of a mercy person. If the primary leader of the church is a mercy person, and he refuses to allow the other gifts to operate as they should, there will be little or no confrontation of sin with a continual emphasis on the need to forgive. In this kind of atmosphere, very few people go on to maturity.

If the pastoral gift is too predominant, a church will remain a small group of people who get to know each other well but live in relative isolation from the world. The people of this kind of church tend to stay trapped in a level of woundedness and sin. This church is of little benefit to the Kingdom. Sometimes it can bring healing to a few, but more often than not, it merely comforts people and coddles them while they stay in their messed up situations.

No ministry is complete in itself. Each of the ministries needs the others or they will end up in some extreme that causes dysfunction in the body. Many churches today lack the personal touch of the pastoral ministry and are dying because of the lack of personal touch. Others are dominated by it, and the people within the church are dying because they have become the center of attention instead of God being at the center. We need each of the five-fold ministries functioning at a healthy level for His glory to manifest!

• What are the outcomes a teacher brings to a church or business?

The final gift listed in the five-fold category is that of the teacher. Again, some try to blend the functions of pastor and teacher as if the two were the same. While a nurturer may do some teaching, teaching is not the core work of the nurturer. The nurturer provides the personal touch. The teacher lifts up the value of study and understanding. A great teacher is a huge asset to any church body—but the gift of teaching should not be limited to what happens inside of the walls of a church.

Some with the calling of teacher may not be gifted in a way to teach a large class, but even playing the role of eager student in a class can elevate the value placed on understanding in a church. The calling of a teacher is more about value and a manner of pursuing life than it is about being polished in skill. However, those who use the gift they have, even if it is simply a student asking questions, will often find themselves teaching before long. When we use a gift, we grow in it. As we grow, we tend to get recognized and used in a greater way. **_"A man's gift makes room for him" (Prov. 18:16a)_**.

Teachers tend to be more logical and often are suspicious of more emotional atmospheres.

Teachers tend to be more logical and often are suspicious of more emotional atmospheres. They want things done in order and by the written code. As such, they bring structure to the body and are a foundational gift. I think that may be what is being conveyed by _**1 Corinthians 12:28**_ when it says, **_"And God has appointed these in the church: first apostles, second prophets, third teachers …"_**.

The apostles are the first ones to go out and set up a basic structure. The prophets follow along with the emphasis on the voice and presence of God. The teachers are next in line setting up a systematic study of the Word of God and also building a much greater level of detail into the basic order that the apostle has established. Finally, the teacher gets it all down in writing, into a policy manual that will establish a universal working code.

Again, the teacher can easily express his gift in a secular setting. He will be the detail person for a business, wanting policy manuals and setting standards for performance according to a

written code. He will press for better training for all of the employees and often will end up being the one to do the teaching. In times of crisis, he will want to "study" the situation, learning all that he can before making a decision. Even as the character gifts mark a person in all that he says and does, so the callings mark a person in every area of his life.

• **What happens if the teacher gift dominates a church?**

If the gift of the teacher takes over in a church, dependence on God can be given a back seat to the written code. Legalism takes over and everything has to be done by the book. Intellectual understanding is given a high value, and the heart condition is less noticed.

That is part of why I said that a pastor and a teacher are very different. They have different core values. The teacher is more than willing to correct if there is a clear written precedent. The person or the situation doesn't matter; the code is given preeminence. The pastor finds it difficult to correct others, and he often puts people above the need for righteousness.

The ultimate end of a church dominated by teachers will be a puffed up, Pharisaical type of church. Head knowledge by itself puffs up *(1 Cor. 8:1)*. The pride that comes with increased knowledge (that is not buffered by an emphasis on the heart connected lifestyle of true righteousness) causes the church to disconnect with God and to live in a more ritual mode.

• **How do spiritual gifts influence worship styles and denominations?**

The teacher, like all of the gifts, even has its own preferred worship style. The more thought centered and organizational types of gifts tend to enjoy the more formal and ritualistic worship styles. To them, the more structured worship is rich and fulfilling. They tend to want any emotional displays kept to a minimum. The mercy/pastoral gifts want a hands on, people oriented service. They like things to be more informal and interactive. The prophet/exhorter/evangelist gifts want to experience a service with some "real passion." An emotionally charged service feels right to them … unless of course they have been schooled otherwise through years of religious training. In that case, who knows which type of service will be preferred!

When we think about the various gifts and worship styles, it is no wonder that we have such a variety within our worship services. And it is no wonder that we have such protracted fights over how to go about our services. I have noticed that entire denominations tend to camp around one or two spiritual gift areas. Everything from worship styles to doctrine often lines up with the values and thinking that comes out of a point of view that lines up with one of the spiritual gifts. It is likely that a few of the key founders of the denomination were able to imprint the denomination with the values and the tendencies that came from their own spiritual gifts. Eventually, a denomination was born that revolved around those same gifts.

> **Entire denominations tend to camp around one or two spiritual gift areas.**

When we realize that this is what is happening, it is much easier to take a step back and reevaluate how we think about denominations. First of all, the denominations themselves might be a little less self righteous in their thinking if they would only realize that they are simply representing one of the spiritual gifts in abundance and not the overall picture. Secondly, those who have judged the denominations might be able to show a little more respect for a worship style different from their own, or they might be able to embrace others for the emphasis that they are bringing to the body of Christ.

After all, I do believe that this is the purpose of the different gifts. Each is created as a piece to the puzzle, a jigsaw puzzle that will ultimately reveal the image of God to the world. When each piece fits in its place, the total picture begins to emerge. As long as each of the pieces is touting its own image as the complete picture, confusion will reign. There are denominations that clearly line up with the gift of the teacher, or of the servant, or the administrator. It is amazing that entire groups of people can be consistent with a single spiritual gift, but it happens more often than not.

As long as each of the pieces is touting its own image as the complete picture, confusion will reign.

As long as each particular group clings to its ability to represent Christ as being superior to others, the body will remain fractured and powerless. We need to see the bigger picture, and value the different gifts, with the preferences for different worship styles. If we would learn to honor one another, we would see an incredible healing of the body and a release of His mighty power. It is because of these divisions that we are weak and struggling. We need to value each other!

Snapshot of the Evangelist

Remember: *The calling gifts are a way we do life. Others will tend to see and identify our calling more than they will see and identify our character gift. However, our character gift does shape the way we approach our calling. Mark items that fit who you are.*

Core Activity: Want to share with those who have not yet heard the good news of Christ's heart; Want to redeem/restore others; tend to continually seek out new relationships.

Skill Set: They are huge visionaries; they ask "Why not here? Why not now?"

How They Operate: Hate negativity! Will minimize those things that might bring conflict or work against a person responding to the call of God on his life.

Tendency: To lose sight of the immediate situation by focusing on what could be; need those who can help them stay more grounded and practical.

Activity for Understanding

Some of the ways we approach life are programmed into us and some are more instinctive. Who do you know that more instinctively approaches life in the manner of the evangelist? What traits do you see in that person that fit the approach of the evangelist?

Are there ways that you instinctively approach life that fit the manner of an evangelist? Are there ways that the evangelistic approach has been programmed into you?

What are things that the evangelist does in a life approach that definitely do not describe you?

Are there parts of the evangelist that are uncomfortable or almost offensive to you? What are they? Are there others you have judged because they are living out their calling?

Have some close friends identify the traits of the evangelist that fit you well. List results:

Snapshot of the Pastor

Remember: The calling gifts are a way we do life. Others will tend to see and identify our calling more than they will see and identify our character gift. However, our character gift does shape the way we approach our calling. Mark items that fit who you are.

Core Activity: Are caregivers and nurturers; tend to stay with the 99 sheep; their lives are defined by the people in their lives.

Skill Set: Build solid, ongoing relationships; tend to have lifelong friends.

How They Operate: When the world of someone close to them is not right, life is not right; they work at bringing peace to people and situations.

Tendency: Often take up an offense on behalf of others when they see one person mistreating another; want people to be "nice."

Activity for Understanding

Some of the ways we approach life are programmed into us and some are more instinctive. Who do you know that more instinctively approaches life in the manner of the pastor? What traits do you see in that person that fit the approach of the pastor?

Are there ways that you instinctively approach life that fit the manner of a pastor? Are there ways that the pastoral approach has been programmed into you?

What are things that the pastor does in a life approach that definitely do not describe you?

Are there parts of the pastor that are uncomfortable or almost offensive to you? What are they? Are there others you have judged because they are living out their calling?

Have some close friends identify the traits of the pastor that fit you well. List results:

Snapshot of the Teacher

Remember: The calling gifts are a way we do life. Others will tend to see and identify our calling more than they will see and identify our character gift. However, our character gift does shape the way we approach our calling. Mark items that fit who you are.

Core Activity: More than any other thing, they seek to understand.

Skill Set: Have the ability to see things from a logical point of view and to see how things fit together.

How They Operate: Want to develop a written code or policy manual to govern how things should be done; want to minimize the emotional side of worship and ministry; strive to establish a value of fairness and doing things in a proper manner; Word driven response in all situations.

Tendency: Emphasize the need to read and study the Word; logic is given precedence over the personal.

Activity for Understanding

Some of the ways we approach life are programmed into us and some are more instinctive. Who do you know that more instinctively approaches life in the manner of the teacher? What traits do you see in that person that fit the approach of the teacher?

Are there ways that you instinctively approach life that fit the manner of a teacher? Are there ways that the teacher approach has been programmed into you?

What are things that the teacher does in a life approach that definitely do not describe you?

Are there parts of the teacher that are uncomfortable or almost offensive to you? What are they? Are there others you have judged because they are living out their calling?

Have some close friends identify the traits of the teacher that fit you well. List results:

More Callings

Chapter 15

• How does a calling end up shaping a generation?

God puts a call on a person's life. That gentle tug, over a period of time develops into a way of doing things, which eventually results in a values system. Because we are egoistic, we tend to value those things that have been repeated patterns in our lives. Even those who go off into self hatred are still giving value to that area by giving it the kind of time and attention that says, "This area matters." Those not responding to the call, who and are fighting it, end up valuing it, if only in a negative way.

Over time, the values system that grows in an individual will begin to influence those around him. Those who are created with a leadership call will have a very significant influence on those around them. Some end up shaping the core family values and a few even shape the family for generations to come.

In the case of founders of denominations, the core value of a single person becomes a core value for an entire community for generations to come. Thus a calling becomes a gift, not just to an individual but to the body of Christ. Our calling is shaping each of us while we attempting to reach out and positively impact others. Entire communities (like denominations) are given a calling to bring a values influence that will cause the body of Christ as a whole to be a complete reflection of His image.

If we could only see how all the pieces fit together and begin to honor one another, what a difference it would make in the way we live. Even those who are not living for God carry the image of their call around with them. They can't help but have a values emphasis consistent with their call, but they often let that value slide to the negative side.

I spoke earlier about the mercy person turning bitter or the organizer becoming a controller. When we understand how it works, it is much easier to pray for those who seem to be totally caught up in wickedness. It is also much easier to pray for those who are coming from a very different place of spiritual gifting and values. It is easier to understand them, and it is easier to pray for them—to pray that they would complete the call that God has for them in a way that honors Him.

The list of callings that we are studying is as follows:

Apostle-Foundation builder, starter, organizer, one sent out to start a work
Prophet-Visionary who sees and hears from God how things ought to be and proclaims it
Evangelist-Proclaims "good news" and sees the good in all
Pastor-The shepherd, the care-taker, nurturer

Teacher-Details and analyzes and seeks to understand life, teaches
Healer-Knows when and how to see God move
Helps-Understands importance of the physical and supports others in ministry
Administrations-Task oriented leadership
Workers of miracles-One given to continually look to the supernatural
Elder, Bishop-Spiritual heads of a given group of believers

• How does the gift of healing work?

The gift is the healer or gifts of healings *(1 Cor. 12:9, 28, 30)*. Because the gifts are given **"for the profit of all" (1 Cor. 12:7)**, it is probably more accurate to say a person does not actually possess a gift of healing. If human beings had that kind of power, they would certainly misuse it in a very grotesque way. It is more accurate to say that God has called a person to work in the area of healing. Because of the call, God tends to work through that person more often in that area than he does those who do not have a calling in the area of healing. It is God who heals and He does so **"for the profit of all."** He chooses when He wants to work, as well as where and how.

Even though a person called to healing does not have control over the gift, the heartbeat of a person with a call in the area of healing is toward healing. He thinks about healing. He prays for it. He believes for it. Where we focus, we grow. When we grow, we become better known for that trait and before long, others are seeking us out when they have a need in the area of our gifting. Of course, we then tend to see it happen more and more.

Especially in this area, I believe it is important to emphasize that anyone can be used by God to pray a healing prayer over another person which will result in healing. And no one "possesses" the kind of healing power that can arbitrarily bring healing in any situation that he chooses to bring healing.

> **Anyone can be used by God to pray a healing prayer over another person.**

• How do the power gifts differ in approach from the gift of healings?

If that is true, what is the call to healing? It is a call, similar to that of the prophetic call. There is a desire to see the power of God show up in a situation. It is very similar to workers of miracles, except that it focuses more on healing. All three of these gifts value the supernatural. They are willing to take the time to fast and pray. They remind us that the natural realm is not all there is, and that in any situation, there is a solution from "outside of the box." While others put time in seeking natural cures, these put heart and soul into entreating God.

That is not to say that a proper use of these gifts would not allow for natural cures. As a part of Hezekiah's healing, Isaiah commanded him to put a poultice of figs on his boil *(Is. 38:21)*. The supernatural has to show up in the natural realm, and those with the gift of healing seem to have a second sense of how to intertwine the two. In fact, the person with the gift of healing isn't so much a healer, as a person who understands God's sense of timing and manner.

Elisha is a great example. He never speaks a word and brings healing the way that Elijah the prophet of prophets would do. Elisha is both a nurturer and a healer. I do find there are some very close parallels between the gift of the giver and the healer. Both understand the right time to help and the right time to refrain from helping in order for the will of God to be accomplished. A healer doesn't just go around healing but uses the gift to nurture others in their faith and to help mature them in God. In many cases, healing is the vehicle that brings a person to faith.

Even as we see with Elisha, the healer will often get the person who is being healed involved in his own miracle. He has the person go wash in the Jordan River (Naaman) or put flour in the poisoned pot of stew. When he is praying for the Shunammite's son, Elisha stretches himself out on the body of the boy and goes mouth to mouth and eye to eye to pray. Elisha fully connects with the situation and when possible, involves the other person.

The healer tends to involve the person being healed in his own miracle.

Jesus does a mixture of the more prophetic style and the healing style. At times, He speaks the word and the healing is accomplished. Other times, He does things like spitting and making mud and applying it to a person's eyes and then tells him to go wash in the pool of Siloam. Sometimes it is a simple word given. Sometimes He asks something of the person.

Those with a call in the area of the gifts of healings have one eye on the growth of the individual and the other eye on the glory of God. When the two can come together, faith is released and His power goes forth.

Those called to a healing ministry can accomplish nothing in and of themselves, but which of the gifts can? It is just more obvious when a healing prayer is not answered than it is when a teacher misses God with his teaching. We all need God to fully carry out our call. The person praying for healing is not called to heal, but to pray. Having been obedient to God, the rest is up to God. If healing does not happen immediately, he should continue to pray.

• How does the character gift influence the gift of helps?

The gift of helps very much parallels that of the servant character gift. Which of the leadership gifts could be effective without followers? The person with a gift of helps is more of a follower who tends to hate being in the limelight. He would rather work behind the scenes. He does need appropriate appreciation expressed to him for his work but wants that appreciation to come in a more private way.

Those with the gift of helps often like to work alone, especially if they are of the servant character gift. However, those with the character gift of the giver often make good helps persons, but they do not like to work alone. They want everyone doing their fair share. A giver will actually become offended and will voice complaints if others are not involved. If a person has a calling in the area of the gift of helps, it is very helpful to know what his character gift is. Whether he works alone or with others, whether he is thanked publicly or privately and how much support is needed for the job will vary with the character gift.

• What are the traits of the administrator?

Another gift listed in *1 Corinthians 12* is that of administrations. In many ways, this is similar to that of the apostle or some of the other leadership gifts, but it has a few unique qualities. The apostle is administrative in style but likes to start new things. He is better at managing things during a startup phase, which often has many peculiarities and requires a great deal of flexibility. The administrator is more of a manager keeping an eye on a well oiled machine. Once everything is in place, they tend to shine keeping everything running smoothly. They usually are not overly fond of change. Change brings chaos, and they prefer order.

The administrator loves having a policy manual and he values fairness. Though they are decision makers, they prefer to make decisions at the general level of policy and then apply those decisions to all. They tend to be organized, on time, and find satisfaction in a smooth road to progress. Most of them are not overburdened with the levels of perfectionism that can push them into micromanagement. The eye is on getting the job done efficiently and well. Perfectionism is actually a stumbling block toward achieving that goal.

• How does a person who is a worker of miracles build his ministry?

The worker of miracles is very similar to the person who operates in gifts of healings. The person seeking miracles is focused on seeing God's power go forth in any and all ways to bring Him glory. This gift tends to be a little bit less personal in nature and often wants to operate more in a public arena. The miracle is not so much for the individual as it is for the body of Christ, to help build the faith of the body … and of course to meet an immediate need. As with the gift of the healer, who can do miracles? No one can, but some are much more in touch with what God wants to do to bring the miracle to pass. They focus on it. They pray for it. They see miracles happen. They are called workers of miracles.

In both the gifts of healings and the workers of miracles, faith is a very important factor. These people have to be able to relate to the unseen world even more than they relate to the natural realm. Otherwise, they would be like most people whose vision is dictated by what they see before their eyes. Both the healer and the worker of miracles have to be able to look beyond the physical reality they see before them and respond to the direction of God in a way that will introduce the supernatural into the natural. God is able to use these persons as a release point for His life into the natural realm because of their faith. Of course, faith is cultivated by spending time with God and seeking Him on an ongoing basis.

> **These people have to be able to relate to the unseen world even more than they relate to the natural realm.**

• What makes a person effective in the leadership area?

A final set of gifts are the leadership gifts. Some of the names are elder, bishop, overseer, or deacon. Though the titles vary, they are all accountability gifts. With the possible exception of deacon, it is hard to separate these four in function. The deacons of **Acts 6** were given the job of overseeing the distribution of food to the widows so that the apostles could continue to focus primarily on ministering the Word of God and giving themselves to prayer. However, before long, the deacons had become significant ministers in their own right. Having served well in the area of the food distribution, they gained favor with the people and soon became more known for their ministry of the Word of God.

It is almost impossible to separate the natural from the spiritual. The deacons who serve well waiting tables will gain the respect needed to minister in other areas. The same is true of elders, bishops, or overseers. The person with a leadership calling who is not willing to get his hands dirty when needed, is not properly exercising that calling. The elder is meant to be a respected leader and a decision maker for the group, but there is a good chance that he got to that place because he exercised his gifts well along the way. Just because he is now in the place of elder doesn't mean he should stop exercising those same gifts. It is his calling.

These leadership gifts are seldom the primary gift of a person.

These leadership gifts are seldom the primary gift of a person but are more like the five-fold gifts that I spoke of earlier. A person is called to do a particular type of work. As he does that work well, he becomes recognized and becomes a leader in that area. In the case of elders, bishops, and overseers, they are being thrust into a position of general oversight of a local or regional part of the body of Christ. Most of them received that call because they had been exercising the gift of teacher, apostle, prophet, or some other gift.

Leadership is a call in and of itself. Some teachers are meant to step into general leadership of the body and some are not. The same is true of other giftings. But the call into almost all leadership positions will not happen unless a person first exercises other areas of gifting in the manner that God has desired. When a person does the more basic things that God has called him to do and does them well, then he gets the opportunity to lead.

• What is the role of spiritual maturity in leadership?

For some people, the leadership call is more primary, and these people tend to try to skip the step of exercising a "behind the scenes" role for a season. These people have an opinion about everything and wonder why they are seldom listened to. They don't understand that there is a time of paying your dues. Some are not so naturally gifted in leadership, but because they have served well, they have grown in spiritual maturity. They are called to serve in a leadership area though it may not be a primary calling.

The ideal, of course, is for a person to have both a leadership call and spiritual maturity. Sometimes the leadership person will get "on the job" training in the leadership area and will grow to maturity through exercising their gift and through making mistakes with other people's lives. It is better for the leadership person to learn by being under authority until the appropriate maturity develops, but that is not always how it happens.

If the church were a little more open to developing leadership gifts in the immature, there would be more godly leaders in the church. However, those with leadership skills but lacking in maturity also need to be willing to humble themselves and sit under someone lacking in leadership skills for a season while they are developing in maturity.

What exactly is leadership in a biblical sense? It is influence. In **Matthew 20**, Jesus describes **"Gentile"** or worldly authority as controlling or dominating. Biblical leadership is best described as servant leadership. It works from the bottom up and not from the top down. It comes alongside. It intercedes. It carries others when necessary. It is an attempt to mold, shape, and influence others toward a walk with Christ. None of this can be done without at least a basic level of spiritual maturity.

People with a call to leadership have a strong desire to influence others. People without that call often feel like they are intruding on others when they are at a point of needing to influence others. Those with a leadership call will be much quicker to exercise influence, but only those with maturity will be able to do so in the biblical manner. All people are called to influence others positively just as all people are called to evangelize others. But some are especially called in this area of leadership. For some, it is a life work. It is a focal point of their efforts. For others, it is more secondary and is only done because there is a need within a local body.

> **Those with a leadership call will be much quicker to exercise influence, but only those with maturity will be able to do so in the biblical manner.**

In the modern church, we tend to give the title "pastor" to the primary overseer of the church. In ministry, the term pastor refers more to nurture. Regardless of the title, the reality is that every church needs a leadership team, preferably with a point person. In biblical times, that person usually carried the title of the elder, bishop, or overseer. Somebody has to be in charge.

If man weren't selfish and sinful, we could determine all decisions by consensus. Unfortunately, man is sinful, and thus we must have a governmental structure within the church. To build that structure, we need to seek out those with leadership gifting, but only if and when they have developed appropriate maturity. Otherwise, it would be much better to install someone with less leadership talents but more spiritual maturity.

• How does God use callings to shape us?

The important thing to remember about the callings is that they are task emphases. The gifts that I have covered are some of the tasks that can be done for Christ. There are many others that I have not covered. In the modern church, we often have worship leaders. Where do we see that in the New Testament? Or what about youth pastors? These are both legitimate calls as are many other jobs that need to be done for a church to successfully minister to its community. I don't believe the New Testament means to give a complete job list. It gives examples and a starting point.

Every person will have a subtle pull within the area that is his call. It ends up being an emphasis and a value. It is a way of going about life. For me, my ministry calling is that of a teacher. I tend to handle life by stepping back to get an understanding, laying out that understanding in a systematic manner, and then proceeding to the task. This is the way I do life. A pure leadership person would approach life much more from the viewpoint of managing people. A helps person would look for a place to contribute, etc. Our calling is a way we do life and that calling is also heavily influenced by our character gift.

If we are not careful, we begin to think our way is right, not understanding that there are many gifts and many callings.

Our calling ends up being a way of seeing and valuing life. If we are not careful, we begin to think our way is right, not understanding that there are many gifts and many callings. When that happens, we are willing to divide the body of Christ over trivial things, over things that if given a proper emphasis would be good. When a calling becomes an exclusive emphasis, it soon loses its goodness. Each calling is meant to bring its contribution to the whole picture. No calling is meant to become the whole picture.

Callings can change. They are more transient than the character gifts, but more often than not, it is not the calling that is changing as much as it is the setting that is changing. A youth pastor gets older and begins to pastor adults. A pastor in America gets a call to go to some distant place around the world. The setting is changing, but the work is similar. What we invest in, we value. As we change what we do, we change. I think sometimes that is the reason for multiple calls. God is using a calling to change our hearts more into His image. After all, both for the individual and for the body of Christ, to be changed into His image is the greatest call of all!

Snapshot of the Next Five

Remember: *The calling gifts are a way we do life. Others will tend to see and identify our calling more than they will see and identify our character gift. However, our character gift does shape the way we approach our calling. Mark items that fit who you are.*

The healer: Tends to be visual in approach; involves the one they are working with; nurtures the one they are working with as a part of the healing; has a good sense of timing and manner for when and how a healing is to occur.

The helps person: Sees what needs to be done; jumps in to complete the task; tends to work alone; and often struggles with his "spirituality" since the promptings of the Spirit generally come to him mostly in the area of things that need to be done vs. words to be heard.

The person gifted in administrations: Understands how things fit together, who fits together, the order that things should be done, and the timing of those things coming together; this gift generally has a leadership feel though being an organizer is not the same as being an influencer; can be more behind the scenes looking to assist with overall organization.

Workers of miracles: Recognize when a demonstration of the power of God will build faith the faith of people; are willing to fast and pray to see God do what man could never do; will seek God to see some form of miracle that captures the imagination of the body and ignites a new passion to serve God.

The elder and bishop: Are called to the work of overseeing others in the body of Christ; the call to leadership is often a secondary calling, which comes with spiritual maturity—after a person has grown up in primary areas of calling; are called to guide, guard, and nurture the body of Christ.

Activity for Understanding

In this section, you can complete the following questions for the one of the remaining five gifts that best fits you or you can repeat the questions for each of the gift areas listed. Fill in the blank with whatever gift(s) you choose.

Some of the ways we approach life are programmed into us and some are more instinctive. Who do you know that more instinctively approaches life in the manner of the _____? What traits do you see in that person that fit the approach of the _____?

Are there ways that you instinctively approach life in the manner of the _____ ? Are there ways that the _____ approach has been programmed into you?

What are things that the _____ does in a life approach that definitely do not describe you?

Are there parts of the _____ that are uncomfortable or almost offensive to you? What are they? Are there others you have judged because they are living out their calling?

Have some close friends identify the traits of the _____ that fit you well. List results:

Opening the Door

Chapter 16

• How is this final category of gifts different from the other two?

I call the final category of gifts the miraculous or the conduit gifts. They come not necessarily out of the character of a person, nor even out of the call of a person, but out of the need of the moment. As I mentioned in the last chapter, God sends forth His gifts for the **"profit of all."** Where there is a need, He delights in using one of His servants to meet that need, whether that person is specifically crafted and called to minister in that way or not. In other words, just about anybody can be used by God in just about any way at any time.

People will be used most consistently according to their call because that is what they are open to and what they care about and focus on. But none of us needs to be limited to a narrow path of a few gifts. We serve an infinite God who is full of surprises. Just when we think we have figured out who we are in terms of gifting, God will surprise us and use us in a way that we had not anticipated. This business of gifting is about Him, His glory, and the needs of the body more than it is about us or our innate abilities!

Before I go into this last category of gifting, I need to talk about what releases the supernatural to operate. Both the character gifts and the callings can and do operate in some fashion, with or without the quickening of the Holy Spirit. Obviously, if there is no quickening of the Holy Spirit, the best a person can do is imitate what God truly wants to happen in his life. The fact that a character gift or a calling gift is a mere imitation is not always obvious to other people. A teacher still makes a stab at teaching. An administrator organizes, an exhorter encourages, etc. The quickening of the Holy Spirit turns a talent into a gift, but at times, the difference between the two goes unnoticed.

> **Without the Holy Spirit, the best a person can do is imitate what God truly wants to happen!**

With the conduit gifts, if a person is praying for healing and no healing manifests, it is quite obvious to all. If there is a crisis, and God does not show up, all that is left are excuses. Since much of the church lives in a manner that is tilted more toward human will power than it is connected to God, the excuses become the norm. We spend a lot of time explaining why God doesn't heal or show up in power.

Some even teach that this last category of gifts are not supernatural, i.e. that a word of knowledge is just knowledge. That way, there is no compulsion to see the power of God manifest in a situation. That way there is no accountability for signs and wonders to follow the believer as the Scriptures say should happen in **Mark 16:17-18**.

However, a non-supernatural view of the gifts listed in **1 Corinthians 12:8-10** makes little or no sense given the context of the passage. The whole context of the chapter is about God intervening in a moment in time to bring a change to a situation. Unfortunately, the

Western church has tended to live in a manner of not actively connecting to God and His purposes—and not depending on nor expecting His power to show up. We accept the fact that He does not intervene as if it were normal. We try to use the Scriptures to explain why the more miraculous things are no longer happening. This should not be! In every situation, God should speak or intervene in some way. If He is not speaking, we should seek Him until there is some kind of word or intervention. For the most part, the Western church does not think this way. We live in the natural realm, hoping that God will cross our paths now and then.

• **What kind of hunger does it take to activate the supernatural?**

So how do we open the door to this supernatural way of living? I believe this list cannot be activated without direct communion with God. The language of *1 Corinthians 12:8-10* emphasizes the direct activity of the Holy Spirit:

> *"for to one is given the word of wisdom through the Spirit, to another the word of knowledge through the same Spirit, to another faith by the same Spirit, to another gifts of healings by the same Spirit, to another the working of miracles, to another prophecy, to another discerning of spirits, to another different kinds of tongues, to another the interpretation of tongues".*

The first gift is called a *"word"* of wisdom. People grow in wisdom through life experiences, but *"a word of wisdom"* is talking about a specific gift of the Holy Spirit to a specific person or group of persons at a specific time. It is something that is supernaturally given. If it were simply a matter of applying general understanding to a situation, it would be called "wisdom," but this gift is much more specific than that. It is a crisis intervention. At a point in time, God shows up supernaturally and something out of the ordinary happens. When that happens, people know that God is involved and intervening in the lives of men. Unfortunately, we tend to provide little space for this kind of activity to happen. We search frantically for any human generated solution and only when we come to a complete dead end do we turn to God.

We search frantically for a human generated solution and only when we come to a complete dead end do we turn to God.

This is the first key to releasing the supernatural. We need to learn to turn to God first. No solution should be sought until we have His solution. His solution may include something very natural, like washing in a river. But are we willing to wait until He speaks? If not, we will seldom see any significant moving of His Spirit. As long as we can manufacture our own solutions, we need not expect God to beat us to the punch with His solutions. He will not try to compete with our ingenuity. That is not how He operates. If He is not being given the first place, He waits until He has that place in our hearts.

Unless we are willing to hunger and thirst after God before and above all other things, the supernatural will never be a significant factor in our lives. In *Luke 11:9-13* it says:

So I say to you, ask, and it will be given to you; seek, and you will find; knock, and it will be opened to you. For everyone who asks receives, and he who seeks finds, and to him who knocks it will be opened. If a son asks for bread from any father among you, will he give him a stone? Or if he asks for a fish, will he give him a serpent instead of a fish? Or if he asks for an egg, will he offer him a scorpion? If you then, being evil, know how to give good gifts to your children, how much more will your heavenly Father give the Holy Spirit to those who ask Him!

This passage talks about seeking God in earnest. The Father wants to release the good gifts to us, but they will not be released until we become a persistent seeker. To say the least, this is not a picture of our culture. We can hardly be described as desperate for God to show up. The Western church could be better described as anxious to show God what we've done.

• What are the different levels of relationship we can have with the Holy Spirit?

A second key to releasing the supernatural is the key that Jesus gives us in *Acts 1:8: "But you shall receive power when the Holy Spirit has come upon you; and you shall be witnesses to Me in Jerusalem, and in all Judea and Samaria, and to the end of the earth."* In *verse 4*, Jesus had been very emphatic, telling the disciples not to leave Jerusalem until they had received the power that comes through the baptism in the Holy Spirit. If the gifts are given completely and totally through a connectedness with the Holy Spirit, it would make sense that some sort of major encounter with the Holy Spirit would open up a person to the supernatural.

I believe that is why Jesus told the disciples to wait in Jerusalem. A significant Holy Spirit encounter was about to happen, and they were not ready to minister the way they needed to without that encounter. Never mind that the disciples had already gone out in ministry and through the power of the Holy Spirit had seen healings and deliverances *(Luke 9:1-6)*. Jesus describes their level of encounter with the Holy Spirit this way in *John 14:16-17*:

And I will pray the Father, and He will give you another Helper, that He may abide with you forever — the Spirit of truth, whom the world cannot receive, because it neither sees Him nor knows Him; but you know Him, for He dwells with you and will be in you.

I call these verses the three "withs" of the Holy Spirit. The first "with" is the Holy Spirit's relationship with the world. Since the unsaved person is not even able to see what God is doing *(John 3:3)*, the unsaved cannot come to God unless there is some kind of convicting or drawing work done by God *(John 6:44)*. It is the Holy Spirit that does this convicting work

(John 16:8). Thus the Holy Spirit is "with" the unbeliever … but in a way that could be pictured as influencing the person from the outside.

Jesus tells the disciples that the Holy Spirit is now *"with"* them in *John 14:17*. This could be interpreted that the Holy Spirit is in Jesus and thus is "with" them, but more likely is talking about the fact that the Holy Spirit has already been there working miracles through them. The Spirit has been *"with"* them, but Jesus says there is more. He pictures the baptism of the Holy Spirit which is yet to come as the Holy Spirit will be "in" you. The Holy Spirit will move from being *"with"* the disciples to being *"in"* the disciples. Being "in" the disciples is the most intimate of the three "withs."

In today's world, I believe the three "withs" still apply. The Holy Spirit is with the unsaved convicting them and drawing them to Christ. He is also with those walking with God. *Romans 8:9* says, *"But you are not in the flesh but in the Spirit, if indeed the Spirit of God dwells in you. Now if anyone does not have the Spirit of Christ, he is not His."* *Romans 8:9* clearly tells us that the Holy Spirit has moved into the spiritual house of the saved. He has set up shop. He is "with" the saved person, and if He has not been allowed to set up shop, the person is not a child of God.

Every saved person has a level of communion with the Holy Spirit, whether he recognizes it or not.

Every saved person has a level of communion with the Holy Spirit, whether he recognizes it or not. Some are more attentive to it than others. Those who begin to pay attention to the Holy Spirit increase the place of influence that the Holy Spirit has in their lives. Those who ignore the Spirit, continue to live under the influence of the sin nature, almost as if they had never been saved. *Romans 8:5* says it this way: *"For those who live according to the flesh set their minds on the things of the flesh, but those who live according to the Spirit, the things of the Spirit."* Communion with the Spirit is not automatic. Salvation opens a door to greater communion, to a closer "with" relationship to the Spirit, but is no guarantee of communion.

- **How does Jesus describe the deepest level of connection with the Holy Spirit?**

However, there is another level of "with" that is beyond salvation. Jesus told the disciples to wait in Jerusalem for the baptism in the Holy Spirit. This baptism would be an intense Holy Spirit encounter, an intense "with" that Jesus said would release His power to flow through them in a way that had not happened before. This is an amazing statement considering that the disciples had already been used by God in healing and casting out of demons. What could be so significant about the baptism in the Holy Spirit?

Jesus gets us started in our understanding of the new relationship to the Holy Spirit by giving us the description that the Holy Spirit will be *"in"* us *(John 14:17)*. The imagery of baptism is a second clue to this new relationship with the Holy Spirit. Throughout the Old Testament, the Holy Spirit could be described as "anointing" a person for a specific purpose. He would temporarily rest on a person and would stay there according to the will of God.

Because Jesus had not yet paid the penalty for sin, the Holy Spirit was not allowed the close kind of abiding that would come after Christ. He anointed people in the Old Testament, but something new was coming.

In *John 7:37-39,* Jesus gives us another description of this baptism in the Holy Spirit experience:

> *On the last day, that great day of the feast, Jesus stood and cried out, saying, "If anyone thirsts, let him come to Me and drink. He who believes in Me, as the Scripture has said, out of his heart will flow rivers of living water." But this He spoke concerning the Spirit, whom those believing in Him would receive; for the Holy Spirit was not yet given, because Jesus was not yet glorified.*

The one who is saved has a well within himself. The Holy Spirit is there for communion and it is good. But Jesus implies that when the Holy Spirit is fully given, the well becomes a river flowing out in ministry. This inner communion will well up and overflow with a power that has never been there before. It is a new level of being connected "with" the Holy Spirit.

When the Holy Spirit is fully given, the well becomes a river flowing out in ministry.

A drink of living water becomes a flowing river that is deep enough that a person can be baptized in the presence of the Holy Spirit in the same way that a person might be baptized in water. It is a very intimate Holy Spirit encounter. It is an immersing in the Holy Spirit, not just a temporary touch.

I believe these Scriptures point to the baptism in the Holy Spirit as the door that opens the flow of the supernatural in a person's life. However, communion with the Holy Spirit is no more guaranteed for the one who is baptized in the Spirit than it is for the one who is saved. The same principle still applies: *"For those who live according to the flesh set their minds on the things of the flesh, but those who live according to the Spirit, the things of the Spirit" (Rom. 8:5).*

Because communion with God is not automatic, there are those who have had key intimacy encounters with the Holy Spirit, but yet continue to live as if they weren't even saved. There are others who have never had a significant intimacy encounter experience, yet still have a much greater level of communion with the Holy Spirit than some of those who are "baptized in the Holy Spirit." In the Christian life, nothing is automatic. We either walk with God or we don't.

- **Is speaking in tongues a necessary part of the baptism in the Holy Spirit?**

On the baptism in the Holy Spirit, many ask, "What does speaking in tongues have to do with the baptism in the Holy Spirit?" Others put it this way, "Do I have to speak in tongues to be baptized in the Holy Spirit?" In our culture, there is a complete aversion to the supernatural.

Most in our culture do their best to make the supernatural as safe or tame as we can. A few thrive on anything that is far out. Neither of these two extremes is healthy.

There are many who have had a significant encounter with the Holy Spirit, who then claimed this encounter as the baptism in the Holy Spirit, but had no experience of speaking in tongues. I will certainly agree that any intimate encounter with the Holy Spirit will increase the likelihood of God's power flowing through that person. Once we open a spiritual channel, we are much more likely to see when God wants to move and respond to His prompting.

D. L. Moody and many others saw a great release in the effectiveness of their ministry after they sought a deeper Holy Spirit encounter. Historically, there are many individuals who have had a "deeper experience" and refer to these encounters as their "baptism in the Spirit."

However, I would suggest that we change the question from "Do we have to speak in tongues?" to "Do we get to speak in tongues?" In *1 Corinthians 14:2*, it says, *"For he who speaks in a tongue does not speak to men but to God."* Tongues gives a person the ability to bypass the normal limitations of the mind *(1 Cor. 14:14–17)* and speak directly to God. A person can intercede or give thanks to God beyond the normal human capacity, even *"with groanings which cannot be uttered" (Romans 8:26)*. The typical Western believer treats tongues almost as if it were some kind of foul tasting cough medicine and not as a privileged kind of communion that is available in Christ.

> **A person can intercede or give thanks beyond the normal human capacity!**

First Corinthians 14:4 also says that, *"He who speaks in a tongue edifies himself"* and *Jude 20–21* says, *"But you, beloved, building yourselves up on your most holy faith, praying in the Holy Spirit, keep yourselves in the love of God, looking for the mercy of our Lord Jesus Christ unto eternal life."* Some would say that the *Jude* passage does not necessarily refer to praying in tongues, but the language is similar to that of *First Corinthians* when it is speaking about praying in tongues. Both books speak of praying *"in the Spirit"* as being something that builds a person up in Christ. Again, it is a privilege to be sought.

Some argue that tongues is not available to everyone. They use *1 Corinthians 12:30* to prove that some do not speak in tongues. Because of the context of the passage, I believe this verse is speaking of tongues being exercised in a public setting (described more fully on p. 170-172). Tongues being exercised in a public setting is very different from tongues exercised in a private setting. In a private setting, tongues could be described as an intimate prayer language given to a person to help him better commune with God.

Peter, describing the incredible tongues encounter that he had experienced, says in *Acts 2:39*, *"For the promise is to you and to your children, and to all who are afar off, as many as the Lord our God will call."* Peter says that this experience with the Holy Spirit is for *"as many as the Lord our God will call."* There is no limiting factor in that statement. *John 7:37-39* indicates that there is a river of God that is supposed to be flowing through us. It is a river that includes a supernatural communion, and it is for the children and great great great grandchildren of the disciples. *"As many as the Lord our God will call"* is still effective even to this very day!

- **If we refuse the supernatural, how does it impact our relationship with the Holy Spirit?**

I believe the aversion that we have had to the supernatural, especially the tongues experience, has shut down the flow of the supernatural in the Western church. Instead of esteeming it highly, which has happened in many other cultures, we have questioned and despised this activity of God. If we approach God as a skeptic, His answer is something like "be it done unto you according to your faith."

We need to seek all that God has for us. Sometimes the supernatural is accompanied by signs like shaking or fainting or even rolling. Early Methodists were ridiculed as "holy rollers." Quakers were given their name because the presence of the Holy Spirit was often accompanied by shaking. Today, such "signs" tend to be despised by many of the more "sophisticated" believers of Western culture.

If we don't embrace God in the manner in which He chooses to work, could we be missing out? Many of the major denominations started with supernatural manifestations of His presence, but as the years went by, the supernatural has generally passed away. It was "embarrassing" in a culture that did not embrace it. When we become embarrassed over the work of God, He will become embarrassed of us and withdraw to a greater distance.

We either choose to fully embrace Him and how He works, or we lose out on the level of communion that is available. Where there is minimal communion, there will be minimal supernatural intervention. Healings will be uncommon. Divine guidance will be rare. People will live as if the Bible were a mere book of philosophy. They will not expect, seek, nor cry out for the supernatural interventions.

That is not the will of God for our lives. *Mark 16:15-18* is clear:

> *And He said to them, "Go into all the world and preach the gospel to every creature. He who believes and is baptized will be saved; but he who does not believe will be condemned. And these signs will follow those who believe: In My name they will cast out demons; they will speak with new tongues; they will take up serpents; and if they drink anything deadly, it will by no means hurt them; they will lay hands on the sick, and they will recover."*

The Western church has, for the most part, acted as if these verses were not even in the Bible. We need to open the door to the supernatural once again. We need to seek the deepest levels of communion with Christ regardless of the cost! Is that your heart? If it is, ask God to give you a new level of faith, a supernatural faith to seek Him like never before.

Walking with God is not just a natural event. It takes the natural and supercharges it! Are you ready to see His power released through you?

Releasing the Supernatural

Chapter 17

• How does a person access or flow in the conduit gifts?

This third category of gifts is sometimes called the "manifestation" gifts because they bring to light the invisible nature of God in some physical form. They typically manifest at a point in time, where a person connects with God and acts as a conduit for the supernatural to show up in real life. Unlike the other gifts, which tend to be almost "owned" by the person, these gifts are much more the property of the body and of the need of the moment.

That does not mean that a person will not be used repeatedly in an area. Once a particular type of gift has been exercised through a person, it tends to increase the faith of that person to see it happen the next time. Positive expectation is powerful and will give a person the sense that he has a gift of healing, prophecy, or one of the other gifts, but the language of Scripture seems to indicate that the person doesn't "have" the gift of healing the way he would "have" the calling as a teacher or "have" the heart of a servant.

The clearest list of these gifts is found in *1 Corinthians 12:7-11*:

> *But the manifestation of the Spirit is given to each one for the profit of all: for to one is given the word of wisdom through the Spirit, to another the word of knowledge through the same Spirit, to another faith by the same Spirit, to another gifts of healings by the same Spirit, to another the working of miracles, to another prophecy, to another discerning of spirits, to another different kinds of tongues, to another the interpretation of tongues. But one and the same Spirit works all these things, distributing to each one individually as He wills.*

It is important to notice that both before and after the listing of these gifts, it is stated that these gifts are clearly the work of the Spirit given at a specific moment according to the will of the Spirit and for the profit of all. A person has a reasonable level of control over his evangelistic ministry. The amount of control a person has over these gifts seems much more limited.

As the last chapter emphasized, what the person *can* do is to open up the spiritual intimacy channel and then wait upon God with faith. A person who is eager, open, and expecting will not likely miss what God wants to do. The person who is closed or who is not closely attentive to God will likely miss what I believe is the key to the operation of all of these gifts: seeing, hearing, or sensing the heart of God. Healing is not about twisting the arm of God as much as it is connecting with the heart of God and then becoming a release point for that healing to manifest.

• What does it mean that God is looking for "release points"?

I say release point because we often have it backwards. We think that if we coax God long enough, He will relent and give us good things. That is a wrong view of God. The reality is that God wants to give us every good and **"perfect gift" (James 1:17)**. What is holding things up is His holy nature and His faithfulness to His word.

When Solomon prayed the prayer about the new temple he was dedicating, it cut two ways: **"Now, my God, I pray, let Your eyes be open and let Your ears be attentive to the prayer made in this place" (2 Chronicles 6:40).** Solomon meant it as a prayer of blessing, so that when the people cried out to God, God would hear and answer. Yet, this same prayer later became the basis of a curse on God's people.

In the days of Ezekiel, the people had set up idols in the temple, and the people's prayers became an offense to God. The same God who promised to be attentive to the prayers in the days of Solomon still was dedicated to be attentive to the prayers of the people in the days of Ezekiel. When the prayers warranted God's hand going forth in blessing, God would move in blessing. By the same token, when the prayers in the days of Ezekiel demanded that God bring judgment, God was forced to move in judgment. Otherwise, He would no longer be holy, nor would He be honoring His word. He would become like us, wavering and unstable. Not trustworthy. Not reliable.

We think that if we can just convince God that something is really, really needed, He will move. I believe He is in heaven saying, "Give Me something to work with! Give Me a prayer of repentance, some humility, or some clear desire for Me, My Word, or My will to be lived out. Give Me something in your temple that will allow Me as a holy God to get past your sins and release My love." I believe this is the heart of God. When we see His heart, we develop the faith needed to be a conduit for the miraculous. We stop trying to convince God and instead learn to cooperate with God.

> **When we see His heart, we develop the faith needed to be a conduit for the miraculous.**

• How do we cooperate with God so that He can use us as a release point?

This may mean that we have to get our eyes off a needed healing or the current crisis of the moment for us to see the hand of God move. Sometimes, God has a clear purpose that He wants to see worked out through the situation. The very manifestation of God's power that we would pray for could, at times, short circuit the thing God wants to do in a situation.

At other times, the purpose of God will not go forth until the supernatural manifests. Again, healing is a good example. Some will not seek God unless the healing is delayed. The lack of an intervention by God causes the person to grow. In other instances, a healing might convince a person that God is real and cause him to get saved. Both in the giving and the withholding of the supernatural, God is at work.

However, at times, it is not God who is withholding, but it is man who is not even looking to God. I am convinced that there are times when God wants to move but has no human release point. We are meant to be the point of the manifestation of His glory. God has limited Himself to work through men. If we are not attentive to Him, or if we don't understand that He wants to move through us, we can stop the moving of God. We need to change our thinking!

Thus, the most significant thing a person can do to activate the supernatural flow of God is to be acutely aware of and actively submissive to the voice of God. When this kind of attentiveness to God is coupled with a faith in His desire to move, the supernatural will begin to operate on a much more regular basis.

• How do we know what God wants to do in a situation?

It is important to remember that the supernatural flows according to His will and His purpose. We need to continually ask God to give us wisdom so that we might cooperate with Him instead of trying to coerce Him into doing something that is out of sequence with His perfect timing. Some of those who believe that God is still doing miraculous works today go to another extreme and assume that God will heal or give some other intervention almost on demand. More than anything, we need to see His heart in all situations!

Perhaps that is why the list of gifts begins with a word of wisdom and a word of knowledge. These two especially highlight the need to hear from God for His power to be released. What is a word of wisdom? Again, some teach that it is merely wisdom that is applied to a specific situation. If that were true, why would the gift be described as *"a word"* of wisdom? Why would it not be just called wisdom?

Solomon certainly seems to have a word of wisdom in the situation where two mothers are both claiming that a baby is theirs. He commands that the baby be cut in half and the real mother immediately offers to give the baby up rather than see her child killed. When Jesus meets the woman at the well, I believe it may have been a word of wisdom when He asked the woman for a drink *(John 4:7)*. This request is not obvious as a word of wisdom, as He may have been simply asking for a need to be met. However, as the situation plays out, this request ends up being the perfect hook to get her interested in the gospel.

A word of wisdom and a word of knowledge are very similar. A word of wisdom is a supernatural level of understanding that comes from God and brings a practical application of knowledge to a situation. A word of knowledge is a quantity of information supernaturally coming from God that is just "known" by the one who receives it. When Jesus is with the

WORD OF KNOWLEDGE VS WORD OF WISDOM

woman at the well, He clearly uses a word of knowledge to finish turning the woman toward God. He tells her that she has had five husbands and that the one that she is now living with is not her husband *(John 4:18)*. Because Jesus knew this information, she assumes that He is a prophet and that He is hearing from God.

• **What was the basis of Jesus' walk in the miraculous?**

As a modern reader looking at Jesus and His interactions, we do have to make a decision. Does He know these kinds of things because He is God and He just knows all things? Or did He fully take on the human role in a way that He had to receive things from the Father in the same way that we would receive them from God?

To me, the answer is obvious. Jesus had to grow in *"wisdom and stature" (Luke 2:52)* just like any other man. He did no miracles until He was baptized in the Jordan River, and the Holy Spirit came upon Him. Until the Holy Spirit came upon Him, He seemed to be just like any other man.

In *Philippians 2:7*, it tells us that Jesus *"made Himself of no reputation, taking the form of a bondservant, and coming in the likeness of men."* To me, it is very significant that Jesus made Himself like us in all ways. He took no special advantages. He had to overcome temptation just as any other man would. He had to learn and grow just as any other man. He had to operate in the spiritual realm just as any other man.

If this is true, Jesus obviously uses a supernaturally received word of knowledge to get the attention of the woman. It provides a confirmation to the woman that He is in contact with God. Jesus takes her understanding one step further and lets her know that He is not just a prophet but the coming Messiah. Both the word of wisdom and the word of knowledge end up being critical to Jesus' ability to minister to the woman.

> **Both the word of wisdom and the word of knowledge end up being critical to Jesus' ability to minister to the woman.**

We can take one of two positions. We can marvel at what Jesus does and feel like His ability to work with people is beyond us. Or we can understand that the Holy Spirit can do very similar things through us, if we will only be attentive to the Spirit and be willing to bring the words whispered to our spirits out into the open. Many times, we are not willing to trust what we sense is happening between His Spirit and ours, and thus we quench what might have been. We must learn to test the Spirit to spirit interactions and then to gain the boldness we need to speak what the Spirit is sharing with us.

• **In Jesus' life, what does His walking in the gifts look like?**

I believe the nine gifts listed in *1 Corinthians 12:8-10* are simply descriptions of ways the supernatural can manifest through believers. Even as I have described with word of wisdom and word of knowledge, they operate very much through a Spirit to spirit interaction that is introduced into a natural world. The list is not meant to be an exhaustive list of what God can or will do, but an illustration of things that happen when we walk with the Spirit of God.

As we survey Jesus' ministry, we find that He frequently acted and spoke beyond a normal human level. He had to have supernatural guidance for Him to be saying or doing some of the things that He said and did ... or He took special privileges since He was and is God. But Jesus shows us how He operates in *John 5:19, "Most assuredly, I say to you, the Son can do nothing of Himself, but what He sees the Father do; for whatever He does, the Son also does in like manner."* A few verses later He adds, *"I can of Myself do nothing. As I hear, I judge; and My judgment is righteous, because I do not seek My own will but the will of the Father who sent Me" (John 5:30).*

In Western Christian culture, we tend to take off and run, doing the kinds of things we think a Christian should do. This kind of life will never manifest the supernatural in any significant way. That is not how Jesus lived. He lived in very close contact with the Father. He said that He could do nothing without seeing and hearing the Father. By comparison, most of us live radically independent lives, lives that only briefly intersect in any intimate way with God. Then we wonder why the supernatural seldom seems to manifest in our culture. But we are very busy doing things that we think a Christian should do!

If these supernatural gifts operate through being intimate with God and then having the boldness to speak and act on what He puts in our spirit is a key to manifesting these gifts—that

Having the boldness to speak and act on what He puts in our spirit is a key to manifesting these gifts!

and greater intimacy with Him. In Jesus' ministry, He did some crazy things. He spit and made mud and applied it to a blind man's eyes. That is hardly a formula for healing, but He had heard from God and saw how he was to activate this man's healing. One time he commands a group of lepers to go show themselves to the priest. The next time He speaks a word, and the healing is done. One time Jesus touches the person and the next He only speaks to them.

Luke chronicles what may be the most important part of Jesus' ministry. Over and over, Luke depicts Jesus departing to be alone in prayer. Intimacy with God is what fuels the supernatural, that and having the boldness to speak and act on what is being directed by God. If a person hears but does not act on that hearing, the release point that God wants to use to manifest the supernatural is shut down.

• What expectations should we have about being used by God?

God uses people to release His power of healing and life. If we shrink back, I believe there are times when the miracle does not go forth. In our culture, we generally respond to the lack of healing by saying, "I guess it must not have been the will of God." The truth is that in many cases it is the desire of God to move, but He lacks an intercessor *(Ez. 22:30)*. When He lacks a release point, most of the time He chooses not to go forward with what His heart would desire. Sometimes He can find a different release point. Sometimes He has to wait for another time and place to do His work *(2 Chron. 16:9)*.

Each of the gifts in this list details a particular way that the supernatural displays itself in this life:

> *For to one is given the word of wisdom through the Spirit, to another the word of knowledge through the same Spirit, to another faith by the same Spirit, to another gifts of healings by the same Spirit, to another the working of miracles, to another prophecy, to another discerning of spirits, to another different kinds of tongues, to another the interpretation of tongues (1 Cor. 12:8-10).*

Notice the different manifestations. Intimacy produces wisdom, knowledge, faith, healings, miracles, prophecy, discerning of spirits, different kinds of tongues, and interpretation of tongues. The last six in the list are clearly the product of the supernatural and cannot be explained any other way unless somehow we reduce a supernatural gifting like prophecy to any kind of proclaiming of the gospel. I do not believe this is the intent of this passage. God wants to move through us supernaturally!

This list is the Spirit's work, and He distributes individually to whom He chooses when He chooses and how He chooses. But He primarily distributes to those who are intimate with Him. He can move through a donkey. He can overpower one who is not in touch with Him, even as He did Saul when he was seeking to kill David *(1 Sam. 19:23-24)*. God can overpower persons to complete His work, but He seldom chooses to do so.

Most of the time, God only works through those who diligently seek Him in faith *(Heb. 11:6)*. If we don't believe that He wants to move supernaturally, or if we don't expect Him to move through us, or if we don't seek to be used that way in our lives, we will frequently quench what the Spirit would desire to do.

It is absolutely vital that we open our hearts and minds to the supernatural moving of God's Spirit. When we walk with God in this kind of expectation, He may quietly speak to us and give us a supernatural faith. When we act on that faith, incredible things can happen—things that can only be explained as being the intervention of God.

People will then be confronted with the evidence that God is alive and at work in the world today. The alternative is to shrink back, with the result being that our only tool in the fight to spread the gospel is human reasoning. We need more than our best effort to touch a doubting world.

• How do we test to see if an impression or a "word" is from God?

Everything we do or say needs to be put to the test of agreement with what God has already spoken in His Word. Anything that contradicts what the Bible says is not of God. We also should consult with others who are walking with God and are mature in their ability to hear God. These people should be demonstrating the outcomes of a godly life in their lives. If someone who walks with God feels that something is not of God, we need to take it very seriously. Generally, it is good to consult with more than one godly person when we are in the early phase of learning to hear from God.

Another test is time. Quite often, letting an impression sit for a while will answer whether or not it is from God. Those with a heart to hear from God will generally get some kind of confirmation one way or another. Those who are headstrong, will twist circumstances to make them fit what they want to hear. Staying in humility and under some kind of spiritual covering is one of the best ways for us to be able to have confidence that we are hearing from God.

• How do the miraculous gifts add to our natural storehouse?

A word of wisdom, a word of knowledge, and faith also illustrate how these gifts work. When a word of wisdom comes the first time, it is a supernatural gift. While it is happening, the person logs it into his bank of experiences, and the next time a situation comes along, he has that past experience to draw from. The person has a storehouse of wisdom, part of which may have come from general life experiences, part from the word of God, and part from a direct supernatural intervention. A person's storehouse of wisdom comes from multiple sources. A word of wisdom arrives at a point in time and is directly from God.

A word of knowledge and the gift of faith are similar. There can be multiple sources of knowledge and multiple sources of faith. The supernatural is only one aspect of the storehouse that a person has for these areas. But it can be a very important source in a time of crisis. When what's in the storehouse is not enough, the spiritual is there to help. If we truly understood life, the natural is never enough. We need Him every day and every hour. We need His light to shine on what is already in the storehouse so that we use it in the way He desires.

A walk with God integrates the human and the divine, the natural and the supernatural. God does not expect us to forsake our storehouse of life experiences. He does expect us to build upon them. The natural and the spiritual continually interact with each other. A walk with God integrates the human and the divine, the natural and the supernatural—in a relatively comfortable way. When the supernatural seems like it is being forced, it probably is. The supernatural can never be driven by a human agenda. It can be sought, but not forced. When we press too hard at a human level, what follows will almost always be something less than the will of God.

God commands us to *"earnestly desire the best gifts" (1 Cor. 12:31)*. The best gift is the one that brings the most glory to God and the most life to the situation at the time. We are to carry His life to a dark and dying world. Our spirit receives from His Spirit and we become a conduit to introduce His life into a world in need. Earnestly seek the best gifts!

Activity for Understanding

Remember: *The conduit gifts flow through us. They don't "reside" the same way that the character gifts or the calling gifts do. The questions in this section will focus on your openness to be used by God in these areas, along with how God has already used you in a supernatural way.*

Who do you know that has been used by God in either a word of wisdom or a word of knowledge? Describe how that gift manifested and how you knew it was from God.

How has God worked supernaturally in your life, speaking something to you that was for you that made a great difference in your life?

What would it take for you to have the boldness to share with someone something that you felt God was saying to them? Share instances if you have shared "words" from God with others.

How do you test words you believe you have for others or others have for you to see if they are of God?

Have some close friends identify times that they have seen God use you to speak to them in a way that they feel was from God.

The Power Gifts

Chapter 18

- **How do the instantaneous "downloads" of the gifts work together with daily growth to produce the result God desires?**

Much of the time, we don't passionately seek God until there is a crisis—until there is an absolute need for a miracle. A word of wisdom is an instantaneous transfer from God at a point in time. It lets a person know how to respond wisely to a situation. It is not a culmination of experience and thought producing a good result but a direct gift from God.

The person who has been reading and studying the Word of God will find it much easier to understand and apply the supernatural download, but the study of the Word does not produce the direct word from God. Someone who has a good foundation of learning is much easier to instruct in new things. They are much more likely to "get it" and to use it in the right way.

The gift of faith comes out of an instantaneous transfer from God, not from a person growing in faith over a period of time.

Similarly, a word of knowledge is not learned information but received information—directly received via the supernatural from God. The gift of faith comes out of an instantaneous transfer from God, not from a person growing in faith over a period of time. A person can live a lifestyle that seeks knowledge of God or has a foundation of walking in faith, but the lifestyle does not necessarily mean a person will have what he needs when a crisis comes.

There are times when we need supernatural faith. The woman with the continual flow of blood *(Matt. 9:20)* received a supernatural faith. She believed that if she just touched the hem of Jesus' garment, she would be healed. She pressed through the crowd, touched Jesus' garment and was healed. It worked!

The gift of faith is almost always paired with one of the other supernatural gifts. For faith to "show up" in real life, it has to have a form of expression. A healing. A miracle. Maybe a spoken word that results in some kind of outcome. By its very nature, faith is internal and invisible. But supernatural faith provokes a word or action which then produces a result.

The Centurion didn't need Jesus to come to heal his servant but believed that all Jesus needed to do was to speak a word *(Matt. 8:8)*. Joshua believed that the sun could stand still and it did for an entire day *(Josh. 10:12)*. Elijah prayed, and there would be no rain in the land *(1 Kings 17:1)*. He prayed again and rain returned to the land *(1 Kings 18:44-45)*. A person is stirred by a supernatural faith to speak or act there is a result according to the faith.

Walking with God, reading His Word, and obeying God lays a foundation for the supernatural faith. But the day to day walk with God does not always give us what we need to face a crisis. Sometimes we need that "right now" download that is the gift of faith.

- ## What is the relationship between physical healing, inner healing, and cleansing from sin?

In this list, it is interesting that gifts of healings follow the gift of faith. Supernatural faith is needed to see healing. Notice that this gift is in the plural: healings. It is not *a* gift but gifts. It is not healing but healings. A person is given gifts of healings. At a point of need, the supernatural shows up. While it is common for a person who has been used in healing to be used in healing again, the person God uses is still not in control of the gift. Having a foundation of faith helps, but it is not a guarantee of an outcome. The "guarantee" comes with a specific word from God and a response to what God has spoken.

Some people value healing more than others and thus will seek it on a more consistent basis. Givers tend to value this area at a high level, as do prophets, though for a very different reason. For givers, healing grows out of a desire to nurture and protect, while prophets enjoy the manifestation of the power of God. Since God tends to move through those who seek to be used in an area, gifts will seem to reside in the person who values that gift. But the Spirit still distributes these gifts to whom He wills and when.

> **Gifts will seem to reside in the person who values that gift.**

One reason for the plural listing of gifts of healings may be that the gift is referring to different kinds of healings. Of course, we immediately think of physical healing first, but healing of inner wounds is just as vital. It is interesting that in some instances, Jesus seems to emphasize the physical healing, but in many instances, He pronounces the person as being made "whole" (usually translated "well"—from the Greek word *sozo* meaning to be made whole or well). To be made whole indicates that something greater has happened than just a physical healing.

The idea of being made whole also implies the close relationship that the Scriptures give between sin and sickness. There was no sickness before sin, and in **Isaiah 53:5**, the Scriptures create a very strong parallel between the atonement for sin and the atonement for sickness. There were times, when instead of pronouncing a person healed, Jesus would simply say **"Your sins are forgiven" (Luke 5:20)**. For a person to gain a spiritual release is a type of healing on the inside that parallels what God also wants to do on the outside.

Gifts of healings will operate more easily when a person understands and cooperates with this relationship between the inner life of a person and the physical life. In some cases, God pours out healing to demonstrate His power to a people who don't know Him or believe in Him. This often happens on the evangelistic field. God uses healing to demonstrate that He is real and to draw people to Himself.

Sometimes a person comes to God because of physical pain, but God's priority is to clean up the inner man first. In these cases, prayer for healing will seldom work. Repentance must come first. Sometimes after repentance, no prayer for healing is even needed. The outer healing comes automatically.

There are times when God simply wants to demonstrate His love and caring toward an individual. In these situations, the direct touch from God often impacts entire families and sometimes for generations to come! If we understand what God is doing through a healing, it can help us pray in a way that is more effective.

• What are the purposes that God has for healing?

The one overarching principle that the Scriptures give for healing is that it should bring glory to God. In *John 9:3*, when the disciples are trying to pin the cause for a man's blindness on someone's sin, Jesus says, ***"Neither this man nor his parents sinned, but that the works of God should be revealed in him."***

While it is important to see what God is doing in a situation, there are times when we have to step back and see an even bigger picture. God has an entire world to manage and if all we see is one man in front of us, sometimes we will not be able to understand why God moves, when He moves, or how He moves. Sometimes, it is not about that person but about a family member, a church, or even a community. And sometimes, it isn't even about the will of God at all. There are times when He is waiting on us to seek Him at a deeper level.

There are times when we look at a situation, and we think healing should show up sooner than it does. By looking at an individual situation, it would seem that God's purpose would demand that the timing for healing is right. But there is always a greater overall purpose of what will bring God the greatest glory.

We need to see these different purposes, not so that we can understand all that God is doing. We never can fully understand. But we need to see what God is doing so that we can more fully cooperate with God in a way that will bring about the healing. Jesus spoke healing *(Luke 5:24-25)*, He spit on a blind man's eyes *(Mark 8:23)*, and He gave people tasks to do *(Luke 17:14)*. He did not give us a patterned approach to heal.

A person who frequently operates in gifts of healings must be open to the variety of ways that God will work. He must be sensitive to finding the right time to pursue healing, as well as the right approach. Sometimes healing is a grand show in front of people, and other times it is done very privately. Sometimes it is closely linked to the inner life of the person, and sometimes it isn't. Mostly, a person being used in this area needs to hear from God!

• How does the natural realm and the supernatural work together in healing?

It is also important to note that healing is not necessarily instantaneous. When it is instantaneous, it is combined with the next gift of the miraculous. In many cases, the healing will show up at a later time. Sometimes it is instantaneous, and sometimes it manifests rather gradually.

Time is not the issue with healing but recovery is. The one who prays for the healing has little or no control over the timing of the recovery. Just because something doesn't manifest immediately doesn't mean God is not at work. If God is directing the process, there is still a point in time that sets something in motion in the person who needs healing. If nothing shows up immediately, the person being used in healing needs to continue to listen for what God is speaking. There are times when God uses a delay to establish one of His purposes in a situation.

How does healing fit with doctors and medicine? In a way, medical science doesn't fit with the gifts of healings because this gift is more about the supernatural transfer from God. There is a natural wisdom that resides more in the heart of a man and there is a word of wisdom that comes more directly from God. Similarly, there is natural healing that depends more on the responses of man and there is a more direct healing that comes from God manifesting His power in a person. Natural wisdom does interact with and support a word of wisdom to make it more effective. Even so, natural health and healing does interact with the more spiritually given healing described in this gift.

Any model that tries to totally separate the natural from the spiritual will break down in its description of how things work. However, this chapter and this gift are not so much about the incremental things of life but about a momentary download from God. Sometimes the manifestation of the download can be delayed for a time. When it does show up, it still is the result of something that has directly come from God.

> **Any model that tries to totally separate the natural from the spiritual will break down in its description of how things work.**

Natural wisdom is needed. Natural healing is needed. Doctors and medicine are needed. The supernatural gifts are not meant to replace day to day living and the growth that comes through ongoing obedience to God. They are meant to supplement it and to help break the hold that Satan has on our lives through the ongoing negative effects of the sin nature which are at work in us. We often need that more instantaneous power boost to break through the bondage which would keep us from fully serving God.

• What is our part in whether or not a miracle happens?

The next gift that is listed is working of miracles. This gift especially emphasizes the time factor. Miracles are things that happen out of the normal course of time. Some call the birth of a child a miracle … and in a way it is. However, that is not what this gift is talking about. This gift is talking about things that show up with a bang.

When Peter's shadow begins to heal people *(Acts 15:5)*, the miraculous has invaded into the area of healing. When Jesus speaks to the storm and it dies down *(Mark 4:39)*, the miraculous has taken place. When a few loaves of bread and two fish multiply to feed the five thousand, a miracle has taken place *(Matt. 14:14-21)*. Again, the key to moving in this gift is hearing from God. God does sovereignly move, but most of the time, someone has set the miracle in motion.

In the feeding of the five thousand, we see some of the same kinds of things we saw with the gifts of healings. There is a purpose and a process to releasing the miracle. Jesus involved the disciples and the people in the miracle. He first asked the disciples to feed the people. He challenged their faith. These are clues to the purpose of God He was using the feeding of the five thousand to grow faith and to demonstrate His compassion for the people.

He asked the people to sit down in orderly groups. We tend to have this idea that miracles just show up. While God can "just show up," most of the time there is a clear order and purpose to what He does, and the miracle will not happen until His purpose is established through the active cooperation of at least one person who is responding to Him. It might be a single person like Elijah or a whole group of people like the disciples, but someone has to be open to what God is wanting to do.

(handwritten margin note: ORDER THAN GLORY P.J. 12/25/19)

- **What is the importance of miracles vs. living daily for God?**

The feeding of the five thousand also illustrates another great point about the relationship of the natural and the supernatural. The people in the crowd had been fed once through supernatural provision. If they then decided that they would not eat again until God provided supernaturally, they would have gotten very, very hungry. The Spirit distributes the supernatural when He wants to and where He wants to. He is not at our beck and call.

The same God who gives us the supernatural also said that those who will not work should not eat *(2 Thess. 3:10)*. Most of the time, the greater purpose of God is worked out by daily obedience to Him. We are to walk with Him in a way that is continuously supernatural, but not exactly miraculous in nature. We "feed" daily on His presence and drink in His words to us. That is supernatural. But this list of gifts goes beyond communion with God. It takes communion with God and explodes it into the natural realm in a way that is beyond what would be expected from regular godly living.

There is a time to wait on the miraculous, but it is always time to pursue the kinds of things that make for good health and healing. Those who refuse to pursue good health may find themselves waiting for a very long time with no "food" coming from God.

We need God to invade the natural world in a way that cannot be explained.

Many times, when God intervenes in a miraculous way, He is using that intervention as some sort of sign. The term "signs and wonders" picks up on this idea. We need God to invade the natural world in a way that cannot be explained by natural events. This boosts our faith in the supernatural. We all need to know that this life is not just a natural occurrence.

Over the centuries, many things were given "sign" status that were simply the working out of natural causes. Sickness was often ascribed to spiritual causes when we now know the role of germs and viruses. We do need to be careful not to make the mistake of thinking that just because we can't see the cause, that there is no direct cause and that the event is supernatural.

Both miracles and healings serve as a kind of jolt or sign gift. They testify that there is something greater out there than man can know or understand. In a way, any of the gifts listed in this conduit category can be a sign gift, but healing and miracles tend to catch our attention more than the others.

God does not want us to sit around waiting for the next miracle. He distributes the signs and wonders when He wants and how He wants. What He does want is for us to walk with Him. That in itself is a daily manifestation of the supernatural. His voice and communion with Him is very supernatural, though it generally arrives in a more subtle way.

We are energized by Him. Our health is renewed by Him **(Rom. 8:11)**. We gain understanding from Him. It is all so … natural and yet so supernatural. As we study His Word, we are quickened in understanding. Because we are studying, it would seem as if it is a totally natural growth in knowledge. But the Word makes it very clear that unless He reveals things to us, we cannot know nor understand.

• Why would God need to slow down or stop the flow of the miraculous?

Most of the time, God chooses not to overpower people because He doesn't want a side show. He wants a relationship with those He has created. When miracles and healings become the center of the show, God shuts them down because it no longer fits His purpose. He doesn't intervene in dramatic ways just to show off. He doesn't want to hand out miracles for the sake of some demonstration of His power. He shows His power to win the hearts of His people. He does it to try to develop a relationship with His people.

When healings are flowing, we tend to make them the center. And it becomes a show. God is grieved. Eventually, the flow stops because the miracles have become the point of focus and not God. However, once the faith of the people has been quickened in the supernatural, the miraculous will generally continue for a season. The power of faith seems to continue to generate the miraculous even though a particular group or and individual is no longer walking with God at a higher level. In the end, anything that is no longer manifesting the heart of God will eventually come to an end.

> **Once the faith of the people has been quickened in the supernatural, the miraculous will generally continue for a season.**

God's heart, more than anything else, is to have a people who will walk with Him. That is His purpose for these gifts. We often miss that. When we lose sight of this, we lose sight of how and when the gifts are to work. We make them an end in and of themselves, and they are not. They are meant to be a power boost for our daily walk with Him. They are meant to be a demonstration of His love or a release point for our faith.

When we understand these purposes, we stay away from the errors of a health, wealth, or power gospel. None of these are God's primary purpose for the gifts. His heart is for us to walk with Him, not for us to have some sideshow happening that will call attention to us or even to Him in a way that does not fit who He is.

Even though the slave girl in Philippi seemed to be giving glory to him, Paul cast the demon spirit of out of the girl who was declaring that he was of the most High God **(Acts 16:17-18)**. The declarations of the slave girl were not about glorifying God but were meant to call attention to the girl and to the demon spirit. Our heartbeat in the area of these power gifts should not be to attract attention to self. It should be to simply manifest the will of God and to bring Him glory.

• How does our tendency to want attention impact the flow of miracles?

When we learn to walk intimately with Him, we are learning the basics of what is needed to release the supernatural. The only remaining step is to know and believe that He wants to release the supernatural in a great way through us—of course in a way that will bring glory to Him. That is a huge asterisk. Few have the maturity to have miracles flowing through them without taking some of the glory to themselves. Even if a person being used by God did remain in a place of humility, others won't let him walk out the will of God. They flock to the "healer" and lose sight of God.

In *1 Corinthians 12:31*, it says, *"But earnestly desire the best gifts. And yet I show you a more excellent way."* That more excellent way is learning the central part that the love of God plays in the manifestation of all things, including the gifts of the Spirit. When we lose sight of God's love for us and of His desire to cultivate our love for Him, we lose sight of the *"more excellent way."* That is easy to do when the supernatural is showing up in a major way.

When we try to force the supernatural because of our immaturity or lack of understanding, we end up making promises on behalf of God that will not come to pass. The one who tries to dictate what God will do and when He will do it virtually forces God to withdraw from the situation. That person has become the center of attention. The focus has shifted to the man. When the promised healing does not come in the way the "man of God" pronounced, people soon become cynics and skeptics. The end result is anything but the glory of God.

The one who tries to dictate what God will do and when He will do it virtually forces God to withdraw from the situation.

He is God. We are not. All we can do is seek to see and hear Him. All we can do is respond according to His leading. In *John 5:19*, Jesus says, *"Most assuredly, I say to you, the Son can do nothing of Himself, but what He sees the Father do; for whatever He does, the Son also does in like manner."* If that is true for Jesus, how much more is it true for us? The one who tries to force the supernatural will never be able to deliver on his promises of what he says God is going to do. Humility is huge.

Even so, we need to learn to be bold when God speaks. He doesn't move until He has a release point. I believe God is waiting on us every bit as much or more than we are waiting on Him. He could do so much more if we were seeking what He is saying and what He wanting to do! God help us not to lose sight of His heart. May we seek to demonstrate His power and goodness to a world that is often blind to Him!

[Handwritten margin notes:]
WORKS WON'T GET YOU THE INVITATION TO SPEND ETERNITY WITH CHRIST BUT RELATIONSHIP IS WHAT GIVES US THE OPPORTUNITY TO SPEND ETERNITY WITH GOD. 12/25/19

If you dont want to be with God now you wont want to spend eternity with him

WAIT ON GOD!

Activity for Understanding

Remember: *The conduit gifts flow through us. They don't "reside" the same way that the character gifts or the calling gifts do. The questions in this section will focus on your openness to be used by God in these areas, along with how God has already used you in a supernatural way.*

Who do you know that has been used by God in either faith, healings, or miracles? Describe how any of these gifts manifested and how you knew it was from God.

How has God worked supernaturally in your life in faith, healing, or miracles, moving in you or through you in a way that made a great difference in your life or the lives of others?

What would it take for you to have the boldness to speak or act in a way that might end up being a release point for a miracle or healing?

How would you know that what you were sensing was from God and not from self? What are some things you could do to test what you were sensing before you spoke or acted?

Have some close friends identify times that they have seen God use you to speak to them in a way that they feel was from God.

Prophecy

Chapter 19

• What does it mean that prophecy is not of "private interpretation"?

The next gift on the list from *1 Corinthians 12:8-10* is prophecy. What is interesting about prophecy is that this is the gift that describes how we received our Scriptures. Prophecy is God speaking His words through a person to another person or a group of persons. God moved on men and gave them the words that were later written down as the Scriptures we have today. When we think about the modern gift of prophecy, we often are quick to distance it from how God moved in the old days to speak to His people, but the gift has not significantly changed throughout time. In *2 Peter 1:20-21*, the gift is described this way:

> *Knowing this first, that no prophecy of Scripture is of any private interpretation, for prophecy never came by the will of man, but holy men of God spoke as they were moved by the Holy Spirit.*

Prophecy is very similar in the way it happens to what I described about both a word of wisdom and a word of knowledge. In these two gifts, a person receives something from God that was not there before. These gifts are not the result of accumulated wisdom or knowledge, nor are they the result of applied wisdom or knowledge. These gifts are inputs received from the Holy Spirit.

In the same way, the gift of prophecy is a received gift. It is not the cumulative knowledge of some wise man. In fact, **verse 20** from above tells us that a prophecy is not **"of any private interpretation."** What does that mean? It means that not even the person giving the prophecy understands what is being spoken. He is being given words to speak that are meant for some other person or group of persons, but his level of understanding of those words may not be any greater than the understanding of others who are hearing them. In fact, sometimes they make sense to the hearer when the person delivering the word does not understand what he is saying to the person. God understands and the people receiving the word understand (or not … in some cases!), but the person delivering the word can be simply a messenger.

Sometimes, the person delivering the word does not understand what he is saying.

Verse 21 indicates that *"holy men of God spoke as they were moved by the Holy Spirit."* While for the most part, God chooses holy men, people like Balaam and Saul were used in this gift. Balaam wanted to use the gift to gain money and was rebuked by a donkey. In *2 Peter 2:15*, *Jude 11*, and *Revelation 2:14*, Balaam is used as an example of having used the things of God in a way that turns good to evil. Even so, the prophecies of Balaam stand as accurate and clear words, one of which is a prophecy that Christ would come out of the tribe of Judah.

A prophecy that is from God is of God no matter how the deliverer of the prophecy responds before or after his prophecy. It is **"of no private interpretation."** The people receiving the prophecy are to judge the word to see if it is from God. They are not to judge the person delivering the word to see if he is of God.

• What are the qualifications for a person to be used in prophecy?

It is true that in most cases, the person delivering the word will be a **"holy"** man (or woman!). Even as I pointed out in discussing a word of wisdom and word of knowledge, those who are sensitive to the Spirit and in continual communion with Him are the ones who are most likely to be used by the Spirit to deliver one of these words.

Holy men pay attention to God. They are open to being used. They desire to be used by God. But if there is no holy man available, and if God can get someone's attention and it suits His purposes, he can and will use whomever He chooses to use. In **1 Corinthians 14:31**, it says, **"For you can all prophesy one by one, that all may learn and all may be encouraged."** It would seem that any and all can be used in this gift if they only set their face to be sensitive to Him.

Certainly, the natural tendency is for the body to give greater credibility to a prophecy given by a **"holy"** man. Those with a track record of having walked with God and having heard from God should be held in higher esteem in the same way that an elder should be held in higher esteem. Yet, that does not change the fact that a word of prophecy stands or falls in and of itself. A godly man can miss God. The unrighteous can be used by God. A word is either from God and is truth or it is not. The key question needs to be, "Has God spoken?"

• Besides determining whether or not a prophecy is from God, what else still needs to happen?

If the answer is "Yes, God has spoken!" that is just the beginning. There are two more steps remaining. There still needs to be an interpretation of the word and then a right application of the word. Caiaphas is a great example of a person who was used to bring a prophetic word to his people but who had a completely wrong understanding of the word that he was bringing. **John 11:51-52** tells us of Caiaphas that **"being high priest that year he prophesied that Jesus would die for the nation, and not for that nation only, but also that He would gather together in one the children of God who were scattered abroad."**

This prophecy was clearly fulfilled by Jesus who died on the cross for the sins of the people, and in doing so, gathered all nations into one body—the body of Christ known as the church. Caiaphas had no clue about the real meaning of the prophecy. In his mind, he saw the Roman government coming down on the Jewish people because of this pseudo-savior-king named Jesus whom many of the people were now following. In his thinking, the only way to save the nation would be to kill off Jesus. So he set out to turn Jesus over to the Romans, to have them crucify him. He completely missed the point of the prophecy, but he still was used by God to carry out His will.

For a prophecy to be effective in the lives of people, it must be interpreted correctly and then applied in the way God desires. In a way, neither of these happened with Caiaphas' prophecy, though in an ironic way, Caiaphas' vendetta to get Jesus killed did help fulfill the prophecy. Some of the words brought by the prophets of old were not understood until hundreds of years later. Not until Christ came did many of the prophecies make sense in the fullness that they were intended.

- **Though a prophecy seems specific to a time and place, how can it have multiple applications?**

WORDS HAVE MULT- IPLE APPLI- CATIONS

Even so, most of these Messianic prophecies had both an immediate and delayed fulfillment. In *Zechariah 9*, the prophet is giving a prophecy about the future, describing when Jesus would ride into Jerusalem on a donkey. Even so, the prophecy also has an immediate application. The entire book of Zechariah has the overtone of God speaking, "I am sovereign. I am over kings and kingdoms. Don't let the powers that seem to be in control worry you." The idea of riding into Jerusalem on a donkey in peace and not on a horse to conquer fits the idea of a sovereign God who doesn't need to fight to be in control. He is in charge, and He can ride in meekly or with power. It makes no difference to Him.

The immediate application in the time of Zechariah was to throw off their fear and rise up to rebuild the temple. They weren't to worry about threats from supposed enemies or governors. God was in charge, and they were to go forward. God had spoken. No horse of any enemy could defeat the power of God, even if all He had was a donkey to ride on. Rise up and build!

In meekness, He broke the power of every authority that thought it could dominate Him.

When Jesus was riding a donkey into Jerusalem, He too was to rise up and build. He was building a church made without human hands. Through the triumphal entry and then His subsequent death, He was establishing the authority of God over His church. In meekness, He broke the power of every authority that thought it could dominate Him, whether that of Caiaphas or that of the Romans.

When a word is truly from God, it can have this kind of depth of meaning with multiple applications. If we are not careful, we pull a Caiaphas and run with the word in a way that perverts it. Most people think that once a word from God has arrived, the job is done. Many times, we need more focus in prayer after we get the word than we had before the word came. We need to seek Him to gain a right interpretation and application of the word. Again, no word is *"of any private interpretation."*

I have seen people take off in some crazy responses to supposed words from God. The first step is always to judge a word to see if it is even from God. Then it needs interpretation and application. Another mistake is that people assume a word means something will happen immediately, when the reality is that there may be a long preparation phase. That often results in a number of foolish choices, when the most important part of the message was to "get prepared!" Many have treated the return of Christ this way. They have gone into the hills to hide out instead of stepping up an urgency to share the gospel or to make needed changes that would better prepare them for the day of His coming.

- ### How do we treat prophecy with honor and yet with a healthy level of discernment?

First Thessalonians 5:19-21 gives us the following instructions: *"Do not quench the Spirit. Do not despise prophecies. Test all things; hold fast what is good."* Because of the potential for abuse and misuse, many have despised prophecies. They have declared that the word of God is all we need and that we do not need any active speaking on the part of God today.

I do agree that the cannon of Scripture is closed. We have a set of Scriptures that are the recognized Word of God which is the standard for all other words. The Scriptures were tested over hundreds of years and found to be the Word of God. Today's prophecies can only be seen from the vantage point of an immediate time period and within the context of a single culture. That limited context means that we cannot view a prophecy in the same way that we view the Scriptures!

> **Today's prophecies can only be seen from the vantage point of an immediate time period and within a culture.**

Instead, we use the Scriptures as the standard for all words that are given. Nothing that contradicts the current Scriptures can be from God. However, that does not mean that God does not still move on men today to bring fresh revelation, insights, and applications to His people. We need to know how the Scriptures speak to us in our day and our culture. Many applications of the Scripture to life need specific guidance from Him. We need revelation to understand what has already been spoken lest we be like Caiaphas and be found to be an enemy of God when we think ourselves to be friends of God.

In *Exodus 18:20*, the Bible gives a command that the prophet who *"presumes to speak a word in my name"* shall die. Because of that warning, we do some funny things with prophecy. We seem to assume that prophetic words magically appear and that they have to be 100% correct the first time and every time. In the Old Testament, Elisha conducted a school of the prophets. If prophecy just "appears," why would there have been any need for a school and what could possibly go on in such a school? The "appears" view of prophecy gives no place for learning to discern a word as being from God.

Instead of that view, we need to give a person room to grow in his ability to hear from God and to test words as being from God. He needs to be taught when a word is truly from God, when it is from self, and when it may even have some demonic influence. *Ezekiel 13* describes the false prophets as prophesying *"out of their own heart" (v. 2)* and having plastered a wall *"with untempered mortar" (v. 10)*. This phrase seems to indicate that

GROWING IN DISCERNMENT

they have not spent the needed time in prayer with God and have simply given an *"untempered"* word from their own heart.

In *1 Kings 22:24-25*, the false prophet Zedekiah confronts the true prophet Micaiah:

> *Now Zedekiah the son of Chenaanah went near and struck Micaiah on the cheek, and said, "Which way did the spirit from the LORD go from me to speak to you?"*
> *And Micaiah said, "Indeed, you shall see on that day when you go into an inner chamber to hide!"*

Again, Micaiah points Zedekiah to needing "temper" for his mortar. Micaiah tells Zedekiah that if he will go into the inner chamber and wait upon God, he too could possibly hear from God. That is not the view we have of prophecy. We think it just "shows up."

Prophecy is simply one more of the gifts in this conduit list that depends on being intimate with God and then translating that intimacy into some kind of practical life application. We can grow in our ability to hear from God and to connect with God. We can grow in our ability to bring a prophetic word. Though it sounds heretical to many, we need to give people space to practice in this area of prophecy. Killing the prophet is not the right response for the immature person who is learning, who realizes that he is learning.

[handwritten: 12/25/19]
[handwritten: TRUE PEOPLE WHO FLOWED IN THE PROPHET-IC WERE IMPRISONED AND GOD USED THE SEPERATION TO SPEAK TO THEM IN THEIR QUIET TIME]

• How do right timing and manner help make a prophecy effective?

Finally, one of the most important parts of giving a prophecy is timing and manner. A person boldly speaking for God and in the name of God is never appropriate, unless the word He brings is absolutely true. In this case, we are at the level of "stoning the prophet" if the word is false ... though I am not suggesting that we actually kill the person.

He definitely needs to be cut off from any other public exercise of the gift until he learns better.

If someone speaks with an Elijah-type of boldness without having clearly heard from God, he needs to be rebuked in the severest way. He definitely needs to be cut off from any other public exercise of the gift until he learns better. It is a serious thing to invoke the name of God. Most prophecies should be given more as suggestions or questions until the person has a track record of hearing from God. While in the learning stage, it is almost always good to test a statement with "I think I am sensing this from God..".

Timing is another huge issue. Those who are more inclined to give a prophecy tend to be those who are more bold in their personality, who are often sure of their ability to hear from God. Once this kind of person gets a word, he often feels a great deal of license to blurt out that word anywhere and anytime.

In *1 Corinthians 14:32*, the Bible tells us that *"the spirits of the prophets are subject to the prophets."* Some people act as if they have no control over when and how they speak a prophetic word. That is not true. The spirit of the prophet is subject to the prophet, and he is responsible for the timing and manner in which he delivers a word.

This means that a person may get a word and have to sit on it for days, months, or even years. If that happens, it is likely because the person is to pray for an extended time before bringing forth the word. In some cases, a word is only for the sake of prayer and is never to be spoken. The "inner chamber" is the key to effective prophetic ministry as it is for all areas of ministry!

Many times, people try to make prophecy fit into a particular mold. They expect prophecy coming in King James English or it has to be done in a church service in a particular format, or it has to have the tag, "Thus sayeth the Lord." Prophecy is when one person "hears" something from God and speaks it to someone else. It is not limited to a style or a location. It may give credit to God or it may not. It may be delivered boldly or meekly. It may be delivered in a spiritual context or a very natural context. And timing is often crucial.

Prophecy is when one person "hears" something from God and speaks it to someone else.

Life is a laboratory of learning. We may get the right word and speak it at the wrong time. We may think we have wisdom from God and be doing nothing more than speaking out of our own heart. It is important for us to grow in our hearing, our interpreting, and our applying of words from God. Then we need to help others to grow in this gift. It is unfortunate that especially in this area of prophecy that we don't give people a model that allows them to grow. If we adopt a new model, I believe we will see much more effective ministry in this area.

- **How should we respond at a personal level to a word of prophecy?**

I also want to give a final warning to those who receive a prophecy from others. Any prophetic word should generally be nothing more than a confirmation of what God has already been speaking to a person. The only problem with that is that some don't seek God and many do not have any understanding how to hear His voice. These people have little or no defense against those who are practicing some form of immature or false prophecy.

If a person receives a prophecy, and he has not been in prayer, it is time to get into prayer and to hear from God. No prophecy should be followed without clear confirmation from God and godly mentors. The cannon of Scripture had to be confirmed by many, many witnesses over a period of hundreds of years. Individual words also need to be confirmed by multiple witnesses, though not over hundreds of years. It may be more a matter of weeks, days or even minutes for an individual.

The basis of all of these gifts in the conduit list is intimacy with God. With true intimacy, they are incredible tools of life. Without it, they are a game of exerting self on others in a way that is loaded with manipulation and control. It is no wonder that we are told to test them. It is no wonder that many take the easy route and despise them. Will you take God's route and earnestly desire them, that you might see His life go forth in a greater way?

Activity for Understanding

Remember: *The conduit gifts flow through us. They don't "reside" the same way that the character gifts or the calling gifts do. The questions in this section will focus on your openness to be used by God in these areas, along with how God has already used you in a supernatural way.*

Who do you know that has been used by God in prophecy (in a way that God used them to speak to you)? Describe how this gift manifested and how you knew it was from God.

How has God worked supernaturally in your life, using your words to speak into the lives of others? How did you know that it was God speaking through you?

What would it take for you to have greater boldness to speak when you do believe you have something from God?

How would you know that what you were sensing was from God and not from self? What are some things you could do to test what you were sensing before you speak?

Have some close friends identify times that they have seen God use you to speak to them in a way that they feel was from God.

The Final Three

Chapter 20

- ## What kinds of things might a person with discerning of spirits "see"?

The final three gifts on the conduit list all are identifiably spiritual in nature. Discerning of spirits is a gift that could simply be good judgment, but the name of the gift moves it beyond natural ability. This gift is very similar to the prophetic in some ways, and often is at work in those with the calling of the prophet.

Discerning of spirits is the ability to "discern" what is happening at the spiritual level. At times the person actually "sees" some kind of spirit being present in the room. Because our culture is not really open to these kinds of visions, the people who have this gift can often be made to feel as if they are psychotic. If a person is told he is crazy enough times, he can be persuaded to believe it, especially when he is seeing something that others do not see.

Our culture has little room for people who have this gift. Probably because of my Pentecostal ties, many people have gingerly approached the subject with me, almost as if they were half expecting to be rebuked again. When I take them seriously, it is amazing how many of them open up as if they have finally been able to breathe a breath of fresh air.

We do seem to recognize that there is more going on inside of a person than meets the eye. There is need for the kind of "intuition" that we call discernment. Even basic communication requires us to "discern" the motives of another person. Motive is about as close to spiritual function as our culture gets. We recognize that there is something deeper than just the thought life in a person, but we have no idea how to get a handle on it. People are spiritual beings and as such have spiritual flows. Their hearts line up with things like peace and joy or bitterness and hatred.

Discerning of spirits picks up on angelic or demonic activity or the activity of God's Spirit. It discerns what is going on at these invisible levels. It also sees the spiritual side of the human heart. Human beings have a spirit that energize their words and actions. A person who is operating in discerning of spirits can pick up on this heart activity.

- ## "Seeing" is only the beginning. What are the next steps?

However, being able to see things at the spirit level is only the first step. If a person is being shown something by God, there is a reason why God is showing it to the person. Just as I discussed with prophecy, there needs to be an interpretation and an application. Once a person "sees" something, he must ask, "What does it mean?" Or, "How do I respond?"

A person who has a tendency to be dominated by a spirit of fear will almost always interpret any kind of vision by giving it an interpretation that lines up with that spirit of fear. It is possible for a person to have some sort of perception or discerning of spirits that is from God, and then run with that perception in a way that God never intended—into fear or bitterness or some other flow. It is possible to start in the Spirit and end in the flesh! *(Gal. 3:3)*.

Some "see" things they believe are true and then run with it in a way that belittles others.

Many people who have a tendency toward being critical of others believe that they are operating in "discerning of spirits." Some people "see" things they believe are true and then run with it in a way that belittles others. Because this gift is so completely "invisible," many are convinced they are hearing from God when they are responding to fear or to a critical spirit in their own hearts.

I have seen people who were dominated by egoism who turned a supposed discerning of spirits into a "look at me" show. I've seen others who used their "superior insight" as a justification for manipulation or control. Similar to the gift of prophecy, there should be appropriate judgment of those who are moving in discerning of spirits. Discerning of spirits should line up with the Word of God. Also, others who are sensitive to God's moving should be able to verify if something is of God.

Just because someone "discerns" something—that is not the final step. Prayer is still needed to find the right interpretation, application, and even timing of a response. Too often people have an immediate, knee jerk response when what is needed is prayer. Sometimes what a person discerns requires an immediate response, though not always.

When one spiritual gift manifests, it often needs another to complete the picture. A person with a gift of discerning of spirits often needs a word of wisdom to know the next step to take. Wisdom majors in right application of information. Sometimes knowing the next step is not enough. If that step is beyond what is humanly capable, the gift of faith may be needed to complete the step. The immature person seldom waits for other gifts to manifest, but instead tries to push through in his own strength and with his own wisdom. The final result is something that dishonors the gift and dishonors God who gave the gift.

Similar to the gift of prophecy, one of the greatest needs for a person who is being used in discerning of spirits is to be shut in with God in prayer. He needs to go into the inner chamber and allow God to cleanse and purify his heart. The selfish heart will almost always use this gift in a wrong way. In fact the selfish heart will likely think he has heard something from God when it is only his own heart creating the vision that he is seeing. The humble and submitted heart will bring glory to His name by walking it through the way God desires.

- ## What is meant by the phrase "different kinds" of tongues?

The next gift in the list in *1 Corinthians 12:8-10* is *"different kinds of tongues."* Many people completely miss the language describing this gift. It doesn't say the ability to speak in different languages. That actually is what happens with the baptism in the Holy Spirit. With the baptism in the Spirit comes an ability to commune with God in a way that is outside of a known language—a kind of private prayer language. The gift in this list is called **"different kinds of tongues."** What could the **"different kinds"** part of this statement mean?

The function of praying in tongues is similar to praying in a known language. Though we don't know what is being said, it is definitely communicating something. It is a transaction between God and man. Calling this gift **"different kinds of tongues"** would be very similar to calling it "different kinds of prayers." It is the difference between talking about prayer vs. talking about different kinds of prayers. Thus, God might give a tongue of intercession or of praise. He might give a tongue of thanksgiving or of confession.

First Corinthians 14:14-16 says, **"For if I pray in a tongue, my spirit prays, but my understanding is unfruitful. What is the conclusion then? I will pray with the spirit, and I will also pray with the understanding. I will sing with the spirit, and I will also sing with the understanding."** These verses clearly tell us that effective prayer is happening even when the mind does not understand the prayer.

This passage suggests a parallel track of praying: in the known language and in tongues. For the two to be in sync, the kind of prayer (thanksgiving, praise, intercession, etc.) could be parallel or the person praying could ask God for an interpretation so that both the known prayer and the unknown tongue matched up. A person can pray in tongues, and it is prayer with or without interpretation. God assures us that this prayer is real prayer, and that it actually builds up the person who is praying in this way **(1 Cor. 14:2, 4)**.

However, the gift of **"different kinds of tongues"** is in a list of gifts to be used publicly in the body of Christ. If in a group, a person feels moved to speak out in a tongue, I believe it should be for the sake of either emphasizing or perhaps changing the spiritual flow of what is happening. I remember one experience like this that impacted hundreds of people. God used an almost agonizing tone of a message in tongues as a part of a call to a deeper level of intercession. We all felt the power of the tongue, and it effectively moved an entire auditorium of people into deep prayer.

> **God used an almost agonizing tone of a message in tongues as a part of a call to deeper intercession.**

If the major part of this gift were about content, why wouldn't God give the gift in the known language as a prophecy? I believe God gives this gift in this form not just to emphasize the content but to emphasize the spiritual dynamic along with the content. We need to become much more attentive to spiritual flow and to what **"kind"** of direction God is wanting to move. On a given day, He might want us to rest in Him. On other days, He wants us to be bold and to launch out in aggressive spiritual warfare. The different **"kinds of tongues"** can help set a tone for this even apart from the interpretation.

- ## How do these supernatural gifts act as a "sign" to others?

Of course, the final gift on the **1 Corinthians 12:8-10** list is interpretation of tongues. This gift highlights that the content of the tongue is very important. In fact, **1 Corinthians 14:28** tells us that if there is not an interpreter present, the one who speaks in a tongue should keep silent. The content of the message is that important. I highlighted the "spiritual dynamic" in the last section, but without content, the gift of tongues can become very much like discernment with wrong interpretation or wrong application. This gift needs to be followed through to God's desired end.

God wants the spiritual dynamic to merge with the interpretation in a way that will move the body of Christ where He wants it to go. He gives this gift in a supernatural way as an exclamation point. He could give the same content and spiritual dynamic in the form of a prophecy and He often does. *First Corinthians 14:5* tells us that a tongue plus an interpretation is roughly the equivalent of a prophecy. So why does God even bother with these gifts of tongues and interpretation? Why not just use prophecy?

I believe tongues and interpretation is not just about content but about the entire dynamic. It is a sign gift. It is God saying "I am here." Of course, in many places within Christianity, it is not received this way. In many groups, it is received more with a sense of "this is weird" or even "that is of the devil." Where people are uninformed about the gift of tongues, it actually becomes something that can create an offense instead of a blessing.

In *1 Corinthians 14:23,* it describes this attitude saying, *"Therefore if the whole church comes together in one place, and all speak with tongues, and there come in those who are uninformed or unbelievers, will they not say that you are out of your mind?"* Those who don't understand how tongues works (the uninformed), or those who don't believe in God see tongues as madness and not as a sign from God.

What is interesting, the very same passage seems to contradict itself by saying, *"Therefore tongues are for a sign, not to those who believe but to unbelievers" (1 Cor. 14:22).* On the one hand, this passage says that the unbeliever will think the people are out of their mind and on the other hand it will be a sign to them that God is present. So which is it? Actually, I believe it is both. In this case, it is in the eye of the beholder. Some who believe in the supernatural will see it as a sign and will be convinced that God is present. Others, who are less accepting of supernatural happenings like tongues, will despise it and turn away.

Through prophecy, the content of God's message can break through to convince even the hardest of hearts.

The conclusion of the passage is that through prophecy, the content of God's message can break through to convince even the hardest of hearts. This can happen regardless of who comes in to the body, whether a skeptic of God's supernatural speaking or not. When a person hears something that seems to be especially for him at exactly that specific time, he realizes that something out of the ordinary is happening. He may not respond as God desires, but he at least has to deal with the fact that something very strange has happened.

There are times when prophecy is more effective than tongues and interpretation. There are times when tongues and interpretation is more effective than prophecy. It largely depends on the people who are responding to the gifts. God will use whatever gift is most effective and whatever gift the people are willing to allow to flow through them. If there is no one present who is willing to be used in prophecy, but there is someone open to being used in different kinds of tongues, guess which one God will use? I'm not sure God always gets His first choice.

- **How does human preference figure into the operation of the gifts?**

In *1 Corinthians 14:31-32*, it tells us, *"For you can all prophesy one by one, that all may learn and all may be encouraged. And the spirits of the prophets are subject to the prophets."* God wants to speak to us. He wants to break into our church gatherings, and He wants to use different individuals to do it. If we are willing, it says *"all"* can prophesy. This clearly says any of us could be used. Anytime. As long as we are sensitive to Him and seeking Him.

However, these verses also tell us that the *"spirits of the prophets are subject to the prophets."* People being used in the gifts often act as if they have no control over the way those gifts are used. That is simply not true. The spirit of the prophet is subject to the prophet.

Human choice has a lot to do with how and when a spiritual gift is manifested. In fact, in the very next verse *(1 Cor. 14:33)*, Paul is rebuking the Corinthians for allowing their use of prophecy to become a competing and confusing mess of voices all wanting to speak at the same time. Instead of having an eye on the purpose of God and how to bring blessing to the body, they were more interested in showing off. That doesn't mean that the people didn't start out by connecting with God. It just means that their immaturity sidetracked them in a way that ended up not being God. Just because we start out connected to God and hearing from Him does not mean that we maintain that connection all the way through to the end of what we are doing or saying.

> **Instead of having an eye on the purpose of God and how to bring blessing to the body, they were more interested in showing off!**

In some churches, the exercise of these gifts becomes a kind of ritualistic happening. It is almost like there is a designated person to perform a specific ritual at a specific time. The sense of God breaking into the service is lost. The spiritual dynamic that might move the church toward praise or intercession is almost non-existent. This doesn't serve the purposes of God any more than a number of competing voices would bring glory to God.

The exercise of the spiritual gifts, especially different kinds of tongues and interpretation of tongues is about emphasizing the active presence of God in a gathering. Dead ritual misses that dynamic. We need to have an eye on what God is wanting to do at any given point in time. We need to spend time with Him and hear His heart. This is much more important than any specific way a person would be used in the gifts.

Those who don't distinguish between tongues as a prayer language being spoken to God and tongues as a gift being used in the church will look at the language of *1 Corinthians 14* and say that everything ever spoken in tongues must be interpreted. I think that misses the point. The first part of *1 Corinthians 14:4* says, *"He who speaks in a tongue edifies himself."* To speak in tongues is to have communion with God which is edifying to the person. It doesn't increase his understanding, but it does cleanse and connect His heart to God in a way that is helpful. It also is effective intercession *(Rom. 8:26)*.

Tongues in PRAYER v.s. Tongues in PUBLIC

The rules of *1 Corinthians 14* apply to the use of the gifts of different kinds of tongues and interpretation of tongues in the church. In fact, it specifically says **"in the church" (v. 28)** when telling the person to keep silent if there is no interpreter present. The use of tongues as a prayer language is valuable, whether it is interpreted or not. Within a public gathering, tongues should only be used in ways that edify the church and not to edify self.

As I described earlier, that means different things in different churches. In some churches, any use of tongues is not welcome and would not be edifying. In other settings, tongues with interpretation is the only thing allowed. In some places, the use of tongues as a part of worship or prayer time is embraced. I believe that the important thing is not so much how the gift is used as it is that the leadership not lose sight of the purpose of God for the meeting.

The will of God must take precedence over the desires of an individual or a subgroup. The way tongues is used needs to take into account who is present, what the overall impact a particular kind of use of the gifts will have, and then monitor that use according to the good of the whole.

Those who want to be used in the gifts more than they want to edify the body of Christ will invariably bring dishonor to God.

Above all, the gifts are given for the good of the body of Christ. Those who want to be edified through the use of tongues still have a prayer closet available to them! Those who want to be used in the gifts more than they want to edify the body of Christ will invariably bring dishonor to God.

The use of the gifts is about learning to walk in a manner that loves others and loves God. The conduit gifts are not meant to be just a communication of content or a display of power but a vehicle toward better relationship, between God and man and between men and other men. May we all seek to be used in a way that reflects His love!

Activity for Understanding

Remember: *The conduit gifts flow through us. They don't "reside" the same way that the character gifts or the calling gifts do. The questions in this section will focus on your openness to be used by God in these areas, along with how God has already used you in a supernatural way.*

Who do you know that has been used by God in either discerning of spirits, different kinds of tongues, or interpretation of tongues? Describe how any of these gifts manifested and how you knew it was from God.

How has God worked supernaturally in your life in discerning of spirits, different kinds of tongues, or interpretation of tongues to move in you or through you in a way that made a difference in your life or the lives of others?

What would it take for you to have the boldness to speak or act in a way that would be a response to the prompting of the Holy Spirit in these gift areas?

How would you know that what you were sensing was from God and not from self? What are some things you could do to test what you were sensing before you spoke or acted?

Have some close friends identify times that they have seen God use you in these gift areas or at least in the areas of discernment or supernaturally using you as a "sign" of God's presence and work. List the results.

Using the Model

Chapter 21

Ecclesiastes 12:13-14

Let us hear the conclusion of the whole matter:

Fear God and keep His commandments,
For this is man's all.
For God will bring every work into judgment,
Including every secret thing,
Whether good or evil.

• How are spiritual gifts present in "seed" form from the beginning?

Many who immerse themselves in studying the spiritual gifts lose what should be their center: to fear God and to keep His commandments. A better understanding of the spiritual gifts should bring a greater focus on God, not a greater focus on self.

So often, spiritual gifts have been taught as if they materialized out of thin air at salvation, came with the baptism of the Holy Spirit, or appeared at some other point of intense seeking of the will of God. One of the most important concepts in this book is the idea of God breathing on human flesh. God has placed in our human frame everything He will ever use during our lifetime. It is there in seed form, but seed form is just that. It is untapped potential. It is life in a dried up form, just waiting for the rain, the sunshine, and the nutrients to awaken it from its sleep.

They are there, lying dormant in every human being until God breathes on that seed and causes it to come to life.

That is a picture of spiritual gifts. They are there, lying dormant in every human being until God breathes on that seed and causes it to come to life. Even as the seed needs continual sunshine, water, and nutrients to grow, so too do we need the continual breath of God to bring to life the fullness of what He has placed within us.

Many approach spiritual gifts as if they were something to achieve or accomplish. They are not. Does a plant achieve growth? Does it labor along the way? Neither does a person work to accomplish his gifts for God. He responds to God's nourishment, and it simply happens. Sure, with human beings there is a cooperation factor. We must actively seek and embrace His nourishment. But that is the point. We stay focused on Him and seek Him, and the gifts just happen along the way.

The greatest key to flowing in the spiritual gifts is intimacy with God. With intimacy, life will just keep right on flowing through an individual, and it might even be difficult to keep a good running description of the "gifts" that are manifesting. After all, these categorizations of the

[handwritten note: GROWTH DOESN'T INVOLVE SEED WORKING ITSELF TO GROW 12/26/19]

gifts are often nothing more than a human attempt to understand what God is doing through an individual. They are descriptions of how God works, but how He works in each and every person is unique. Every person is a new picture of His glory.

We do need to let Him water the seed. Most of us are too busy trying to water our own seed. We study the gifts to chart a plan of action, to set a direction for growth. That is the wrong model. Only He knows when the season is right. A seed growing out of season will suffer a premature death. We need to know His timing and wait for Him.

- **Why does a study of the gifts often end up in confusion? What can be done to minimize any confusion?**

I have taught on the gifts many times. Virtually every time I have taught on the gifts, I have seen significant points of confusion during the process. Invariably, the confusion comes at a point when a person is pressing the self part too hard and is not willing to wait for God to speak, for Him to reveal His heart to the person.

If you have completed this book and you are at that place of confusion, I challenge you to back off and to wait in His presence. When you cease striving and start resting in Him, He will grow that plant in you. Suddenly you will discover that it is not so much a process of awakening something within you as it is observing what He is doing in and through you. The wise man learns to look for the activity of God. When we see His breath on some kind of human activity, we are seeing spiritual gifts at work.

More often than not, confusion actually seems to be the norm in this area of spiritual gifts. There is a reason for that. In *James 3:16* it says, *"For where envy and self-seeking exist, confusion and every evil thing are there."* Most of the time, when people are studying the gifts, there is a very strong focus on self. They begin to compare themselves to other people and invariably it does slide into some form of envy and self seeking. If there is envy and self seeking, what will be the state of the person? Confusion.

The best way to avoid confusion is to keep the right focus. Fear God and obey His commandments. Generally, if God opens a door for a chance to serve others, take it. There are a few people who become compulsive about taking on ministry opportunities. Those who have this tendency toward being compulsive need to take the opposite advice. They need to hold back and make sure something is God before moving. Again, the best advice is to look for the breath of God in your life, that place where God is moving and blessing, and focus there. When the breath of God is at work, there will be greater results with a lesser amount of energy input on our part.

The best way to avoid confusion is to keep the right focus.

I am one of those individuals who tends to press … way too hard for too long and too often. I am one of those persons who lived in confusion … until I learned to rest. I had to learn that apart from Him I could do nothing *(John 15:5)*. I had to be "put on the shelf" for extended periods of time because I was busy striving to accomplish. In the end, all of my striving netted me nothing (but stress and headaches!).

When I rest in Him, I am able to give His life to people. When I see people's lives touched, I light up. When I try to touch people's lives, I become stressed. When I watch Him work, I rejoice. Even though I have a call as a teacher, when I force the issue of understanding, I become a fool. When I wait on Him and I listen, it is amazing what God will flow through me. Because I am intelligent or special? Hardly! If I were highly intelligent, it would be a product of me. It would bring Him no glory. No. In the moments when I truly realize how little I know, He speaks so much. When He speaks, I truly appear to be wise … but it is not my wisdom. It is His breath.

> **In the moments when I truly realize how little I know, He speaks so much.**

When I stop trying to be a mighty man of God and focus on Him, it is amazing what just seems to happen. I respond to what He is speaking, and not necessarily in dramatic ways, but things just start working out. I think you could even call them miracles … though they often are just a bit like good luck or ordinary life in a good flow. Relax. Enjoy life and it will be all but impossible to miss His call.

(handwritten margin note: OBEYING BEFORE FULLY UNDERSTANDING 12/26/19)

• How does obedience clarify our understanding of spiritual gifts?

Generally, if a person is active in serving others, he will begin to see the life that God desires to flow through him lived out in real time. It will not be a matter of seeking his place in God so much as it will be a matter of observing his place in God. If he obeys God, he will actually see the will of God being lived out in him before he fully understands the will of God for his life.

Life in Christ is like that. If we learn to hear and obey, so much of the rest of life takes care of itself. One of the greatest dangers in studying the gifts is to become too self focused. I generally tell people that this study needs to be taken in smaller doses, and that if you ever catch yourself becoming obsessive over this area of gifts, it is time to put it down for a while.

> **When thoughts about "my gift" becomes too obsessive, it is time to put down the study of the gifts for a while.**

The irony is that some of the greatest blessings of my ministry have come out of helping others see their place in God through this model of the gifts. It is an incredible and powerful tool. It sows value into others. But when the model or thoughts about "my gift" become too central or too obsessive, it is time to put down the study of the gifts for a while. It is very much like the principle Jesus teaches in *Matthew 10:39, "He who finds his life will lose it, and he who loses his life for My sake will find it."* One of the best ways for a person to find His gifts is to just forget about them for a while and set his eyes on serving God. Once that has happened for a season, life will become much clearer.

It is a great thing to be able to speak to someone and to give him a vision and a hope for his future. Once we begin to understand the concept of core values and how it manifests through the gifts model, we can often see a person's purpose, even if it is being manifested negatively at the moment. It is actually easier to see this for others and to speak it over them than it is to see things for ourselves.

I have also found that it is better to hold the model loosely, staying more at the core values area. Nailing down a precise description of a person's gifts is difficult, even with people I've known well. It often is like trying to get a good grip on a glob of slime. It's messy, and it's very imprecise.

That's because the gifts are descriptions of groupings. They are summaries and people are individuals. No two individuals are created alike. Core values are impacted by the generations and by life influences, both of which write upon a heart individually created by God. Which of us is able to get a good handle on that level of complexity and feel like we have it nailed down for sure?

- ### How do core values give us a more practical approach to understanding our spiritual gifts?

The general core values of a person become obvious rather quickly ... usually within minutes. Fine tuning the picture can take years because different events in life trigger different parts of the heart, and thus different responses. If a person allows himself to be drawn into a game of seeking full understanding of self, before long the result becomes confusion.

Once a person understands the basic core values, he has the big picture. The best thing to do from that point on is to fear God and obey His voice. Of course, obeying the general commandments of God lays the foundation for being able to hear God's voice in the day to day issues. If a person focuses on following God in all things, he will begin to see the more detailed picture of his calling and his character lived out. Then, he will understand.

Once a person understands the basic core values, he has the big picture.

God loves His children and will direct them into the perfect place. We don't need to know that place to go there. We just need to know His voice and to trust Him. If we respond to Him, everything else will take care of itself. When Solomon got caught up in self, he lost the meaning of life. If we allow a searching out of self to cause us to become too focused on self, we too will lose our way for a season.

We do need to study the gifts. We do need greater understanding of self, but even more so, we need to use it to bless God and others. That is our purpose. In the words of Solomon, ***"Let us hear the conclusion of the whole matter: fear God and keep His commandments, for this is man's all" (Eccl. 12:13).***

Activity for Understanding

Are you at a point where you need to back off from your study of the gifts or to press in for better understanding? How do you move away from being self focused and toward being God focused?

Are you able to see the gifts of others in a way that you can encourage them? How can you grow in being able to do that?

What are your deepest core values that show up most often and create the strongest responses in you?

How do those core values point you toward one or more of the gifts as being your character or your calling?

Looking back, can you see the "seed" form of your gifts at times in your life when you were not walking with God?

What helps you move from the more "human effort" seed form of the gift to where you are truly walking in partnership with God?

When you walk in obedience, where does the "breath of God" show up most often? Give an example of God producing supernatural results through your words or actions when you thought you were just doing basic obedience to God.

A Brief Scriptural Basis for the Model of the Gifts

Appendix

I still remember the question, "Where did Paul get his understanding of the spiritual gifts from?" It has been over 30 years since I first heard that question posed by Derek Prince on a tape that had been loaned to me about the spiritual gifts. It is a very good question.

At best, Paul had a very limited exposure to Jesus personally, and if he did have any exposure, it was from the negative perspective of seeing Jesus from within the thought world of being a Pharisee. That leaves three sources for Paul to have drawn from for his understanding of the spiritual gifts. One was the revelation from God. A second would be real life experiences of the gifts. The other was the Old Testament. Given his background, the Old Testament had to be a very significant part of the foundation for Paul's writings on the spiritual gifts.

There are those who see the Old Testament as an entirely unfit place to be studying spiritual gifts which they see as purely a New Testament dispensation. Many people think that what happens in the New Testament is so qualitatively different from the Old Testament that they see the Old Testament as having little relevance on how things work today. Of course there are those who believe that at least some of the gifts only operated while Jesus and the apostles were alive—which would mean that even the New Testament doesn't really apply to what is happening today!

Derek Prince's question was a challenge to my thinking because he pointed to the Old Testament as Paul's source. How much weight can we put on the Old Testament in the area of spiritual gifts? Over time, I have adopted an approach that minimizes the differences between the two testaments. I also definitely believe that what God was doing in the days of the apostles is still available and relevant to our lives today!

How much weight can we put on the Old Testament in the area of spiritual gifts?

In the Old Testament, God used the system of sacrifices to get the people to look forward to the death of Christ on the cross. In the New Testament times, we look backwards to Christ's death on the cross. God made it clear throughout the Old Testament that the sacrifices needed to be mixed with faith. Today, we still need to mix our confessions and commitments to Christ with faith. There is less difference between the two than some want to make.

Much more significant to the topic of the spiritual gifts is the role of the Holy Spirit in the Old and New Testaments. In the Old Testament, the Holy Spirit had a limited access to the people to work in their lives. I believe Paul explains the reason for the limited role of the Holy Spirit in **Romans 3:25b-26** when speaking of the death of Jesus on the cross, he says,

> *"This sacrifice shows that God was being fair when he held back and did not punish those who sinned in times past, for he was looking ahead and including them in what he would do in this present time. God did this to demonstrate his righteousness, for he himself is fair and just, and he makes sinners right in his sight when they believe in Jesus" (NLT).*

Even though God absolutely knew that the death of Jesus would atone for all sin, God limited His interaction with sinful men until the debt for sin had been completely paid. He did not freely pour out the work of the Holy Spirit until He had demonstrated Himself to be righteous in His passing over of the sins of those who interacted with the Holy Spirit.

The sin debt had not yet been paid. For God to freely disperse the Holy Spirit in the Old Testament times would have left God on shaky legal ground. We see God being challenged on this in **Zechariah 3**, when the devil is disputing for the body of Joshua. God is God, and He had promised to pay the debt, even from the time of the Garden of Eden. But until the debt was actually paid, it was as if God was borrowing on His own promise every time He interacted with sinful men.

Thus the work of the Holy Spirit is limited in the Old Testament. The relationship of the Holy Spirit with men in the Old Testament is described as the Spirit coming upon a person in a kind of anointing, not with a permanent abiding as there is in the New Testament. This makes sense in that until the debt for sin was paid, God chose to limit the closeness with which the Spirit could abide with men.

In the Old Testament, as men were holy or full of faith, they opened the door to a greater work of the Spirit. While holiness and faith are still important today, God is able to abide more closely for a more extended period of time, even when we are not responding as we should. The sin debt is paid and so there is more freedom on God's part to press harder in His work of drawing men into relationship with Him.

As we see the Holy Spirit flowing through the lives of many of the prophets, we are often seeing something that looks a lot like the New Testament relationship that is available.

While the closeness of the relationship of the Holy Spirit to men is certainly different in the Old Testament, we can still learn a great deal from the Old Testament. As we see the Holy Spirit flowing through the lives of many of the prophets, we are often seeing something that looks a lot like the New Testament relationship that is available.

The prophets clearly hear God speak. Miracles are done through the prophets and healings. Discernment is given by God as well as divine wisdom and knowledge through the power of the Holy Spirit. The Spirit's work is limited to a few individuals in the Old Testament, but where we do see the Spirit at work in the Old Testament, it is very much like what happens in the New Testament.

All of this is a foundation for the fact that I use the Old Testament to establish an understanding of many of the spiritual gifts. I don't believe that people have significantly changed throughout history. The only thing that has changed is the freedom that the Holy Spirit has to work in humanity as a whole.

Once the death of Christ was completed, Peter quotes what God had said in the book of **Joel** saying that, ***"I will pour out my Spirit upon all flesh" (Acts 2:17).*** Listen to that language. It is almost as if God is rejoicing at His new ability to be excessive in His giving of the Holy Spirit. He will ***"pour"*** the Holy Spirit ***"out"*** upon the people. It will be a lavish outpouring and it will be for ***"all flesh"***—that is for all people of every station in life all around the globe. And God is excited about it.

Man was never created to live without being connected to the Holy Spirit. From the beginning, man was designed to be completed by the presence and empowering of the Holy Spirit. Throughout the Old Testament, the Spirit's freedom to do the work that He wanted to do in men's lives was limited. We still get to see glimpses of it through the stories of when God interacted with the people. The design God had for men has never changed. Access to the Holy Spirit changed radically after the cross—though you would never know it by the way some people live today.

From the beginning, man was designed to be completed by the presence and empowering of the Holy Spirit.

Some people believe that in New Testament times, it works completely different from Old Testament times. They believe that in some mystical way, at either salvation or the baptism of the Holy Spirit, there is a kind of download of spiritual gifts into men. In other words, the unsaved have no spiritual gifts. Then they get saved and suddenly something is poured into them or perhaps is activated in them or … I'm not quite sure exactly what the thinking is. In truth, most have not thought it through. Mostly, the idea is that spiritual gifts can happen now, but they could not in the Old Testament times.

If that were true, where did Paul get his understanding of spiritual gifts? I believe that spiritual gifts are what happens when the Holy Spirit joins with human beings to produce something that is greater than would have been possible if the human being had continued to live at the natural human level. We see a minimal level of that joining of God and man in the Old Testament. There is a much greater level of joining available in the New Testament. While there are differences between the two, I believe there is still much to learn from seeing how the Spirit operates in the Old Testament.

In fact, if we want to see the Spirit operating at a real life level, we almost have to turn to the Old Testament. With the exception of a few life scenes in the book of Acts, most of the New Testament is doctrine. We don't see many scenes of life with the Holy Spirit at work in individuals.

After studying the first group of gifts, the character gifts, you should be able to see why life scenes are so vital to the understanding. Without the life scenes, the ability to clearly see the character gifts would be very limited. This means that we need to go to the Old Testament for instruction. To me, using the Old Testament is not a liability for this study since the way human beings function is not significantly different between the two testaments. The key difference between the two testaments is the access to the Holy Spirit, and the prophets definitely had access to the Holy Spirit.

I also want to comment briefly on the basic model of spiritual gifts that I am using. It comes out of the language of **_1 Corinthians 12:4-7_**, where it says, "

> **_There are different kinds of gifts, but the same Spirit. There are different kinds of service, but the same Lord. There are different kinds of working, but the same God works all of them in all men. Now to each one the manifestation of the Spirit is given for the common good (NIV)._**

The first verse starts it off by telling us that there are **_"different kinds"_** of gifts. Most models of the gifts don't take seriously that the gifts are not all of the same kind. They deal with them as if there were no differences between, and the result is confusion.

In English, the next three phrases sound rather bland. We have gifts that are **_"service"_** gifts, gifts that are **_"kinds of working,"_** and gifts that are a **_"manifestation of the Spirit."_** In the Greek, these phrases carry much more depth. The **_"service"_** gifts are ministries. They are something we do. The word used for the **_"working"_** kind of gifts is related to our current word of energy or in the Greek, *energema*. We are energized by certain kinds of things. We have a core set of values that we care about. I call these the character gifts. The Greek word for the final type of gifts is *phaneros*. The basic meaning of this word is "to appear or to make visible." With this set of gifts, something that is invisible (God) is made visible through a supernatural happening.

These categories are clearly described through the main text of this book, but this is the biblical basis for the grouping. With limited textual support, this grouping of the gifts has to be called a model. It is a human construct that makes sense and brings greater understanding. It is not clearly delineated in Scripture but is arrived at through a process of inductively studying Scripture.

I do believe that you will find that it is consistent with the Scriptures and that it has a definite ring of truth with many life applications that demonstrate its validity. But I also give the caution that any time inductive processing is involved, a writing needs to judged accordingly.

I understand that this very limited amount of detail explaining the scriptural support for the model does not measure up to an academic proof. It is, at best, a philosophy that has guided my thinking. Not just with spiritual gifts, but in all things I try my best to study the whole counsel of the Word of God. I find that the more I understand about the Old Testament, the more I understand the New Testament. When I minimize the difference between the two, both make more sense. Together, they are the Word of God.

The best picture of spiritual gifts is the breath of God waking up and sustaining the dormant seed within.

For me, the best picture of spiritual gifts is the breath of God waking up and sustaining the dormant seed within. Without the breath of God, we are not even alive. His breath enters our being, and we become a living being. When it leaves, we die **_(Eccl. 8:8)_**.

Our spirit may be more of a seed form that some would describe as being dead spiritually, but there is at least something there. As human beings, we range from being "dead" spiritually, even as a seed is dead, to being fully alive and fully in partnership with God.

That partnership is what spiritual gifts are all about. It moves a human being from being dust to being something much greater than just a collection of cells. Throughout the Scriptures, we see so many pictures of all the dynamic ways God intervenes in the lives of people. Plus He uses one person to impact the next. We partner with God and with one another in His work. That is not just a New Testament work. It started in the Garden of Eden.

God intervenes in the lives of men and women. Spiritual gifts are a part of that description of how He works. If you don't like the model presented, at least grab hold of those parts which reflect the truth of God's work in people. He uses us to complete His work in a way that brings Him glory. Partnership. That is such an amazing concept!

God wants to partner with you to accomplish His purposes and to bless His people. I hope this study challenges you to grow beyond where you are now and to increase your partnership with God to greater and greater places. God has a vision for each person, but the true picture of the gifts is about us together as one and not about a gifted individual.

God wants to partner with you to accomplish His purposes and to bless His people.

Partnership. God. You. Me. Us. Drawing people from all ages since the beginning of time into one body. This is God's purpose. Truly the vision is much *Greater Than* we could ever think or imagine. Empowered for a purpose. All one. Together. In unity. For His glory. Amazing.

Other Books by David A. Case

Heart Change Handbook: Practical Principles for Life Transformation

Going Deeper: Insights Toward Intimacy with Christ

Study Guide for Going Deeper

Becoming Lifegivers: Bringing God's Life to a Dark World

Releasing God's Life through the Hearts of Men: Transforming a Broken Generation into Men and Women of God

Dead Dogs on the Highway: Overcoming the Stench of Unforgiveness

Biblical Counseling: Pointing People Toward the Plans, Purposes, and Power of God

A Biblical Approach to Conflict

Journey of Discovery: Knowing the Voice of God

Cross Steps: The Upward Climb of a Spiritual Walk

Blog

David publishes a blog at effectiveheartchange.com. Books, videos, and other materials can be accessed or purchased at that website.

Books Available from:

Live Free Ministries
201 S. Chestnut
McPherson, KS 67460

620-241-1371

livefreeministries.com

livefreemin@gmail.com

Information about the Omega Project is available at omegaprojectks.com or the above listed address and phone.